REINVENTING
POLITICAL SCIENCE

REINVENTING
POLITICAL SCIENCE

A Feminist Approach

Jill Vickers

Fernwood Publishing • Halifax

Editing: Lee d'Anjou
Copy editing: Donna Davis
Design and production: Beverley Rach
Printed and bound in Canada by: Hignell Printing Limited

A publication of:
Fernwood Publishing
Box 9409, Station A
Halifax, Nova Scotia
B3K 5S3

Fernwood Publishing Company Limited gratefully acknowledges the financial support
of the Ministry of Canadian Heritage and the Nova Scotia Department of Education
and Culture.

Canadian Cataloguing in Publication Data

Vickers, Jill, 1942-
Reinventing political science.

Includes bibliographical references.
ISBN 1-895686-78-4

1. Political science. 2. Feminism. 3. Women in politics. I. Title.

HQ1236.V54 1997   320'.082   C97-950031-1

CONTENTS

Acknowledgments

I first began teaching courses about women and politics more that two decades ago. Consequently I have accumulated many debts, since this book has been germinating that long. Many people helped me work out its ideas; others have supported me in my belief that feminist political science was a project both doable and worth doing.

I owe a special debt of gratitude to Carleton University, which has allowed me to pursue this project for most of my career. While not all of my colleagues have understood or valued the project, I have had the support of many others, which made its completion possible. In particular, I wish to thank Dennis Forcese and Rick Clippingdale, who made it possible for me to do my work in the Institute of Canadian Studies; my colleague and mentor Teresa Rakowska Harmstone for her support and advice; the late Pauline Jewett for her example and support; and my friend and departmental chair Vince Wilson for his support and for thinking up the title.

I have also been blessed with many generations of wonderful students, some of whom have gone on to play a role in creating feminist political science themselves. I wish to acknowledge the contribution made to my learning by Christine Appelle, Michèline Arseneau, Isa Bakker, Janine Brodie, Cheryl Collier, Mary Lynn Doonan, Jessie Gibbs, Kiera Ladner, Lisa Marshall, Marcella Munro, Elissar Sarouh, Jay Smith, Fraser Valentine, Lisa Young and Lisa Woodward.

I have also been fortunate to be associated in both mainstream and feminist politics with many women from whom I learned a great deal, although in a less academic way. I wish to acknowledge as political mentors my friend Doris Anderson, Rosemary Brown, Marion Dewar, Evelyn Gigantes and Audrey McLaughlin. Also in terms of practical politics, I wish to acknowledge what I learned from the women of the National Action Committee on the Status of Women (NAC) in the five years I served as their parliamentarian.

I have also had the support and intellectual encouragement of a number of generous colleagues in the emerging field of feminist political science. In particular I wish to acknowledge the teachings and friendship of Mary O'Brien, Carolyn Andrew, Angela Miles, Michèline de Sève, Thelma McCormack, Jane Arscott and especially Pauline Rankin. I also owe my friend and colleague Vanaja Dhruvarajan a great debt for help in learning what 'difference' and racism really means. I also wish to acknowledge those women who have struggled through the "chilly climate" controversies at universities across the country, and the men who supported them. I hope the insights of this book will make political science an easier place for women to work in, and I want to recognize the courage of those students and faculty who have attempted to make it so.

A project that has taken over two decades has needed funding. My thanks to Sue Findlay, then of the Secretary of State Women's Programme, who funded my initial research in the 1970s. For the last six years, I have enjoyed a grant from the Social Science and Humanities Research Council, which I wish to thank for its confidence in me. Tangible support has taken other forms as well. I wish to thank Gaby Levesque for her word processing when my own machine failed me. Special thanks to my publisher Errol Sharpe who persuaded me that "now's the time" for this book to see the light of day, and to Lee d'Anjou whose editorial skills made this a much better book.

Finally, my husband and friend Keith Johnson has supported this and every other project I have undertaken in our twenty-five years of marriage. He has my eternal thanks and love. The book is dedicated to my mother Patricia Pryor, who has been both my inspiration and the burr under my saddle my whole life long.

Woolf House, Portland-On-Rideau, March 1997

Chapter 1

REINVENTING POLITICAL
SCIENCE: A FEMINIST APPROACH

In January 1988, when the Supreme Court struck down Canada's restrictive abortion law, effectively decriminalizing abortion throughout the country, a student in my course on women and politics told me that, for the very first time, she understood that the state could influence her life in a significant and intimate way. A male colleague, discussing the decision with me the same day, argued that the decision was unfair because Madam Justice Bertha Wilson, a woman, had written the opinion for the court. To him, the court's decision-making had been tainted because a woman had taken part. He assumed Wilson could not be objective because she could not be detached from the circumstance of at least potentially having experienced an unwanted pregnancy.

Each of these observations tell us something important about the official politics of the state and how political science has shaped citizens' views of those who participate in political decision-making. My student's observation reflected the alienation many women feel from institutions such as the courts, the bureaucracy, the military and even parliament—institutions that for centuries have been dominated by allegedly objective male persons. She was fiercely interested in what she called women's politics; that is, the activities of women who were trying to achieve change. But with few women involved in decision-making within the institutions of the state, she had found it hard to see how they affected women.

Chilly climate: The effect on the working and learning environment for those excluded from an activity or discipline, when the activities and values of a dominant group are portrayed as the norm in the activity or theories of the discipline. Previously excluded groups experience this effect long after they are allowed to enter a field.

My colleague's response illustrated the intellectual **chilly climate** political science often presents to women and other students who, because of their race, poverty, sexual orientation or disability, don't resemble the discipline's image of the 'political man'.[1] His view was that activities such as judging must involve 'rational' thinking supposedly untainted by self-interest. This idea let him conceptualize the men, mainly white, who usually made such decisions as if they had no self-interest or had special powers to rise above it. Men, who created and ran the political institutions in question while women were excluded from participating by both law and custom, not surprisingly made male attributes and values the norm, presuming them to be universal or even natural. Women's characteristics, values and activities just don't fit, as many women discover when they try to find space for themselves and their interests in political science. Racial minorities and people marginalized because of poverty, disability or sexual orientation face similar exclusions.

In this book, I explore why political science has been particularly resistant to feminist approaches that try to include women's political activities in the discipline's course of study. I also consider some of the reasons why most strains of feminism have great difficulty accepting the validity of the politics of the state.[2] My main purpose, however, is to provide an alternate vision of political science for students who want to make space for themselves and the political activities they want to study.

Thus, this book presents a new framework within which a feminist account of politics is being developed. I call it a *feminist political science* because this framework deliberately builds bridges between political science and feminism, allowing for a women-centred analysis of both **official** and **informal politics**. The framework incorporates radical redefinitions of politics that can open up space for us to study **identity politics,** oppression, exploitation and the struggles against sexism, racism, ablism and homophobia, as well as women's attempts to influence state decision-making by conventional means. In brief, the book is a survival guide for women and other students currently faced with trying to reinvent political science on their own. (I discuss in more detail below how it can be used.)

> What a feminist political science must do is to invent a new vocabulary of politics so that it can express the specific and different ways in which women have wielded power, been in authority, practised citizenship and understood freedom. Kathleen Jones, 1994

In this introduction, I have three objectives. First, I want to introduce you to the basic ideas that led me and others to conclude that political science needs to be reinvented through a major infusion of insights that come from viewing politics and government from a *women-centred perspective.* Women are still much less likely than men to be ministers, judges, generals or senior bureaucrats (see Exhibit 1). They are more likely to be the ruled than the rulers the judged than the judges. A similar situation prevails in the main institutions of *civil society* (see Exhibit 2). This difference has given women a perspective on official politics that comes from the bottom up and the outside in. And although the situation is changing—quite slowly in some countries, more quickly in others—the **paradigm** within which political science works reflects the many centuries when politics and government were male activities.

In this introduction, I briefly outline four reasons why the political science **paradigm** has made its practitioners resistant to feminist insights and women-

Exhibit 1. Power in the Institutions of the Canadian State.

Courts ♂

Cabinet ♂
Prime Minister ♂

Legislature

Senate (appointed) ♂

House of Commons (elected) ♂

Crown corporations

The Bank of Canada ♂
CBC ♂

Coercive branches

Military ♂
Police ♂

Civil service

Decision makers ♂
Clerical ♀

♂ Majority male
♀ Majority female

Exhibit 2.
Power in Canadian Social and Economic Institutions.

Banking, Insurance etc ♂

Media ♂

Unions ♂

Education

Postsecondary ♂
Secondary ♂
Elementary ♂

Professions

Law ♂
Medicine ♂
Nursing ♀

♂ Majority male
♀ Majority female

centred theories. I also explore briefly the reasons why most strains of modern feminism reject the politics of the state. (I discuss these issues in more detail in Chapter 1. My purpose here is to whet your appetite.)

My second objective is to suggest how this book can be used. You will use it differently if you are facing a chilly climate than if you are in a more hospitable environment. Its uses will also differ depending on whether you are in women's studies or political science courses and on your particular interests.

> Paradigm: A set of concepts, theories and assumptions accepted and widely used by scholars in a field; includes assumptions about proper methods, units of measure, theory of knowledge, and so on. Most scientific fields have a single dominant paradigm; in the social science fields, several may compete for dominance.

My third objective is to illustrate how the alternate vision of political science presented here can provide a platform to foster other approaches to reinventing the discipline.

The Need to Reinvent Political Science

Before I was a feminist, I was trained as a political scientist. I became an insider, a member of an intellectual community that shared basic ideas about the nature of politics and how government works. The price of admission to this community was to accept its basic worldview and check my sex at the door.

For some years, I was unaware of the second requirement (there were very few women in political science three decades ago). The field presented its subject matter as universal: therefore, like race, disability and sexual orientation, sex and gender were considered irrelevant to the study of politics and government. The assumption that the discipline's theories and concepts are also gender-neutral and apply equally to both sexes was never challenged, not even by the few women working in the field. In reality, these concepts are profoundly gendered and rarely apply to women.

It strikes me now as inconceivable, but it wasn't until after I received the PhD, which certified me as an 'expert' in political science, that I found out much of what I had learned didn't apply to me because of my sex. I realized that the ancient democracy of Athens, so revered by my colleagues in political theory, would have excluded me because of my sex. I discovered that until this century I would have been denied the right to be educated, own property, serve on juries, vote, sit in the legislature or be a judge in most countries of the world. I also learned (but was never

> What feminists are confronted with is not a state that represents 'men's interests' as against women's, but a government conducted as if men's interests are the only ones that exist.
> R. Pringle and S. Watson, 1992

taught) that women had struggled and some had died for the simple right to vote. Because the community of which I had become part saw no connection between my sex and the great issues of politics, I simply hadn't noticed the fact of my exclusion or sought to uncover the political history of my sex. To be a political scientist, I had had to become an abstract, detached person who didn't notice the contradictions between my own experience and the received wisdom of my discipline. It took me almost as many years to unlearn these assumptions as it had to learn them.

What's Wrong with Political Science?

I have written elsewhere about my personal journey of unlearning many of the assumptions of the political science community as I worked to develop a feminist understanding of politics based on women's political activism and women's struggles for equality (Vickers 1983, 19829a, 1993). What I learned in that journey is that four basic characteristics of the political science paradigm make it difficult to focus on women within it.

1. The paradigm focuses on the official politics of the state and on politics between states. It pays little attention to any other form of political activity, including that which occurs in local communities or institutions outside of the state where most women do most of their politics. Women remain rooted in their home locale more than men because the division of labour between the sexes in *patriarchal* societies assigns women most of the responsibility for child care and family and community maintenance. Most women are thus not as available as men to move to the central locations where state institutions are commonly placed.[3] Nor do they have as much disposable time as men who are generally freer of these responsibilities.

2. The paradigm accepts as natural a split between *the public and private spheres,* which derives from the past exclusion of women (and slaves or servants) from the public sphere, which was maintained by law and custom. But it was also ultimately maintained by force, as becomes evident when women are still punished, often by rape or diminished status, for entering into exclusively male space, occupations or fields. Although the exclusion of women has been challenged, they continue to be subordinated in the public sphere.

3. The paradigm defines as political only activities that take place within the public sphere and excludes activities that take place in the domestic sphere and in civil society, considering them non-political. This line is often confused, however. For example, what is usually called *private enterprise* occurs in space that is not domestic and that is conventionally understood as public. The distinction between *private* and *domestic* is especially unclear, as is the scope of **civil society.** Until the challenge of feminism in the 1960s and 1970s, power relationships within families were usually

12

considered private within liberal societies, although the development of the **welfare state** involved the state in extensive regulation of some aspects of family life. **Sexual politics** are still excluded from political science's understanding of the political, and women-centred analysis of public policy is still resisted.

4. The paradigm assumes that the basic structures and processes of state politics are sex- and gender-neutral as well as race- and class-neutral. It further assumes that its own concepts, theories and methods are also neutral; that is, it understands itself as a science working with universally applicable concepts and units of measurement and with testable theories capable of validation.

We could find exceptions to each of these characteristics, just as there were exceptions to the centuries-long exclusion of women and other members of enslaved, oppressed or dominated groups from government and the politics of the state. Nonetheless, as a general account of the theories, concepts and assumptions that shape political science, the list is accurate.

The strong biases that exist within political science should not surprise us. As I describe in detail in Chapter 2, the roots of the discipline in the western tradition go back almost 2500 years to political theorists such as Plato and Aristotle. Modern states, composed of specialized structures for performing the tasks of governing, adjudicating and administering a society so that internal conflict is managed and minimized, are the result of an historical development that goes back centuries earlier. And all states of which scholars have knowledge have been patriarchal in character. That is, as the historical work of Lerner (1986) and others explains, the exclusion of women from participation in state institutions and activities and the suppression of conflict between the sexes were part of the long process of making the state form stable. Giving men control over the women, children, servants and slaves in each household and **legitimizing** that control in the laws of states produced forms of government and politics from which the assumptions of the paradigm were derived. The powerful concept of **patriarchy,** developed by feminists as the basis of their challenge to male rule sanctioned by the state and legitimized by law, religion and custom,

> Patriarchy: As the term is used in feminist political science, is political system characterized by institutionalized male dominance, in which men are dominant in all state institutions and favoured by the balance of power in other important social institutions. Patriarchy is historical; that is, we know when and how it was invented. It takes different forms over time and place. All known historical states have been patriarchal in form; some non-state political systems, such as village republics, have not, however.

> Legitimize: To justify; to make acceptable and in accordance with a prevailing set of rules.

refers to a form of state that has existed for more than ten thousand years.

Since all known states show patriarchal characteristics, it is clear that all states are masculine to a greater or lesser degree. The question that provokes debate among feminists is whether the state form is essentially and inevitably patriarchal in nature or whether it can be reconstituted to achieve women's goals.

To develop a framework within which a feminist account can develop space for women's understandings of politics, the patriarchal assumptions underlying the political science paradigm must be challenged. Some feminists believe that this venture is impossible—that feminist political science is a contradiction in terms. They see states only as oppressors of women and enforcers of patriarchal laws and relationships. They also see political science as a discipline that perpetuates patriarchy, legitimizing oppression in its theories, concepts and methods. As I discuss in detail in Chapter 2, this view derives primarily from **radical/cultural feminism,** which associates the state and formal politics with maleness and rejects out of hand the private/public split. Some **left-wing feminists** argue that a feminist approach to conventional politics in existing states is unnecessary since they believe only revolutionary change could truly liberate women. Both these feminisms (explored in more detail in Chapter 2) see women's virtual exclusion from existing political systems as all the more reason for them to seek radical and fundamental change that would include the end of politics.[4]

Not all feminists, however, view states as inevitable oppressors. Indeed, in countries such as Norway, Sweden, Finland, Australia and New Zealand, many feminists see state institutions as potential allies that women can mobilize to help them achieve the changes they want and need. Some feminists in Canada also take this view, with most franco-Quebec feminists believing it quite strongly about the Quebec state.

The dominance of US, UK and French theories within western feminism has, however, until very recently inhibited the development of feminist approaches to politics and political science because women's movements in these countries have little influence on the state (Sawer 1994). Women who have faced hostility from their government for decades not surprisingly focus on the oppressive character of the state in their theories.

By contrast, women who have succeeded in achieving some desired policy and programs or changes in the nature of politics or government are more likely to believe that women can usefully take part in politics. Thus they are more prepared to engage in the official politics of the state while they retain the belief that the politics practised outside of the official sphere also needs to be studied and understood. Women in some countries choose to find space for themselves and their concerns mainly within the official politics of parties and legislatures. For others, the nature of their political system suggests other choices, such as developing a feminist presence in the bureaucracy, as has occurred in Australia and New Zealand. Canadian women have developed a mixed approach that includes the activism of strong women's movements, efforts to get more women into senior decision-making positions, the development of status-of-women machinery within governments and efforts to achieve constitutional protection.

Critiques of political science and its paradigm have developed out of these varied feminist experiences with politics. Building on the insights of women active in both conventional politics and oppositional movements, feminists working on the margins of political science have begun to develop a new framework within which to view politics. Recall that until very recently women were as scarce in political science as in parliament, the courts or the senior bureaucracy. While I was studying for my first degree in political science in the early 1960s, for example, Grace McInnes was the only woman member in the Canadian House of Commons. I was almost as lonely as one of three women students in my political science program. Now, by contrast, women equal men in most undergraduate political science programs, and the numbers are approaching equality in graduate courses as well.[5] Numbers of women in the key institutions of the state have also grown.

The result of these changes in a relatively short period of time has produced a disjuncture between the political environment as students experience it and the paradigm within which most political scientists work. It is this disjuncture and controversy over efforts to change it that have produced the chilly climate experienced by some women in the field. It would be unrealistic to expect changes to occur easily or without conflict, however, since in political science the ideas being challenged are both central to the paradigm and hallowed by long-standing tradition. Nor have the facts that the paradigm explains changed significantly. Men, mainly white men, still dominate the institutions in which major decisions are made, just as they still dominate political science as a discipline. Despite some change, neither women nor other marginalized groups are yet a powerful enough presence to dislodge long-sanctioned assumptions or relationships.

It is my hope that outlining a theoretical framework on which a feminist political science can be built can help students develop an understanding of politics from a woman-centred perspective. Other visions of political science are also needed, however, and reinventing political science will be a long task. It will also be a collective task to which many women (and men) can contribute.

What Is Different about a Feminist Vision of Political Science?

For the past decade, women in many counties, largely in isolation from one another, have been thinking about ways to view politics from a women-centred perspective. In this book, I make their ideas available to political science and women's studies students. My hope is to promote the integration of some of these ideas into the mainstream discipline.

The challenge is considerable. As I've already begun to explain, women-centred ways of understanding politics don't fit easily within the discipline's existing paradigm. Feminist scholarship, which insists that treating women equally doesn't always mean treating them the same as men, isn't easily incorporated into a discipline that continues to believe in a universal 'rational' man, driven by self-interest, as the basis of all politics.

Many of the women attempting to develop a feminist understanding of politics were often forced to work outside of the discipline. In Canada, for example, "founding mothers" such as Mary O'Brien and Angela Miles found that their work wasn't considered political science and had to accept employment in other fields. Much of the early work of this group was presented first at the meetings of women's studies groups and, since conventional political science journals would not print it, much of it was published in small feminist journals or newsletters. Some of the research was done for government agencies, but this research could be (and was) simply shelved by government. In some cases, research findings were reportedly even changed in the public document from the author's original work (Burt 1995).[6] Few other sources of funding for research concerning women's politics existed until very recently. Nonetheless, the field has emerged despite these barriers.

The framework I present challenges many of the assumptions and methodological practices underlying the current disciplinary paradigm. It rejects the idea that politics is only about activities within or directed to the institutions of states. Instead, it reconceptualizes what is political to reflect insights drawn from the centuries-old struggles of women and others against oppression, domination and marginalization.

Thus, in my definition of **politics**, activity is political if it involves collective efforts to change power relationships in society, its communities or its institutions—or to prevent change or maintain the status quo.[7] Politics certainly includes the way a country is governed, but it goes further to embrace organized attempts that focus not on the state itself but on social institutions and communities.

> Politics: All activity aimed at changing, maintaining or restoring power relationships in a society, its communities or its institutions; usually involves activity undertaken within a collective or group context.

Examples range from the strike women staged in Iceland, withholding services from both their families and societal institutions, to struggles to establish child-care centres, and to the efforts of anti-war groups such as the Raging Grannies who fought to keep nuclear submarines out of Vancouver harbour. What my definition of political does not include is matters that intrinsically involve only personal relationships, such as the negotiation of household duties between individual partners.[8]

In addition to applying feminist insights to many concepts, theories, assumptions and methods drawn from mainstream/malestream political science, I also critique some feminist assumptions about politics. My purpose is to build conceptual bridges between political science and feminism that allow for a woman-centred analysis of both the formal politics within and between states and the informal politics of women's activism in grassroots groups, movements and local communities. It is not my purpose to use women as a vehicle to prove or disprove any particular theoretical approach. (Both political science and feminism represent worldviews within which a number of theories compete.) Instead I set out a framework with a set of concepts, units of analysis and methodological assumptions that can orient women-centred research coming from different theoretical positions.

It is also my hope that male students who see little space to explore issues of concern to them within the mainstream paradigm will find the book and the framework it develops useful. In developing, in Chapter 3, the methodological assumptions that underpin the framework, I pay particular attention to the importance of **contextualizing** issues so as to highlight the similarities and the differences among women. In particular, I make a case for comparing women's experiences both within and across jurisdictions and locales. My methodological insistence on comparing women with other women suggests the parallel need to compare men's experiences within and across jurisdictions.

This approach challenges the idea of a universal 'political man', always 'rational' and pursuing self-interest in the same way, and opens up space for comparing the impact of such things as race, sexual orientation and disability on differently-located men's political values and activities. For example, such an approach lets us discover that the gender gap often attributed to all populations does not apply to the black population in the US because most black men, like most black women (but unlike most US white men), support state activism and liberal values.

My basic purpose, however, is to develop a framework that allows us to find both the room and the voice to navigate political science and help reinvent it. As at least half of every country and as half of humanity, women should not be considered just another special interest group. Nor should they be ignored or silenced and their interests trivialized or neglected. They are entitled to a tradition within political science that puts women at the centre of analysis instead of at the margin. This need does not, however, preclude the development of other accounts that aim to reinvent political science from a race-centred perspective, for example. Indeed, this book should show the need for such multiple approaches to reinvention.

A Challenge

My main purpose in this text is to provide you with an alternate vision of political science, one that makes space in the mainstream discipline for women and others currently marginalized by such things as racism and homophobia. I also hope to provide you with some thinking tools to guide your analysis of women's politics. By putting not the state but women's political activity, wherever it occurs, at the centre of our inquiry, we can begin to reinvent political science on a new base. This new approach also offers a new vocabulary of politics and a new, broader understanding of what is political.

I am not implying that you should treat the power of the state as illusory or conclude that I believe women should reject involvement in state politics. Quite the contrary. It is because I know the power of the state to be real that I encourage you to decentre and demystify it. And it is because I find persuasive the evidence that women's presence in state institutions as a **critical mass** can reduce the biased nature of their decisions and make them more responsive to women's needs and interests[9] that I encourage you to pursue feminist political science, rather than reject the sphere of politics out of hand as inconsistent with feminism.

When I began this project, which is based largely on the material I have used to teach about women and politics over the past twenty years, I was not sure there existed enough basic work on an alternate paradigm that I could legitimately call feminist political science. Frankly, I had not expected the wealth of new sources that I quickly uncovered as I expanded my analysis beyond the subfields in which I usually teach. In the field of international politics, for example, the explosion of material stimulated by a resurgence of feminist internationalism and supported by UN agencies and feminist non-governmental organizations (NGOs) alike is astonishing. In fact, this book could easily have been three times as long as it is. Since being more exhaustive would have increased the cost three times, I have resisted the impulse. Nonetheless, you should realize that the sources I report on represent only a fraction of the work available as you begin to study politics from a women-centred perspective and, I hope, decide to make a contribution to building feminist political science.

It is clearly possible to practice feminist political science—that is, to undertake political analysis from a women-centred perspective that recognizes the forces that shape and move political systems as well as those that shape and constrain women's lives. By reorienting the framework of analysis, feminists can uncover far more ways in which women participate in politics than they knew about before.

At a number of points in the text, I show that aspects of the discipline's paradigm that marginalize women or render them invisible have a similar effect on racial minorities, aboriginal peoples, people with disabilities and gays and lesbians, to identify only a few of the main groups marginalized or oppressed worldwide. A reinvention of political science that puts women's political activity at the centre of study is not incompatible with reinventions in which race or disability is the focus. But it is no substitute. In the years ahead, more **standpoint analyses** of political phenomena will be developed so that we will be able to identify, for example, aboriginal accounts of politics. I have designed the framework of this book to make you open to such developments.

New frameworks often have short lives; some parts of the scaffolding I have presented to you as feminist political science are more solid and will bear more weight than others. In all areas of political science, however, it is now possible to do useful work within a women-centred framework. If nothing else, this small book proves that fact. If anyone tells you it isn't possible, tell him (or her) that you know better.

The question of whether practising feminist political science is desirable, on the other hand, is hard to answer so simply. Women who critiqued male-dominated political systems were not wrong when they determined that official politics was hostile to them and their interests and needs. Their decision to remain apart from official politics was based on the apparently obvious conclusion that by staying outside women could transform state systems. The lack of results from many decades of women's practical testing of this proposition suggests that it needs to be revised. State politics is simply too powerful and exerts too much sway over women's lives for them to ignore it deliberately. But neither should women abandon their activism outside of official structures. As I show, both approaches are essential.

Challenging the established paradigm of a powerful academic discipline like political science is not for the faint-hearted. Nor is it comforting to realize that other challenges, such as those within left-wing movements, also often prove hostile to the project of feminist political science. Yet everywhere women are struggling to come to terms with the politics of states and striving to make useful political choices. Women can neither abandon politics nor simply be absorbed into male-defined politics as usual. Nor can they afford the luxury of ignoring political science or the surrender of assimilation that renders them unable to speak in their own interests.

Many of the women now doing the research, teaching and writing that constitutes feminist political science are part of a second generation of feminists who struggle to create a space for women within the field. Women have not yet become a critical mass, however, despite impressive growth.

Power, even the surrogate power of advisors and academics, is rarely surrendered or shared easily. Ultimately, the reinvention of political science will depend on the failing power of its paradigm as an explanatory tool. The more apparent it becomes that the paradigm cannot explain many aspects of politics actually experienced by politicians and students of politics alike, the easier the task of reinvention will be. It will also be helped along by less isolated and more collective efforts on the part of those who wish to do the reinventing. This poses an important challenge to us all.

It falls to your generation of students to ensure that feminist political science grows and prospers despite the chilly climate that signals the passing of old ideas. The time is right and women's insights are sorely needed in a political world on the brink of enormous change.

How to Use This Book

How you use the book depends on your circumstances. You can use it on its own as a women-in-politics text or as a supplement to the male-centred readings you

are assigned in most political science courses. It provides you alternate definitions, explanations and ways of understanding methodological issues that you
can use as tools to enrich your experience in mainstream courses and to question,
critique or resist the patriarchal assumptions underlying most political science
writings (and many others).

If your political science instructor has assigned the book, you can assume that
she or he wishes you to explore its challenges to the dominant paradigm. If you
are using it as a subversive text in a chilly climate, however, I recommend that
you form a group with three or four classmates to study together and provide one
another with support. You can use the questions at the end of each chapter in
your support group or suggest them to your instructor or discussion group
leader.

Students in women's studies courses may also find the book useful. For
reasons I explore in Chapter 2, most feminist scholarship is weak on political
analysis. The book can help you understand the nature of both the official
politics of the state and women's politics. You may also find useful the method
of comparing women to women, and the techniques for contextualizing difference so that minority women's concerns in politics are treated seriously. I hope
the book also opens up space within feminist analysis for various perspectives
on political questions. You may also find the discussion questions and readings
helpful.

If your women's studies professor has assigned the book, you can assume that
she or he wants you to explore its challenges to some common assumptions
about politics found in the feminist literature. If politics is absent from your
course, however, you may find it useful and enriching to form a small study
group to discuss the issues the book raises.

Outline of the Book

Whatever your situation, you should be aware that I have constructed this book
so you don't have to read the whole thing (though you may find it useful to do
so).

Generally speaking, the outline is as follows:
- Chapter 2 discusses why the political science paradigm makes women and
  their activities invisible most of the time, why many strands of feminism
  resist conventional politics and whether a feminist political science could
  bridge the two worldviews.
- Chapter 3 outlines a framework for a feminist political science, one that
  includes official politics but also activity in other areas in which women
  often work, including women's movements. This chapter also provides a
  methodological discussion of the importance of both comparing women
  with women and contextualizing to encompass the implications of wom-
  en's differences as well as their similarities.
- Chapter 4 looks in detail at the ways the basic concepts used in political

science must be reinvented in order for us to look at politics from a women-centred perspective. The text here can help you understand political theory from a women-centred perspective. It also provides insights for understanding how to address conventional politics within feminist theories.

- Chapter 5 considers how we can understand and compare women's political activism, agendas and movements in different political systems, including which political strategies work best for women in terms of outcomes. This chapter can provide you with insights to use in a course dealing with a single country or in a comparative politics course.
- Chapter 6 examines what women want out of politics and how we can conceptualize differences among women on issues of public policy, especially between women living in affluent countries and those in poorer countries. It also explores women's activism in the global arena, contrasting it with their exclusion from the conduct of official international politics.

Be aware that each of Chapters 4 through 6 applies to a different part of political science—theory, comparative politics and public policy (including development studies and international politics). Once you've read Chapters 2 and 3, you can move to the chapter most relevant to you.

Aids within the Text

No matter how you are using this book, it offers a variety of aids to help you grapple with the material. At the end of each chapter is a list of readings that further explore the issues raised, and a list of discussion questions that can be used as essay topics. There is also a bibliography, which gives full information on every work cited in the text, and a glossary, which provides definitions of many basic concepts.

Finally, throughout the text, I mark some words and terms in special ways. They are:

- **bold type face** is used to denote terms that are defined in the glossary. Be sure to check these terms. Some may sound familiar, but my definitions may differ from those you have learned in other courses.
- *italic type face* is used to emphasize particular words and phrases and to draw the reader's attention to them.
- words and terms set inside single quotation marks denote terms whose meaning is problematic or controversial.

Further Readings

McCormack, Thelma. 1975. "Toward a Nonsexist Perspective on Social and Political Change." In M. Milman and R.M. Kanter (eds.), *Another Voice*. New York: Doubleday.

Smith, Dorothy. 1978. "A Peculiar Eclipsing: Women's Exclusion from Man's Culture." *Woman's Studies International Quarterly* (4):281–96.

Vickers, Jill, and June Adam. 1977. *But Can You Type? Canadian Universities and the Status of Women.* Toronto: Clarke Irwin.

Questions for Discussion

1. What are the symptoms of a chilly climate in a field or department? Are those symptoms evident in your environment?
2. If you are taking or have taken a political science course, look at the table of contents and index in your textbook. Is there an entry for women? for women's politics? for the women's movement? Are policy issues of particular concern to you being discussed? What about violence against women? abortion? pornography? If these issues are being discussed, are all women being lumped together or are differences among women being explored?
3. If you are taking or have taken a women's studies course, look in the index and table of contents for entries on politics. Is there a discussion of women's efforts to become involved in government and the politics of the state? Is government viewed as an inevitable enemy of women everywhere? Or is it also portrayed as a potential ally for women in some countries?
4. What are the major ways in which the current political science discipline makes it difficult to study politics from a women-centred perspective?
5. Investigate the current female/male representation in your provincial or state legislature, local government and university or college. How has the representation of women in these institutions changed over time? Are women's groups working to increase representation?

Notes

1. See page 21 for an explanation of my special use of single quotation marks and other graphic devices.
2. Within mainstream political science, the terms *politics* and *political* generally refer to the *official* or *formal* activity that occurs within or in relation to state institutions. Feminist political science expands the definitions of *politics* and *political* to also include the many forms of *informal* or *unofficial* political activity.
3. The development of communications technology could eventually reduce this effect by diminishing the impact of space and distance. Before the development of specialized institutions for government and politics, women participated more easily—as, for example in the Igbo village republics in what is now Nigeria.
4. Another reason many feminists have rejected the project of trying to create a feminist political science is their aversion to the methods of science.
5. The proportion of women teaching political science has grown more slowly, however; few departments have women as more than 20 percent of faculty, with most of those at junior ranks.
6. In 1975, the federal government funded the two reports, "A Basic Statistical Mapping of Female Candidacies in Federal and Provincial Politics, 1945–75" and

"Private Lives and Public Responsibilities: Women in Politics in Canada," which formed the basis for my first "Women in Politics" course in 1977. My contract prevented me from publishing the reports, but it is unlikely that any political science journal would have accepted them in 1975 in any event. Sue Findlay, then director of the women's program, was responsible for initiating that research, for which I am most grateful.

7. In other words, my definition of politics includes activities that are aimed at change in which women are heavily involved but that are conducted outside the arenas of formal politics. It does not, however, cover potentially all personal relationships. Thus, although this definition is broader than the definition that is part of the disciplinary paradigm, it is much narrower than the one used by radical/cultural feminists, for whom *all* aspects of *all* relationships are political.

8. Although the action of a group of women who decide to demand wages for housework *is* a political action.

9. Later in the book, I explore the concept of **critical mass**, which is associated with Drude Dahlerup.

Chapter 2

THE FEMINIST CHALLENGE TO POLITICAL SCIENCE AND THE CHALLENGE OF POLITICS FOR FEMINISM

In this chapter, I explore three questions basic to efforts to create a feminist political science. First, I discuss why political science cannot "see" women, especially women acting as **sexed and gendered** people. Several feminist political theorists consider this point in depth. Canadian Mary O'Brien (1981) demonstrates that the separation of women from politics and government had already taken place in the Greek city states of the fifth century B.C. and was **legitimized** by the writings of theorists such as Aristotle. Kathleen Jones concludes that the main consequence of building political science on this ancient split between the private and public realms has been to make "women and their political interests invisible" (1988:12). Australian Carole Pateman argues that when women attempt to be active in politics as sexed and gendered beings, they are by definition excluded from **liberalism's** "central category of the individual" (1988:6).

The political science **paradigm** also incorporates liberalism's original justification of the private/public split. When democratic ideas were eventually added onto liberalism and women were permitted to enter politics as voters, "[c]itizenship was defined as a genderless activity" (Jones 1988:16). Thus, political science can deal with women only if they check their sex at the door and take on the characteristics of political man. Political scientist Sandra Burt concludes, for example, that public policy analysts can see Canadian women only when they claim to be treated the same as men.[1] Because political science and other disciplines adopted the idea of "rational, self-interested man" early on "as the reference point for both policy development and policy studies", she maintains,

> You may not care about politics, but politics cares about you.
>
> Walter Karp, 1988.

political scientists and policy-makers can "see" women only when they move into the public sphere and become like "good men" (Burt 1995:357). In the first part of this chapter, then, I explore the characteristics of the political science

24

paradigm that make women invisible in official politics unless they function as political men.

I then turn to consider why some strands of modern feminism resist engagement with the politics of the state. This trend was evident early on in the work of US radical feminist theorist Kate Millett, who defined sex as a "status category with political implications" but defined politics so broadly that it encompassed "all power structured relationships" (1969:32–33). Declaring that "the personal is political", *radical feminists* urged women to create their own politics out of their lived experience and argued that the only way to transform *patriarchy* was to transform consciousness and culture by withdrawing from mainstream institutions and creating a counterculture with their own separate institutions. This alienation also characterizes the newer *cultural feminism,* which sees the politics of the state as a masculine preserve women should try to dismantle or ignore rather than enter. *Left-wing feminisms* also have created a scholarship with the deconstruction of state politics and

Sex/gender: Sex identifies biological characteristics. They are differently expressed in different places and times. For example, menstruation is a biological characteristic of human females. In circumstances of adequate nutrition, it is a regular occurrence of physically mature women for much of their lives. In times of nutritional inadequacy, however, it may cease or occur infrequently. Moreover, its onset and cessation vary significantly even within the same place and time. How sex is experienced also varies according to such things as class, race and sexual orientation.

Gender describes the social behaviours and roles societies (and groups within them) assign to men and women because of their sex. The characteristics of gender, therefore, also vary across cultures and time, although there are some commonalities. That women bear children is a dimension of sex; that they are assigned responsibility for childrearing is a dimension of gender. My use of the compound term *sex/ gender* indicates that my approach is interactionist; that is, indicates that some aspects of sex are socially constructed, while others are not.

government as its goal. This scholarship built on women's experiences with powerful, hostile states and produced incisive critiques of existing political systems. I explore these critiques, which have limited modern feminism's engagement with conventional politics, but I also contrast them with ideas developed by feminists in less hostile and less powerful states where women have organized with some success to implement feminist goals.

In the final section of the chapter, I consider whether such radically different perspectives on politics can build any useful relationship. The challenge is considerable because feminism seems to threaten political science more than it does other disciplines. One reason may be the great antiquity of the ideas in the political science paradigm, which makes them seem natural and proper to most men who currently hold power. As a team of Scandinavian political scientists concludes:

> "Political science is reinforcing the invisibility of women by keeping the domestic sphere apolitical and at the same time neglecting to see as a problem the absence of women outside the home. Thus the field of political science reaffirms the status quo" (Halsaa, Hernes and Sinkkonen 1985:xvi)

(Turn back to Chapter 1, pages 12–13, if you don't recall the four problematic characteristics of the paradigm. This chapter will refer to them over and over again.)

Only a few years ago, I thought no useful bridge could be built, and I wrote, "It is unlikely that a mature, feminist paradigm will emerge within political science proper in the foreseeable future" (Vickers 1993:155). Although some of my pessimism is still warranted, three things now make me believe that we should try to achieve this difficult task. First, an increasing number of students in political science are demanding changes in the field. While this stance causes more overt conflict and an even chillier climate for some, it also marks an important departure. Further, a *second* generation of feminist political scientists is now actively working to build the approach. Finally, the fundamental changes political systems are undergoing as the world's overwhelmingly male political leaders respond to *globalization* and *economic restructuring* make the task more urgent than ever before.[2] Political science is too central to the forces that maintain patriarchal government to ignore. Critiques are not enough. It is essential to develop a feminist framework that can challenge the paradigm of political science and thus contribute to its reinvention.

Why Can't Political Science See Women?

Academic disciplines shape what their practitioners can "see". Like a hologram in which an image is invisible except when your sight line is exactly right, the mainstream, male-centred paradigm of political science lets people see women only from a very precise vantage point—when they look like men or when the fact that men and women live quite different lives doesn't matter.

Clearly, the paradigm is not accurate. Neither is it current. Nonetheless, most male-led governments are today bent on dismantling much of the **welfare state** as part of their response to **globalization** and **economic restructuring,** based on economic theories that ignore the substance of women's lives (Bakker 1994, 1996). These theories and the political science paradigm ignore the facts that the actual division between private and public is constantly in flux and that most states use laws, programs and entitlements to intervene extensively in families. Thus, our first task is understanding how the political science paradigm makes its users sex- and gender-blind unless the sight line is precisely right.

I begin by discussing what role a paradigm plays. Next I examine the basic problems with the political science paradigm, and then I consider why it so resists feminism.

The Paradigm: Some History

Within the intellectual division of labour of the twentieth-century bureaucratic university, disciplines are relatively self-contained, autonomous units, shaped primarily by their research enterprises. The development of the modern discipline of political science is interesting—and telling.

The process of fragmenting knowledge, especially research, into disciplines, each with its own turf, began in the sciences in the sixteenth century. Carving the social sciences out of the humanities was a much more recent phenomenon, starting in the nineteenth century, and political science in its current form developed even later, after the Second World War.

Of course, many approaches to the study of government and politics have, appeared over the centuries. Consider theorists as widely separated in time and philosophy as Aristotle, Thomas Aquinas, Niccolo Machiavelli, Thomas Hobbes, John Locke and John Stuart Mill. But the modern focus of political science first took shape in the United States in the 1950s.[3]

What made this new incarnation of the field different was that it aspired to create a study of politics based on scientific principles that could lay claim to the mantle of the natural sciences. Its adherents believed that, like their colleagues in the physical sciences, they could make authoritative statements for which they could claim proof and universal validity. In particular, they were eager to prove that democracy and free-market capitalism were superior to communism and state planning, which characterized the United States' superpower competitor, the Soviet Union. They were also eager to prove that 'third world' or 'underdeveloped' countries were poor because they had not yet 'modernized' or 'developed',[4] not because they

> Americans respect technology and science; political scientists envy authority that can be based on experiment not argument. Harold Lasswell, cited in Crick 1959

were exploited by imperialist or neo-imperialist capitalist powers (as the communists argued while competing for influence with countries around the world).

The new political science took its efforts to be scientific very seriously, relying heavily on quantitative techniques, including statistical analysis and mathematical modelling. This attempt at scientific rigour and 'objectivity' allowed political scientists to compete successfully for research grants and become advisors to governments and corporations, and they were eager to be viewed as experts who offered evidence and proof, not opinions. Debates about the morality of public policies were left to philosophers and citizens.

27

Not surprisingly, when political scientists focused on state-centred activity, elections, public opinion and other things that could be studied quantitatively, the discipline's frame of reference and definition of politics became increasingly narrow. Political activities not focused on the state and even those geared to the local level of government were ignored or left to other disciplines to study. Although earlier studies of politics had left only limited space for studying women, the creation of a discipline self-consciously imitating the natural sciences reduced that space further, since few women were in positions of power and the paradigm dictated that what can't be counted can't be seen.

This aspiring scientific discipline naturalized observations about state-focused politics, assuming it had a universal form. In essence, US scholars studied their own environment and assumed it was (or ought to be) a worldwide norm. For example, looking at US women's political activity in the 1950s, they constructed theories that purported to explain why women were 'naturally' apolitical or apathetic. These observations, based on the US political system with its low rates of citizen participation and on an atypical historical period, were then assumed to apply elsewhere.

The general export of the "American science of politics" was part of the United States' cultural dominance after the Second World War. By the 1970s, the new paradigm, including its assumptions about women, was being taught in most Canadian universities. In schools throughout the 'first world', in fact, this new, US-based political science became an influential force, often transforming small departments that had studied government and political thought into larger departments with funded research and graduate programs (although as discussed later, there were also scholarly movements which resisted this export).

The Importance of a Paradigm

One of the keys to the success of the postwar reinvention of the discipline was its acceptance of a division of labour that significantly narrowed its focus (even though it still considered itself the "master science" because of its antiquity and breadth). Such divisions of labour fragment the natural and social sciences so that the practitioners of each discipline view the world through a different lens, using different concepts and theories and different units of analysis. This method of **analysis** involves breaking things into parts for detailed and controlled study. The academics who inhabit the various intellectual compartments view the world differently, often ignoring knowledge from other disciplines and even understanding little of their specialized language or jargon. Each discipline, then, is a more or less self-contained **cognitive com-**

Cognitive community: A group of people who interact with one another through a common set of ideas about their subject matter. They almost literally "see" their fragment of the world through the same intellectual eyes. Each new generation is socialized early into the community's worldview so that it seems natural.

28

munity (Douglas 1986).

Although agreement on the content of a discipline's paradigm is rarely logically rigorous, it is not just a self-sustaining illusion. Its assumptions bear some reasonable resemblance to the commonly observed field of activity its theories claim to explain. Most members of the community learn the discipline's assumptions, basic ideas and methods almost unconsciously when they are students. Unless the picture portrayed by the paradigm significantly conflicts with the real world as students experience it, they are unlikely to question it.

It is thus difficult for students of political science to challenge effectively the paradigm within which they are being educated. Few students have enough experience in formal politics to challenge the unspoken assumptions that are part of what they are being taught. In fact, few professors communicating the ideas of the discipline to students are conscious of all of the assumptions of the paradigm or its implications. For this reason, efforts to critique elements of the paradigm from a women-centred perspective may provoke genuine incomprehension. As a supportive male colleague said to me recently, "A lot of men just don't get it". Obviously, those of us who seek change have a responsibility to make clear what it is about the discipline's ideas and methods that suppresses or distorts women-centred knowledge. It is also our challenge to begin to construct alternate ways of understanding politics in which women as sexed and gendered people do not disappear.

The Paradigm Today

Even without the feminist challenge, the paradigm of mainstream political science would now be under considerable stress because of major changes in politics in recent years. The modern discipline was constructed at the beginning of the cold war era of ideological conflict between the United States as the champion of democracy and free-market capitalism and the Soviet Union as the champion of communism and state planning. The collapse of the Soviet empire has shaken its moorings. The resurgence of nationalisms, the revival of religious fundamentalism around the world and the democratic transformation of South Africa are also events that have changed the political world radically but that political science neither predicted nor could explain. In a single year, much of the discipline's basic terminology became obsolete. And as globalization and economic restructuring proceed, political units and structures that transcend the state are becoming increasingly important. In the slogan "think globally, act locally", citizen activists construct a new picture of politics as state governments find themselves increasingly limited in what they actually can do to achieve (or prevent) change in many crucial areas from the environment to the economy.

The increased citizen activism in many states is linked to a decline in the trust citizens place in politicians or political institutions. Race, sex/gender and ethnicity are important in the organization of that activism, but the discipline's paradigm offers little insight into the new phenomenon of **identity politics.**

Even the discipline's methodological premises are being challenged as critics question whether a *science* of politics that aims at universal explanations is possible, let alone desirable.

The Paradigm Close Up: Basic Assumptions and Methods

Clearly, the political science paradigm fails women. We owe its adherents and ourselves, however, somewhat more specificity about *why* and *how* it fails. In this section, I examine two of the central problems of the paradigm. Along the way, I describe how some traditions that oppose the mainstream also fail women. Because they accept some of the paradigm's basic assumptions, they are only slightly more able to generate women-centred understandings of political life.

Patriarchal Political Systems

From a women-centred perspective, the central problem with the political science paradigm is that it fails to recognize the fact that all state-based political systems are **patriarchal**—that is, in no country in the world are women equal participants in the institutions of the state or equal beneficiaries in its distribution of power or in the norms and values sanctioned in law and enforced by those institutions.

The perplexing question is how the discipline can proceed as if the exclusion or marginalization of more than half the citizens of every otherwise democratic country is little more than a minor flaw in an otherwise splendid (or at least acceptable) political system. If we can understand how the paradigm induces such profound blindness in its practitioners, we can pinpoint key issues a feminist political science must address to reinvent the master science.

> Women are poorly represented in the ranks of power, policy and decision-making. Women make up less than five percent of the world's heads of state, heads of major corporations and top positions in international organizations. Women are not just behind in political and managerial equity, they are a long way behind. United Nations, 1991

Look at Exhibits 1 and 2 in Chapter 1. They illustrate the profound point mainstream political science ignores: men hold power; women do not. Nowhere do women constitute a majority of power-holders in the key institutions of the world's political and economic systems (although women serve as heads of state—as presidents or prime ministers—in a few countries and lead a few business corporations, schools and other institutions).

The central reason political science accepts women's exclusion from or marginalization in government and the politics of the state as almost natural is that its paradigm has embedded in it the centuries-old conception that women should be limited to the private sphere and excluded from the public one because they lack the independent rationality believed to be needed for political decision-making. This idea was challenged by subsequent theories and by women's activism, which gained them the right to vote. But when women were admitted to citizenship it was on the same basis as men, not as *sexed and gendered women*.[5] Most women's lives differ from most men's, however, making it possible for only a few privileged women to gain political power. Because women have had

> The major concepts of Western political thought are built on the idea that the public is fundamentally distinct from the private and personal. This . . . shapes the analytic tools of traditional political science. Kathleen Jones, 1994

to act like political men to participate in political decision-making, their presence has effected little change in how political systems work. And although women are by far the largest group of people excluded this way (Karl 1995:5), political science is little interested in the phenomenon that it can explain only with theories of women's disinterest or their 'deviance' from male norms.

Of course, most men were also excluded from political decision-making throughout most of history, yet the identification of political rule and authority with maleness has been so long-standing and endemic as to seem almost natural. Carole Pateman concludes:

> [p]olitical theory is so thoroughly patriarchal that one aspect of its origins lies outside of the analytic reach of most theorists . . . [that is that] the 'individual', 'civil society' and 'the public' have been constituted as patriarchal categories in opposition to womanly nature and the 'private' sphere (1989:34).

When women finally won the vote and could legally take part in the politics of the state,[6] the discipline did not rework the fundamental concepts of its theories to explore, much less resolve, the profound contradictions between institutions that had served male interests for many centuries and the presence of new female citizens.

Moreover, women often made their claim to citizenship on grounds of strict equality; that is, they argued that they wanted to be treated just the same as men. Indeed, in some countries, the dominant strains of feminism required women to flee femininity and reject motherhood and domesticity so that they could actually be more like men.

It has taken women some time to recognize that being treated *equally* need not mean being treated *exactly the same* as men. We have also been slow to recognize that women who live sexed and gendered lives in the private realm cannot easily live unisex political lives. Nor do many women wish to behave like

31

men in politics, since the major reasons why women engage in political activity reflect their experiences of living as women. Nothing in the political science paradigm, however, helps us understand the behaviour of political 'woman'.

Some Opposing Traditions

Feminist political theorists have needed several decades to unravel the many patriarchal assumptions embedded in the mainstream paradigm of political science. To the surprise of some people, many of these assumptions are also buried in the discipline's oppositional traditions.

Political philosophy is one tradition that operates within the field more or less in opposition to the "American science of politics". Feminist political theorists now demonstrate that this tradition shares the paradigm's underlying assumptions about the private/public split and the maleness of authority, assumptions that stem from Greek, Hebrew, Christian, conservative and liberal political thought (O'Brien 1981; Pateman 1988).

The other main oppositional tradition within the field is inspired by *Marxism*. This left-wing tradition critiques many aspects of the political science paradigm and the liberalism that heavily influences it. But, as many feminist political theorists demonstrate, most aspects of the mainstream paradigm that effectively limit the ability to see women are also embedded in left-wing political thought and practice (for a survey of the extensive literature on this point, see Bryson 1992). In particular, feminist scholars point to Marxism's acceptance of the division of labour between the sexes as natural rather than man-made and its idea that the reproductive and domestic labour women perform has value only when performed outside the family. Many women active in left political movements argue that societies built on left-wing ideas also replicate patriarchal power relationships and that left-wing movements are as sexist as other male-dominated movements. Some have developed the idea of "the struggle within the struggle" to describe their need to fight against patriarchal ideas and practices within movements designed to achieve their **liberation.**

> [M]any *companeros*, who are revolutionaries and good *companeros*, never lose the feeling that their views are better than those of any woman in charge of them. Rigoberta Menchu, cited in Burgos-Debray 1984

What basic ideas do the political science paradigm and its oppositional traditions hold in common about women and politics? First, they accept the idea that the public realm is fundamentally different from the private, personal or domestic realm. Second, they believe that women's marginalization in the public realm reflects their roles as actual or potential reproducers. While many conservatives operating within the political theory tradition believe that absence is appropriate, mainstream political scientists and left-wing scholars share the more modern view that women can overcome their "disadvantage" by entering the public realm and becoming more like men.

Scholars influenced by Marxism attribute women's "disadvantage" explicitly to their privatization in the home performing child care and domestic work. They recommend those tasks be socialized (performed collectively by society), but they do not question why women not men or both women and men are assigned such work in all known societies and are still expected to perform it when it is socialized.

Mainstream political scientists basically ignore questions about the division of societies into private and public spheres. They simply cannot understand many of women's demands on political systems, such as the demand for birth control or protection at work from sexual harassment, because the framework treats individuals as interchangeable—and these are not the kinds of demands made by men.

Political science also assumes that individuals are interchangeable in that they operate on the basis of *rationality* and *self-interest,*[7] which have been defined by men out of male experience but are assumed to be transferable to women. When women act in sexed and gendered ways, the discipline cannot see them; indeed, they are usually considered to be acting inappropriately.

The Locus of Political Activity

A second basic problem in trying to see women through the lens of the political science paradigm is its almost exclusive focus on **politics** within institutions of the state or between states. Although mainstream political scientists have a variety of definitions of politics, in practice few study community-level movement activism or other activities through which women try to achieve or resist change. The left-wing tradition takes a somewhat broader view, including in its framework economic relationships in which women appear as workers and consumers.

Much of women's political activism, however, is found in three other arenas. First, women are active in achieving and resisting change, which affects their lives collectively within the institutions of civil society: for example, fighting for pay equity, organizing against sexual harassment, demanding the right to become priests and creating women-centred cultural institutions (from newspapers to women's studies programs). Second, women are active in mixed-sex movements focusing on change. Peace movements, environmental groups, community-development organizations, gay and lesbian rights and disability rights movements all involve women as activists and sometimes as leaders; so do similar groups and movements opposing change. Finally, women have created autonomous women's organizations and movements, some traditional with decades of history behind them, others are more recent and often more radical.[8]

Women's political activism in such arenas is extensive and increasingly well documented, which makes political science's neglect of these activities a sign of the paradigm's gender-blindness. Expanding the focus to include economic relationships as the left-wing frameworks do is useful, but they cast the net too narrowly and accept too many male-centred assumptions about politics. What is needed is a framework that incorporates the arenas where women's political activism is evident.

Gender-Neutral Actors?

A third problem with mainstream political science (and its two oppositional traditions) is that the basic images of figures such as leader, judge and citizen embedded in it are all infused with implicit male content. As a consequence, key concepts such as **power** and **authority** are implicitly male.

The abstract concept of 'political man' is assumed to be unbiased. Like many of the other concepts and theories that are part of the paradigm, however, the abstract political person is *not* sex- or gender-neutral. The assumption is, for example, that both citizens and decision-makers use a 'rational' calculus that emphasizes the importance of efficiency. This supposedly neutral concept is actually infused with the characteristics of male behaviour to which few women can aspire unless they become like men.

Rather than acting out of 'rational' or 'self-interested' relationships, most women are engaged more in **altruistic** relationships with their children, families and communities. Women are expected, and indeed trained, to act in self-sacrificing *not self-interested* ways, especially in their relationships with their children. Thus, in the terms of the paradigm, women cannot be 'rational' citizens and also 'good' mothers, partners and community members. Yet to many women, the values of empathy, compassion and altruism are as important in political decision-making as the pursuit of self-interest and efficiency. A study of Canadians, for example, finds that women conceive the ideal democratic citizen as caring for others, sharing and offering friendship, while men stress the need for a citizen to act rationally to "really make the vote count" (Burt 1988:56–57).

Altruism: Unselfish behaviour in which the self-interest of the actor is overruled by the needs of the person acted for.

Politicians and the Common Good

Political science derives the idea that the structures and processes of state politics are neutral from the liberal ideology that has shaped western thinking from the seventeenth century to the present.[9] It is also a basic idea of the paradigm that those who hold decision-making power within the state use it 'for the common good' or 'in the public interest'.

In this framework, feminist demands for more women in decision-making roles seem unnecessary or inappropriate. The example of anti-feminist women leaders, such as Margaret Thatcher, is used to advance the argument that women behave no differently than men in decision-making positions, so having more women in such roles would make no difference.[10] These ideas have been powerful barriers to women's analysis of the actual consequences of their exclusion from positions of political power and influence.

Testing the idea that male decision-makers act 'in the public interest' or 'for the common good' and that women decision-makers make no difference has become an important task of the newly emerging feminist political science. I detail some findings in later chapters. Here I note just three, to whet your interest.

1) When the UN's Human Development Index (HDI)[11] is adjusted for gender disparity, the HDIs for countries with larger proportions of women in their governments improve while those for countries with smaller proportions fall. For example, the rank of the HDIs for Sweden and Denmark, each with women comprising more than 30 percent of its government, goes from 5 to 1 and 16 to 7 respectively. But Canada, with fewer than 20 percent of decision-making positions in most legislatures filled by women falls from number 2 to 11 and Japan, with a government of fewer than 5 percent women goes from 1 to 17 (UNDP 1993:16).

2) In the US, even women legislators who do not consider themselves to be feminist are more likely than male legislators to support the introduction and retention of state programs and entitlements of benefit to women (Susan Carroll 1984).

3) Men's and women's levels of dependence on state entitlements and state employment differ significantly in most countries.[12] Where more women play decision-making roles in state institutions, the interest of most women in retaining an expanded welfare state is more easily defended.

In short, the intuition that having a significant number of women in a decision-making body makes that body more able to understand their concerns is confirmed in a preliminary way. As Linda Trimble, an Albertan feminist political scientist, argues, the characteristics of decision-makers matter if for no reason other than that the critiques of even "a few good women" can dispel the myth of the neutrality of state institutions and processes and present women-centred views on matters of public policy (1993). No magic charm makes institutions run by men into the neutral bodies assumed in liberal thought and the political science paradigm. Women legislators are more likely to respond to women's interests and needs (although they are also influenced by such things as their own class interests and racism).

Conclusions About the Paradigm

Given the problems just described (and others), feminist political theorists conclude that the political science paradigm has embedded in it assumptions about the nature of the public sphere and ideas that are used to try to legitimize women's exclusion from it. They also show the great influence of liberal thought in the paradigm.

Liberalism not only assumes the positive value of the *private/public split,* it also draws a sharp line between the institutions of the state and those of **civil society.** Because liberalism values freedom, it also emphasizes the importance of government not interfering in economic, religious and cultural institutions. Most early liberal thinkers argued for a strict hands-off policy summed up in practices such as the separation between church and state in the US constitution and the freedom of the press from government censorship.

Early liberals wanted government to be a minimalist affair with representatives acting as agents for the small class of men who enjoyed the right of political participation. A more positive concept of freedom did not emerge until the nineteenth century, when the mass of people in many countries began to demand greater equality under the influence of democratic ideas.

In brief, the negative concept of 'freedom from interference' was the freedom valued by affluent men who had little need to depend on anyone else. They wanted the state to enforce contracts and protect them and their property from external threats and internal conflicts. The positive concept of 'freedom to', as in to be an equal citizen, was the value of less powerful men and of women who sought to somewhat level the playing field by using the state—the collective power of society—to provide education and public health services.

In the Nordic countries, the ideal of equality emerged as more important than the value of freedom, supporting a much more activist state or social democracy. During the twentieth century, especially after the Second World War, however, both the **liberal democracies** and the **social democracies,** developed activist or welfare states. The push for suffrage for women and their demands on their states as citizens shaped this development. Today, however, throughout the affluent world, women are faced with efforts to contract these welfare states.

In brief, the political science paradigm contains within it a mix of ideas: some drawn from Greek and Christian thought, some from liberal thought about politics and some from democratic thought. The paradigm does not deal with the conflicts among these ideas, especially conflicts between the liberal ideas about freedom and the democratic ideas about equality. For example, the conflict that arises when your freedom (to be a macho husband, for example) deprives me of my right to equality is not resolved. Another example: the state is seen as a neutral set of institutions, and the institutions of civil society, especially the churches and the media, are supposed to be free of government direction; yet under the welfare state, institutions of civil society, such as the economic market, have been regulated, although the paradigm assumes that the market is private. The paradigm also assumes the value of **representative government; direct democracy** in locally controlled communities is not explored as a possibility.

A Particularly Resistant Paradigm

The question remains of why the paradigm makes political science much more resistant to feminist interpretations than most other disciplines. In history and sociology, for example, extensive feminist work has had considerable impact on core ideas. In anthropology, the work of Ruth Benedict and Margaret Mead dates from before the Second World War; explicitly feminist work followed in the 1970s, and feminist analysis is now considered part of the discipline's intellectual tool kit. Even in geography, a feminist subfield examining gender/space relationships has emerged and is having a growing impact on the core discipline. What then is different about political science?

First, the discipline's understanding of what constitutes valid knowledge about politics sets it apart from other disciplines. Part of the discipline's paradigm is its **epistemology,** which is a philosopher's word to describe a theory of how people know and what should be considered reliable or valid knowledge rather than opinion. In political science, the

> Epistemology: Any theory of how human beings know and what constitutes valid knowledge.

ideas admitted as knowledge are primarily those about government and politics from the perspective of the powerful. The ideas of the powerless, or even the less powerful, are rarely accepted as knowledge. (Even in left-wing critiques, testimonials of women such as Guatemalan rebel leader Rigoberta Menchu[13] are rarely accorded the status of expert knowledge. Most oppositional theories are the product of affluent, secure academics, not poor, death-threatened revolutionaries.) The ideas of the judged, governed and administered, if admitted at all, are accorded far less standing in political science than the ideas of judges, governors and administrators. In postwar democracies, the governed are, of course, often asked how they will vote or for their opinions on hot public issues. What they think about political matters is rarely categorized as knowledge, however, unlike the opinions of the powerful.

This underlying limitation on the knowledge base of political science is self-imposed, the consequence of the discipline's adoption of a very narrow conception of politics. Most feminists have a healthy suspicion of the abstract knowledge of powerful people and self-designated experts. Their conceptions of what is political are much broader, and their epistemology places more importance on lived experiences. Indeed, an important task of feminist political science is to broaden the understanding of what is political and expand the view of the kinds of people who have reliable knowledge about politics.

In other disciplines, like anthropology, history and sociology, by contrast, the paradigms define the discipline's subject matter much less narrowly and are more open to knowledge drawn from the less powerful or powerless.

Another reason the discipline's response to feminist challenges has been one of incomprehension and resistance is the perception that women are absent from its field of study. What isn't there, can't be studied. In subsequent chapters, I demonstrate that a broader and more accurate conception of what is political reveals much political activity by women, which can be studied to provide the basis for a broader paradigm. By expanding the understanding of what is political, we also expand the understanding of *who* can provide reliable knowledge.

Why Do Some Strains of Feminism Resist Politics?

While we seek to lay bare the biases within political science, it is equally important to understand the biases within some strains of today's feminism that alienate adherents from the politics of the state. Both the *radical/cultural feminisms* and the *left-wing feminisms* have conceptual and methodological aspects that direct their adherents firmly away from politics and government as understood by political science.

These strains of feminism emerged mainly from women's political experiences in the 1960s and 1970s. By contrast, earlier waves of mobilization, beginning in the nineteenth century, had fostered different ideas about politics, most of which had focused on women's struggle for political representation.[14]

Radical/Cultural Feminism

A set of feminist ideas became dominant in the 1960s–1980s period, when the current political science paradigm achieved dominance. Each had considerable influence in many parts of the world because each formed part of the intellectual and cultural influence of the US as a world superpower. In former European colonies, such as Canada, Australia and New Zealand, British and French feminist ideas were also influential. The dominant feminist traditions in the US, the UK and France were alienated from the politics and governments of their states, although in each country some feminists and their organizations continued to engage in state politics.

Radical Feminism
Elements of **radical feminism** have influenced all contemporary strains of feminism. The powerful concepts of *patriarchy* and **sexual politics** have their origins in the radical feminism analysis of systems of male dominance. So does the idea of women withdrawing from all mainstream political institutions.

Before the rise of the **women's liberation movement** in the United States in the late 1960s, most feminists in that country and elsewhere were not opposed to interacting with state institutions. Indeed, women's struggle to gain the right to vote had mobilized many women. Although male left-wing thinkers often declared the vote irrelevant to the working-class struggle or even a distraction from it, many left-wing women saw the vote as a way working women might gain some control over the conditions of their lives.

Radical feminism developed in the late 1960s. It was a period of turmoil and conflict. In the US, the black movement for civil rights challenged white Americans' sense of themselves and their country. The Vietnam experiences further shook US confidence.

Meanwhile, the **New Left** arose in the US, the UK and France; fiercely anti-state, it focused on the practices of direct democracy and mass demonstrations and fiercely individualist, it was op-

> Radical feminism: A version of feminism based on the belief that women are oppressed by men as part of a universal sex/gender system maintained by culture, economic and political power and coercion (force). Radical feminism also holds that women were the first oppressed group and that patriarchy is a universal system in which men always oppress women on the basis of women's sexuality and reproductive capacity.

posed to existing institutions. Around the world, movements for national liberation called people to throw off their bonds of oppression.

Then well-educated and mainly white women in the United States, angered by the sexism they found in the mixed-sex groups of the New Left and other oppositional movements, began to form women-only groups. But these radical feminists adapted the New Left's theory of change, which was based on a process of **consciousness-raising.** Perhaps the best illustration is the popular notion of "the great refusal", summed up in the slogan "suppose they gave a war and nobody came?". The movement sought to change individuals, not the community or institutions or government (Vickers 1993).

In its early years, radical feminism was politically activist to the extent that it shared the New Left's commitment to a revolution that would transform the United States by ending both patriarchy and capitalism. But radical feminists quickly became politically quiet when an immediate revolution began to seem impossible to achieve because of the enormity of state coercive power. Deployed to fight both opposition to the war in Vietnam and the race riots that erupted regularly in the wake of unsatisfied civil rights claims, it was ruthlessly used.

The idea of a cultural revolution, however, also offered possibilities for change, the radical feminists believed. Communes would replace families, and decentralized, local decision-making in small communities would replace conventional politics. Feminist theatre, women's bookstores and newspapers and women's studies programs would also contribute to the change.

Cultural Feminism

Radical feminism has generally been replaced by an offshoot, called **cultural feminism,** which emerged in the 1980s. It also rejects engagement with male-dominated institutions and politics, but focuses on pornography, violence against women and women's cultural specificity. It lacks any sense that revolutionary change may be possible because it attributes violence and war to men's basic nature and qualities like empathy and peacefulness to women's

> Cultural feminism: A theory that involves the belief that violence, conflict and competition are part of men's nature and that peacefulness, cooperation and nurturance are part of women's nature. This form of feminism is usually alienated from the politics of the state and other male-dominated institutions. In practice, most radical/cultural feminists have organized in women-only groups that operate by consensus, designate no leaders and reject representative forms of democracy in favour of direct forms.

basic nature.

Many cultural feminists are active in anti-violence and anti-pornography movements. Some are themselves survivors of incest, rape or battering. Many project the negative features attributed to male nature onto male institutions, especially political institutions. The slogan "pornography is the theory, rape is the practice" illustrates cultural feminists' idea that cultural manifestations, such as depictions of violence in sexual practice, cause men to act out the practice in rape.

Cultural feminists also identify patriarchal representations in religion, the media, art, literature and scholarship as major causes of the oppression of women. In some cases, they argue that sexuality is the locus of male power. Catharine Mackinnon, for example, thinks that male dominance and female submission are built into the institution of heterosexuality (1982). She links this idea to her proposition that the state is essentially and unchangeably patriarchal in character, designed to enforce male dominance and female submission.

Radical/Cultural Feminists and Feminist Political Science

Radical/cultural feminism's ideas about the politics of the state create major barriers to the development of a feminist political science. First, this worldview uses the concept of patriarchy to describe a universal form thought to be caused by the very nature of the human species. This approach prevents comparison of the different ways in which patriarchy, as a changing political form, has been organized over time since its invention. It neglects the fact that patriarchy as **institutionalized male dominance** was invented by human beings in a particular place at a particular time (Lerner 1986) and that non-patriarchal cultures have existed, although not in the form of complex societies organized by states.

R.W. Connell, an Australian sociologist, argues that it is more accurate to consider the state as a phenomenon that is historically but not essentially patriarchal (1987), and that it is more valuable to examine the extent to which state institutions are masculinized than to use patriarchy as an on/off description (1994). Nonetheless, it was valuable that radical feminism's formulation of the concept of patriarchy directed attention to the importance of sexuality and reproduction in the human scripts of male dominance. As long as things men had declared 'private' were not subject to political scrutiny, the legitimacy of this oldest and longest-lasting political system remained unchallenged.

The second way in which radical/cultural feminism poses a barrier to creating feminist political science lies in its insistence that *all* states are instruments for *all* men to oppress *all* women *all* of the time. Historian Gerda Lerner's *The Creation of Patriarchy* (1986), an account of the emergence of the patriarchal form in the states of ancient Mesopotamia about four thousand years ago, gives the patriarchal state form a history and concreteness the earlier, ideological version lacks. She also noted the important point that some women were actively involved in the creation of the state and have always benefited from it over the centuries. Likewise, she demonstrates that many men have experienced oppression within patriarchal states. Feminist anthropologists have also noted that female power often co-exists with male dominance (Sanday 1981) and that women have resisted male dominance by exercising **counterpower.**

These insights—that women's experiences range from collaboration and cooperation to marginalization, oppression and exploitation—require that we question the utility of a theory that describes all women as victims of institutionalized male dominance. Similarly, the demands of racial and ethnic minority women that we understand the differences in women's experiences challenge both the image of a common experience of oppression and the concept of universal sisterhood.

The third basic aspect of radical/cultural feminist thought that inhibits the development of a feminist political science is its belief that the institutions and practices of conventional politics are invariably oppressive and therefore, by definition, cannot be employed by women to achieve their goals. In the first place, this claim overlooks the fact that many women joined in the mass movements to achieve change through the state. In the United States, Britain, France and Italy, for example, mass grassroots demonstrations brought women greater reproductive and sexual freedom by getting state decision-makers to change laws.

We also need to take into account the fact that state institutions are seen as sources of services and protection by some women in most countries and by most women in some countries. Nonetheless, when radical feminism was emerging during the 1960s and 1970s, many women and men experienced the oppressive faces of state institutions. As Connell notes, for example, during this same period gay men "experienced the state as a direct oppressor since their own sexuality was criminalized" (1994:144). Meanwhile many young women and men who were white, middle-class and raised to expect respect and protection from the police also directly experienced state oppression. Many women encountered demonstrations of male dominance in rape, battering and sexual harassment and found that agents of the state could not or would not protect them.

Radical feminism identified its way of doing politics as an essential part of what it meant to be a feminist, and cultural feminism adopted this outlook. "Feminist politics", in this definition, is politics conducted only in small groups that operate without leaders, and in which tasks are shared by all and decisions

Consensus: A general agreement of opinion, usually achieved by extensive discussion that continues until those who originally disagreed are persuaded or until a new position emerges that all participants can accept.

are made by **consensus,** not by majority vote or a leader's will. If no consensus emerges, the groups often split.

These small, intense groups have been important in generating feminism's political agenda out of women's lived experiences. But they tend to be homogenous in terms of their members' characteristics and opinions, a situation that limits debate between majority and minority women, whose points of view differ on many issues. These collectivist groups are also ill-fitted to interact effectively with the official political system, even when they want to, and most have proved short-lived. To the extent that radical/cultural feminists have conceived of their goals as involving the state, they have had to rely on more conventional women's organizations or mass demonstrations to achieve them.

Overall, all strains of contemporary feminism have been influenced by the critiques of politics developed by radical/cultural feminism. Many theorists were influenced, for example, by Kathy Ferguson's analysis in *The Feminist Case against Bureaucracy* (1984) and Catharine Mackinnon's argument that not only the institutions of the state but also the supposedly neutral apparatus of laws, constitutions and the judiciary are patriarchal (1982). In discussing whether a feminist state is conceivable, R.W. Connell concludes:

> A feminist state that is a structure of authority, a means by which some persons rule over others, is self-contradictory. A feminist state that is an arena for a radical democratization of social interaction may be a very important image of our future (1994:166).

The project of creating a feminist political science itself can be a very radical venture, provided that the critiques of mainstream politics and the contradictions that emerge when women's participation as sexed and gendered people can be moved into the core of the field's development, instead of continuing to be marginalized.

Critiques of Anti-State Radicalism
Many other feminists have conceptualized women's complex relationships with conventional politics differently. For example, in the Nordic countries, Canada and Australia and New Zealand during recent decades, women have found state institutions more open to change and women's involvement than they have in the more powerful United States, France and UK. Even in the US, women organized the National Organization of Women (NOW) to lobby governments in the same environment that also produced radical feminism. (US women willing to engage in the ordinary political process, however, were scorned as tradition-

42

alists, and the radicals even refused to describe them as feminists.)

In Australia, many in the women's movement undertook a **femocrat** project in which women influenced by radical feminism entered the public service to develop women's policy units that would subject all proposed policy to feminist scrutiny. In each of the Scandinavian countries, women now constitute more than 30 percent of the legislature and are a significant minority in the citizen's agencies that administer many of the programs of the welfare state. In Canada, status-of-women machinery has been established, and the proportion of women is increasing in the regular public service and the judiciary.

It certainly makes little sense to talk about politics in these countries as unremittingly patriarchal, male and oppressive to women, when increasing numbers of women are playing roles in decision-making, albeit constrained still by their numbers and male power. Because of the dominance of US radical/cultural feminist theory, however, we have few theoretical accounts of how women can interact with state institutions to achieve feminist goals. Nor do we have much serious discussion of whether the existence of almost 40 percent female legislatures and cabinets in Sweden, Norway and Finland has had an impact on politics and state institutions in those countries. That is, we have few theories that explore the questions of whether states can cease to be patriarchal and at what proportion women decision-makers can begin to transform them.[15] Nonetheless, as I noted earlier, there is significant empirical evidence to suggest that the presence of women in decision-making bodies does make some changes in their outputs and how they operate, even if the state remains patriarchal overall. The effect of different degrees of masculinization or feminization of institutions, therefore, becomes the interesting question for feminist political science to explore.

Left-Wing Feminists

Left-wing feminists rely on more complex theories of the state than radical feminists, but these theories also restrain the development of feminist political science because they direct women to deny importance to the politics of existing states.[16] Left-wing feminists focus on the sexual division of labour and the state's role in maintaining or restructuring the relationships between the economy and the family — for example, by conceptualizing women as part of a reserve army of labour who are drawn into paid work in boom times and sent back into unpaid family work in times of recession and depression.

Left-wing feminists may also be interested in understanding the role played by states in shaping and restructuring economic patterns, which they consider basic to women's oppression. Most left-wing feminists believe that states advance male and capitalist interests by organizing the **hegemonic** or dominant ideas over subordinate groups that find their interests co-opted and distorted by state actors. Patricia Marchak, a feminist political economist, concedes, however, that a major problem with the theoretical tradition is that it provides "no coherent theory of politics and government" (1994:263–64). That is, left-wing tradition critiques the mainstream paradigm of political science but offers no alternate theory of government and politics.

Can We Bridge the Two Perspectives?

Clearly, women's experiences with state institutions and official politics are much more complex than the simple description of them as oppressive reveals. In most countries today, state institutions have two faces: they regulate women's public and private lives, often enforcing patriarchal laws, but they also provide legal rights, policies, programs and entitlements that make a more equal life possible for many women. In social democratic states, feminist scholars write about the "welfare state citizenship" of women, arguing that the rights, services and employment women have extracted from state institutions make it possible for them to assume their roles as equal citizens.

We could thus try to build a feminist political science without radical/cultural or left-wing feminisms. Yet they are too important as part of the overall feminist challenge to political science to ignore as misguided. Each has provided important critiques of the political science paradigm and the liberal democratic thought and practice embedded in it. It is now hard for any feminist studying politics to deny that the state is patriarchal, for example (although the definition needs historical context). Likewise, it is difficult to deny that states allow for the exploitation of many women and men as their labour is extracted under sanction of the law and regulated by public policy.

Clearly, feminists wishing to understand politics from a woman-centred perspective cannot ignore state politics, although they must insist on a definition of politics that goes well beyond the state. Nor can they ignore the critiques of state politics provided by feminists who reject engagement with it.

What is essential for bridging the gap is a methodology that permits focus *both* on how women might operate in existing political systems and how they might act to transform political systems given the legitimate and telling critiques developed by second-wave feminists. Canadian feminist political scientist Angela Miles expresses the point this way: "[We] must continue to insist on our right to participate fully in public life, but must at the same time challenge its very shape and underlying logic" (1982).

The critical methodology that makes the bridging of these two contradictory traditions possible insists on the importance of starting where women are, accepting as valid their self-knowledge about politics *as they define it* and putting together the contradictions that emerge from men's and women's accounts of politics so that they can be explored and theorized. We must make room in our analysis for knowledge that comes from the standpoints of the powerful, powerless and less powerful. To develop feminist political science, we must, as Canadian sociologist Dorothy Smith puts it, "begin where we are" (1978) by focusing on where real, concrete women are practicing what they consider to be politics (even if they don't call it that)—any collective activity that aims to achieve or resist change.

Our framework cannot ignore the macrostructures of state and international politics, however, or the current challenges of economic globalization. In the chapters that follow, I present a framework that incorporates insights from the political science paradigm and from feminist critiques. I also present an alternate understanding of methodology that gives status to women's experience of politics and considers them experts on their own theories of experiences. In this way, the analysis presented both "begins where women are" and maintains the parallel vision necessary to at least present the contradictions between the different accounts of political life.

Further Readings

Burt, Sandra. 1988. "Different Democracies? A Preliminary Examination of the Political Worlds of Canadian Men and Women." *Women and Politics* 6/ 4(Winter):57–79.

Connell, R.W. 1994. "The State, Gender and Sexual Politics: Theory and Appraisal." In H. Lorraine Radtke and Henderikus J. Stam (eds.), *Power/ Gender: Social Relations in Theory and Practice*. London and California: Sage.

Jones, Kathleen. 1988. "Towards the Revision of Politics." In Kathleen Jones and Anna Jønasdøttir, *The Political Interests of Gender: Developing Theory and Research With a Feminist Face*. London: Sage.

Vickers, Jill. 1993. "Sexual Politics and the Master Science: The Feminist Challenge to Political Science." In Geraldine Finn (ed.), *Limited Edition: Voices of Women, Voices of Feminism*. Halifax: Fernwood.

_____ . 1989. "Feminist Approaches to Politics." In Linda Kealey and Joan Sangster (eds.), *Beyond the Vote: Canadian Women and Politics*. Toronto: University of Toronto Press. Reprinted in Paul Fox and Graham White, *Politics: Canada*. 8th ed. on Primis, Toronto: McGraw-Hill Ryerson, 1995.

Questions for Discussion

1. Discuss how expanding the definition of politics also expands understanding of who has valid knowledge about politics and government. Have each member of the group ask a *differently-located* woman (perhaps a mother, grandmother or aunt) what she thinks politics is and how she has been politically active. Try to include the views of women from racial and ethnic minorities too.

2. What are the basic elements of the political science paradigm that can keep people from "seeing" women in politics at all or only when they act like political men?

3. Why are *radical feminists* alienated from the official politics of the state?

What valuable insights does their critique offer?
4. How do the critiques of *cultural feminists* and *left-wing feminists* differ from the critique of *radical feminists?*
5. In which countries are women's movements mainly hostile to state politics? In which countries are they more state-focused? Can you think of any reasons for the difference?

Notes

1. Women also become visible when they make the claim that all women are not the same and that some women ought to be treated differently than others. In such cases, however, policy-makers, political science and the media often declare that "women" don't know what they want, that they are fighting among themselves and, therefore, that their claims can be ignored. Either women are said to know what they want but are not entitled to it, or they do not know what they want and so entitlement need not be considered. Were it to be acknowledged that women do know what they want *and* that they are entitled to it, feminist political science would be well on its way to the transformation of politics.

2. The impact of these processes on the anglo-Canadian women's movement is well analyzed by feminist political scientist Janine Brodie (1995).

3. The circumstances are explored in Crick (1959). During his 1930s tenure at Cornell University, British political scientist George Catlin first offered a system-atic account that aspired to being scientific, but his ideas were not picked up until after the Second World War.

4. These concepts are now highly controversial. Given the fall of the Soviet empire, even the phrases 'first world' (the West), 'second world' (communist or socialist systems) and 'third world' (everyone else) have become meaningless and are often now replaced with the terms of North (the affluent countries) and South (the poorer countries). This nomenclature also has problems given the location of some wealthy countries—Australia, New Zealand—in the southern hemisphere and of poor ones, such as China, in the north. I use the old terms when I am writing about the paradigm that prevailed from the 1950s to the present but put them in single quotation marks to remind you of the problems. Similarly, I put contested terms such as 'developed' in single quotes. In later chapters, I outline alternate ways of conceptualizing these divisions.

5. Notice my use of both *sexed* and *gendered* here, and many other times in this book. As explained in the definition of sex/gender early in this chapter, the two words do not mean the same thing. Male-female differences important to our understand-ing of politics and public policy come *both* from the fact of reproductive sex and from gender as socially constructed by different societies. See Vickers (1994a) for a full discussion of the problem of dealing only with gender.

6. Women in 104 countries gained the legal right to vote only between 1945 and the present. In almost 20 others, women regained the right in this period, having won and lost it before the Second World War. In another 11, majority women won the vote earlier but minority women won the right only since 1945.

   An even more complex pattern marks women's struggles to gain the right to participate in other ways. The right to run for office, for example, was rarely achieved at the same time as the vote.

7. I explore these and other contested concepts later in this chapter and in Chapter 4.
8. I further explore these arenas in Chapter 3.
9. It is not shared by left-wing critics, who believe that these structures and processes embody the interests of the ruling classes.
10. Left-wing critics argue that most women in government are privileged women who will not represent the interests or identities of those oppressed and exploited.
11. The UN's Human Development Index measures the quality of life and of human development in each country.
12. Because women as a group are everywhere poorer than men as a group and are culturally assigned responsibility for child care, elder care and home care of the ill, they rely on both state services (where they exist) and state employment more than men.
13. Menchu is one of the leaders of the Guatemalan Indian peasants organized against the landowners and the Guatemalan military, which has been supporting the landowners. This oppressive regime has spawned a movement of indigenous peoples, attempting both to resist exploitation and oppression and to protect their traditional cultures and language. See Burgos-Debray 1984.
14. Which is still incomplete. Women still lack the legal right to vote or hold governing power in at least two countries (Kuwait and the United Arab Emirates), while no woman has yet been elected to the legislatures of at least eight more countries despite a legal entitlement (Karl 1995: Table 4.4).
15. Although a willingness to engage with the state and participate in official politics is often used to categorize feminists as liberals, this usage can be misleading for two reasons. First, conservative and left-wing feminists may also engage with their states, if the opportunity arises. Second, it assumes the state interacted with is also liberal; that is the definition reflects only the experiences of 'first world' women.
16. Within the left are two major traditions: *Marxist feminism* and *socialist feminism.* The former believes that class is more important than sex in explaining women's oppression, and the latter that each plays a more or less and equal role. Both see state institutions as maintaining class dominance, although socialist feminists are also concerned with how it maintains male dominance.

Chapter 3

A FRAMEWORK FOR A FEMINIST POLITICAL SCIENCE

In this chapter, I develop the foundations for a feminist political science and provide a map for discussions I develop more fully in the chapters that follow. First, I highlight the elements of the existing political science **paradigm** that have to be changed to transcend male politics as the norm and give standing to women's political experiences as valid knowledge. Second, I explore several important methodological principles that need to be established to develop a women-centred approach to political science: *starting from where women are,* maintaining a *parallel vision,* comparing women with women and *contextualizing* for differences in women's geographic location, class, collective or communal differences (race, ethnicity, region or nation, language or religion) and personal status (age, disability, sexual orientation, and so on). A key issue is how to practise political science and politics, taking into account both the things women have in common and the things on which they differ. Third, I map the *major arenas* in which most of women's political activism occurs, differentiating between *official politics,* as I call the politics of the state, and *unofficial politics.* I begin to expand the framework to include women's involvement in international politics, in movements that transcend state borders, in international civil society and in the worldwide processes of economic and social change.

Throughout, I urge you to keep in mind the basic questions of the book: Can conventional politics actually be transformed enough to let women work within the institutions of the state to achieve their goals? Can political science encompass a new understanding of politics and government based on the experiences of the powerless and the less powerful?

Transcending Male Politics as the Norm

Feminist political scientists have formulated a generalization about women in official politics around the world: the higher the fewer. It refers to the decreasing number of women found at successive levels of politics, with the most women at the least powerful levels and the fewest at the most powerful. Because all states are patriarchal, men dominate most of the powerful offices in state institutions. And because this situation has existed since such institutions were created, this power relationship between men and women is endorsed by most cultural, religious and even purportedly scientific ideas.

48

Yet setting up male experiences in politics as the norm and comparing women only with men leads to missing other equally important parts of the picture. For example, such a frame makes people ignore the powerful roles women play in unofficial politics in many societies and the fact that women constitute quite large minorities in some political institutions, including the Norwegian cabinet, the Swedish parliament and the Canadian Supreme Court. It also ignores some women's exercise of supreme power and responsibility as state leaders, conducting wars and pursuing peace.

> Women are the world's largest excluded group. Even though they make up half the adult population, and often contribute more than their share to society, inside and outside the home, they are frequently excluded from positions of power.
> United Nations Development Program, 1993

Writing Women In

The key to reinventing political science on a women-centred foundation is to keep seemingly contradictory propositions in mind at the same time, using methodological techniques discussed below. As we try to resolve contradictory propositions, we'll see how feminist political science must revise our understandings of politics. We must reinvent political science so it can explain politics and government without making half the adult population disappear because women don't fit a model that is already long out of date.

In this section, I consider six ways feminist political science challenges political science and its oppositional traditions (see Exhibit 3). First, I explore what political life looks like from a traditional, state-centred point of view. Exhibit 4 gives a rough picture of this outlook, in which politics occurs almost entirely within state institutions such as legislatures and courts. Local and communal politics are largely ignored, as are the political dimensions of non-state institutions. The whole of civil society, including mass movements, is considered social, not political.

Most mainstream political science involves analysis of the impact of different ways of organizing the state or parts of the state including:

1. The form of the state on how it functions; for example, how having a **unitary state** affects the functioning of state institutions especially in contrast to a **federal state** (in which the power to make collective decisions is divided between two levels of government).
2. The kind of state **regime;** that is, the effect of having a **democratic** regime, a *state socialist* regime or an *authoritarian* regime.[1]
3. Ways of organizing legislatures, (for example, **parliamentary** or **congressional), bureaucracies** and the **electoral system** (for example, first past the post, single member plurality, proportional representation).

49

Exhibit 3.
Six Ways Feminism Challenges Mainstream Political Science.

Mainstream political science	Feminist political science
1. Considers the patriarchal form of states—that is, institutionalized male rule—to be natural, unproblematic or the result of some deficiency in women, which they could cure if they were more like men.	Asserts that institutionalized male dominance is "man-made"—that is, socially constructed and maintained—and that women should be able to "do politics" as women—that is, as sexed and gendered people.
2. Accepts the division of societies into private and public spheres as a given that is natural and even provides protection of freedom and privacy.	Asserts that the split between private and public is socially constructed and always in flux, and that the state often interferes in "private" institutions, including families.
3. Assumes women now enjoy equal citizenship in a gender-neutral political system.	Asserts that women's citizenship lets them participate in a male-centred political system only if they behave like men politically.
4. Views power relationships from above—from the vantage point of the powerful—especially of those who hold state power.	Asserts the need to focus also on power from below—that is, on the viewpoints of the powerless and less powerful.
5. Puts power relationships within the state at the centre of its analysis.	Makes sex/gender, wherever it occurs, central to political analysis.
6. Considers women, in comparison to men, making male experience the norm.	Considers women's experience on its own terms, making female experience a norm, too.

4. Ways of linking people to the state (for example, through two-party or multi-party systems or through mass/cadre arrangements) and ways of organizing the expression of organized interest.
5. **Political cultures** (the distinctive elements of a country's, region's or group's values and beliefs about politics) in relation to elections, protests and governmental functioning.
6. International politics and international institutions.

Finally, because the mainstream **paradigm** originated in the cold war compe-

Exhibit 4.
A Traditional, State-Centred View of Political Life.

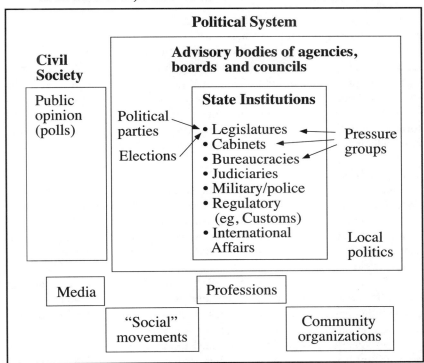

tition between the US and the USSR, the discipline studies 'third world' or 'modernizing' countries separately. (Left-wing political scientists attack this aspect of the mainstream paradigm, seeing the whole area in terms of conditions of **underdevelopment** and *dependency* created by imperialism and colonialism.)

Mainstream Questions, Pertinence to Women
To many feminists, the areas of study just listed seem almost useless to women since they all deal with different ways of organizing male power in the official politics of patriarchal states. The work of feminist political scientists, however, reveals that each of these areas does have importance for a women-centred reinvention of political science. For example, feminist studies reveal that gender ideologies are important aspects of different regimes. All three kinds of regime are patriarchal, but they construct women as citizens and potential decision-makers quite differently. Each provides different opportunities for women to participate in official politics and a different scope for women's politics in arenas outside the institutions of the state. Consequently, what kind of govern-

mental regime is in place matters from a women-centred point of view. (There is little study of this question in the mainstream discipline or oppositional traditions.)

The relevance of some aspects of state organization to women-centred analysis is more apparent than others. The governmental regime clearly affects women—their experiences worldwide suggest that democratic political systems, although patriarchal, give women more opportunities than authoritarian regimes to participate in both official and grassroots politics outside of the state.[2] The implications of other aspects of political science's traditional areas of study for women are less obvious. For example, having a unitary or a federal form of the state did not seem relevant until feminist analysts began to explore how "which government has the power to do what" affects women as women.[3]

Some Key Differences

The main areas that preoccupy mainstream political science, then, are also important areas for feminist political science. Yet several differences exist. One is that feminist political science must also explore aspects of politics that the mainstream discipline currently ignores or neglects. A second is that women-centred approaches must challenge the basic assumptions that currently structure the field.

Third, the radical feminist critiques of the patriarchal nature of the state and bureaucracy and the feminist legal scholars' critique of the male-biased nature of law and judicial decision-making make us focus on parts of state functioning that were abandoned to other disciplines when the current political science paradigm emerged. In particular, we need to reconceptualize the role of the bureaucracy from a women-centred perspective. Although filled through appointment rather than election in most countries, bureaucracies involve major decision-making power that must be opened to feminist scrutiny. Similarly, aspects of global politics neglected under the current paradigm, including transnational movements for change and activism within the structures of international civil society such as churches, unions and other **non-governmental organizations (**NGOs**)**, must be brought back into focus as we develop a feminist political science. And as politics increasingly becomes a matter of "think globally, act locally", we must reintegrate local, community-based politics into the framework, especially since this is where women are most active.

A fourth main difference is that a feminist political science needs to focus explicitly on the coercive instruments of state power, particularly the institutions of the military and police. Violence (and the threat of violence) is an important dimension of the organization of patriarchy, both in the family and the state. (Indeed, radical and cultural feminists argue that a continuum of violence links violence in intimate relationships with the state's exercise of violence in wars and in the oppression of minority populations.[4]) It is important to explore in detail how political institutions would work without male-female or interracial violence. Clearly, some coercion will always be necessary to ensure the security of life for each of society's more vulnerable members. What feminists need to explore is how much coercion is required, how it should be regulated and how women can participate in its exercise and control.

Challenging Male Politics as the Norm

Although feminist political science has not yet explored all aspects of the issues just described, it is now possible to map out basic conceptual and research agendas. Most important, feminist political science challenges the mainstream discipline's assumptions.

Feminist political science asserts that men and women experience political life quite differently and that this fact must be taken into account in political analysis. One reason is that women's experiences of politics must be treated as valid in their own right, not simply compared to men's experiences and found inadequate because the two differ.

Men's and women's experiences of politics differ partly because their lives differ everywhere and partly because politics occurs in state institutions that are male-dominated and have the maintenance of institutionalized male rule as an underlying, if implicit, function.

Note that I am not making a cultural feminist argument that men and women differ *by nature:* that men are aggressive and dominant while women are nurturing and peaceful because their genes or hormones hard wire these characteristics into them in some essential and unchangeable way. These assumptions are **stereotypes,** whether they are used by conservative thinkers to justify excluding women from the public realm or by feminists to argue that men are unfit to rule. Of course, stereotypes sometimes seem to be common sense but they are usually preconceived, oversimplified ideas about the characteristics of a group. For example, the assertion that "men are warlike by nature" seems right. The world has many images and accounts of men fighting in wars and committing acts of violence against women and children in the process. Women, however, have mostly been excluded (or protected) from fighting wars, so, not surprisingly, the accounts of their fighting are few. Thus, the idea of women making war seems 'unnatural'.

> **Stereotype: A preconceived, oversimplified idea of the characteristics of a group; it is often used to 'justify' oppression or discrimination, as in "women are too emotional to be judges".**

Some feminist thinkers assume that men's and women's characteristics are completely socially constructed and that the goal ought to be a politically unisex world in which neither the **sex** nor the **gender** of the citizen matters. French social scientist Chantal Mouffe (1992, 1993), who takes this view, argues for a massive decentralization of all political systems to make this outcome possible. Political theorist Mary O'Brien (1981), by contrast, maintains that most men and women will always have some different experiences because of their different roles (or potential roles) in reproduction. US philosopher Iris Marion Young concludes the problem actually lies in the liberal idea that equality among individuals means their receiving the *same* treatment, rather than *appropriate* treatment. She maintains that this belief has led people to accept the liberal myth of a universal, undifferentiated citizenship. In its place, Young (1989, 1990) argues for a differentiated citizenship that recognizes men and women as differently related to the state not because of their natures but because of the differences in their lives.

This point is a matter of considerable debate among feminist political scientists, theorists and philosophers. Some are unwilling to use the idea that women differ from men in relation to politics because difference has been used historically to defend the discrimination, marginalization and oppression of women and others who are different from the dominant majority, and our intellectual frameworks provide little help in understanding that people may be equally valuable even if they differ. On the other hand, to assume that men and women have the same experiences and that those experiences relate them to the state in the same way denies reality. I certainly cannot resolve this important debate for you here. Instead, I explore briefly the main ways in which women and men are differently related to states now.[5]

State Interest in Women

State decision-makers have some interests in women that differ from those they have in men. Because all existing states are patriarchal, most decision-makers are men. Even where women are a sizeable proportion of decision-makers, however, they have interests in the fact that most women are the physical, social and cultural reproducers of the next generation.

How states act in relation to women's reproductive potential varies considerably. Governments may want more population and be pronatalist, encouraging more births through offering women incentives or denying them access to contraception and/or safe abortions. The government of Quebec, for example, provides financial incentives for births because it fears a declining birthrate threatens the viability of its francophone population, which is a minority in Canada, although it is a majority within the province. Other governments wish to limit population and provide incentives or offer threats to gain compliance. In China, a one-child policy involves heavy sanctions against women's having more than one child[6] (nevertheless, because Chinese culture favours boy babies, many women risk a second pregnancy to produce a son). Although men are usually directly involved in the conception of children and their fertility continues longer than women's, reproductive policies are usually targeted at women.

States may also be interested in *which* women are reproducing. In apartheid South Africa, for example, black and mixed-race women were encouraged or forced to limit births while a Babies for Botha campaign provided white women with incentives to have more white children for the fatherland, symbolized by then Prime Minister Louis Botha. In many affluent countries, women with disabilities and from racial minorities are discouraged from having babies or even sterilized while the considerable sums are spent on fertility clinics so that 'normal' couples of the majority race and culture can have children. These sorts of situations make it important to contextualize the experiences women have in relation to both the state and reproduction.

States see men more often as workers and potential soldiers, and women more often as reproducers.[7] Many states limit women's work to locations that are physically safer than where men work, keeping women out of mines or labs with radioactive materials. The fact that one man can theoretically impregnate millions of women, whereas women rarely bear more than five children in a one-year period, makes men reproductively the dispensable sex.

That the state has little interest in men as reproducers makes a crucial difference. Not only are women the physical reproducers of children; the culturally-sanctioned division of labour everywhere also assigns them the responsibility of rearing children. Men are encouraged to absent themselves to go to war or to the cities to find work, leaving women at home to feed, clothe, house and educate "their" children and to look after other dependants.

What Difference Do the Differences Make?

What are some of the consequences of the fact that states are interested in women, but not men, as reproducers? One result in affluent, democratic societies that developed elements of a welfare state is that women are more dependent than men on state action. Women are more likely to depend on government programs and entitlements because they are poorer than men and bear the responsibility for caring for children, the elderly and the ill. Women are also more likely to be workers in state institutions since, when state activities expand to provide new programs, women are most often hired, especially in clerical and nurturing jobs. As a consequence, policies that increase or decrease the scope of state activity affect women more than men. When the state contracts, they may lose both their jobs and the entitlements they need to maintain independence of a male earner (such as child care and elder care).

Women are also less independently mobile—that is, able to move from place to place—than men. Because men generally earn more than women, few women raising children in partnership with men can afford to move to where there is work (or better work and conditions), or they are forced to move to follow their male partner when they would prefer not to.

Being more tied to locale by responsibilities for parents and children, women are more affected than men by which government has the responsibility for different functions. Some feminists believe women are best served by decentralized government structures in which they can influence decisions. Others point to the fact that they and their children may be moved to a totally different state, province or country and need standard programs and entitlements across a country or in larger units such as the European Union.

Men and women relate to states and experience politics differently in many other ways. By treating male politics as the norm while not examining women's political experiences, activities and values on their own terms, mainstream political science has been unable to explain how women act and think politically.

Four Issues of Methodology

The political science paradigm includes assumptions about appropriate methodology as well as the nature of politics. In this section, I explore four ways in which feminist political science differs methodologically from mainstream political science:

1. Starting from where women are, giving legitimacy to their lived experiences.
2. Maintaining a parallel focus on the realities of existing systems *and* on the potential for transformation.
3. Comparing women with women to transcend the assumption of male politics as the norm.
4. Contextualizing for difference to ensure that we *actively* seek knowledge from women of different races, ethnicities and personal status and explore how that difference affects their political experiences, values and goals.

This section is not intended to be a full treatment of feminist critiques of methodology. (I list books and articles that do this at the end of this chapter.) My goal is to guide you to the major ways in which feminist political science differs methodologically from mainstream political science. I also suggest some ways in which bridges can be built between the two approaches.

Starting from Where Women Are

Studying politics in a women-centred way must challenge the idea that what men do in politics is the norm. If we do that, where do we find women? Remember the mainstream paradigm lets us "see" women only when they are acting like political men. So if we do not change our methodology, we study women mainly as voters. Alternatively, we may examine the few women who make it into the male-dominated world of legislatures, courts, bureaucracies, the media and political science, although women who pioneer in male-dominated institutions are rarely representative of the majority of women.

This dilemma led many feminists in political science over the past two decades to engage in what I call **barriers research,** which is what results from studying women in politics and government without changing methodological assumptions. Because women in government and politics, as defined by mainstream political science, are so few, what these analysts end up studying is the absence of women and the barriers to women's integration into official politics on the same basis as men.

This important research helps feminists understand how such things as different electoral systems limit or maximize women's opportunities for influence in the institutions of the state. It does not, however, challenge the division of society into private and public spheres or the division of labour that assigns to women physical and social responsibility for reproduction and the care of the old and infirm. Once we identify the fact that women's child care, elder care and community responsibilities act as barriers to their being elected to legislative roles, for example, what do we do?

Some argue that women who wish to be active in politics should transfer those responsibilities to other women, as men have always done. Others think that institutions must be changed (as, for example, Canada's federal parliament now has a child-care centre attached to it and has ended night-time

> All research into the role of women in politics will in the foreseeable future remain research into the absence of women's power, or at any rate, their lack of influence. E. Haavio-Mannila et al., 1985

sittings). For most women living women's lives, however, these changes do not alter the fact that they can't aspire to decision-making roles in official politics. Nonetheless, such women have been engaged in doing politics in movements for change, local government and community politics, and other grassroots and ad hoc political activities — actions that need to be considered political when we construct our framework.

What the principle of starting from where women are dictates is that we expand the definitions of what constitutes politics and study women's political activism wherever it occurs. This does not mean ignoring women's activism within state institutions or giving up efforts to identify and lower barriers to it. Rather, it assumes that studying where women are now active will reveal something about their political values and how they conduct politics when they are in charge, as they are in autonomous women's groups. This approach can aid in identifying women-centred norms for political activity based on what women are doing, rather than on their absence. It can also help us discover what facilitates women's political activism, rather than just barriers that inhibit women.

The implications of this methodological principle are both conceptual and practical. First, it means that we must give standing to women's statements about their experiences in both *official* and *unofficial* politics. But how do we do so in practical terms? Political scientists usually work by gaining information from people in official positions, thereby giving the status of knowledge to the views of the powerful. How do we gain knowledge from the powerless and less powerful? Mainstream political science gathers information about the opinions of ordinary citizens through surveys. Although survey data can be quantified, opinions are not treated as knowledge. Indeed, most surveys are conducted to inform those in power about the views of the less powerful and rarely tap the knowledge of the powerless and less powerful about what their political experiences means.

Re-defining our concepts of politics . . . necessarily challenges the assumed bifurcation of the public and private into two radically isolated realms.

Kathleen Jones, 1994

How can political science move from surveying opinions to gathering knowledge from those who don't occupy positions of power or influence? One method many feminists use is qualitative research, in which women researchers discuss political experiences with women citizens active in grassroots political groups. This inquiry is engaged research, not spectator research, with researchers sharing a "conscious partiality" with those they are interviewing, rather than taking a distanced and supposedly 'objective' approach (Mies 1983, 1991).

In brief, a key methodological principle to guide the development of feminist political science is to start from where women are because the very study of women's political activism, wherever it occurs, asserts that women's experiences of government and politics in patriarchal states are as important as men's. Locating and studying the political activism outside of official politics gives status to the knowledge of all groups from which political science has not heard because of their marginalized or oppressed circumstances or because of activism that does not fit the discipline's conception of what politics is about. In this way, our reinvention of political science will get a radical kickstart.

Maintaining a Parallel Vision

European sociologist Maria Mies (1983) argues that feminist researchers should have a "double-consciousness" in which the researcher replaces the view from the top (spectator research) with a view from below. Some feminist historians first formulated the idea of a *doubled vision* several decades ago, and it has passed into the general consciousness of feminist research, although it is not always clear how the concept should be implemented as a methodological rule.

The concern of these feminists was that the search for women doing things in the public, male-dominated world should not result in abandoning a women-centred understanding of activity in the domestic and community spheres where women traditionally have been found. Consequently, the approach I call maintaining a **parallel vision** requires a focus on both. In other words, feminist political science must simultaneously gain a better understanding of women's activism within official politics and in groups away from or alienated from official politics, including those who would radically transform politics.

How do we put this principle into operation? First, we must focus on women's political activity in women-led organizations and arenas where women were active before they had the legal right to participate in the public realm. Canadian sociologist Thelma McCormack argues that women "live in a different political culture from men" (1975). She believes that part of this difference stems from women's awareness that government and the politics of the state are a male preserve. Part of it also reflects a different "design for political living", which women create on the margins of the public sphere. This realm of women's associations and institutions, com-

> Parallel vision: A principle of feminist method that requires focus on women's activity *both* in traditionally male fields and traditionally female fields and use of norms based on the view *both* from the top and from below.

munity services and movements has its own norms and values, which reflect women-centred experiences. I describe this women-dominated sphere as involving "the politics of getting things done" (Vickers 1989b). Simultaneously, we must look to women's experiences in the public world.

In brief, to follow the principle of parallel vision in this project, we must focus on the politics of both the male-dominated arena of state politics and the female-dominated arena of communal and women's politics, realms for which I often use the terms **official politics** and **unofficial politics.** (Below, I explain the importance of greater precision since the realm of women's politics now includes local government in some countries but not in others.) In our analysis, we must look particularly for norms and values that flow out of women's experiences. In this way, when we are exploring how to reconstruct the basic concepts of political science, we will always have insights from at least two distinct points of vision.

Comparing Women with Women

To date, most attempts to understand women's political activism focus on why women are different from men in the realm of official politics. The fact that all political theories and approaches to the study of politics emerged after states based on institutionalized male dominance were invented means that male experience has provided the norms and values for all forms of political analysis. Yet when analysts try to understand women's political activism by comparing women to men, women's values and norms are swamped by men's, and the focus ends up primarily on women's absences and 'inadequacies'. Instead, the method being developed by some feminist political scientists compares women with women whenever possible.

What happens when such a method is used? First, we can begin to ask questions such as why only one in five Canadian MPs are women while the comparable figure for Norway is two in five. Or we can ask why significant numbers of women are elected as mayors in Canada and the US while this office is rarely held by women in France. In other words, we can ask questions about women that are useful in understanding how male-dominant political institutions work and how women find space to act within them. For example, when do women become a large enough minority—a **critical mass**—to begin to transform male-centred structures and processes?

Comparing women with women is also useful in explaining why women predominate in some forms of political activity, such as protests and short-lived groups organized to achieve new services or avert the loss of existing ones. This approach helps us link the sexual division of labour to women's choices about their political involvement. When we explore women's rich history in anti-slavery, anti-war and environmental movements, we begin to get a sense of how women's political values may lead them to prefer involvement in groups and activities they see as having moral importance or touching on issues of survival or quality of life.

By comparing women's political activism in different jurisdictions, we can also begin to identify which political structures, such as electoral systems, impede or facilitate women's involvement in both official and unofficial politics. For example, there is now good evidence that electoral systems that use some forms of proportional representation facilitate the election of women legislators (Rule 1987; Lisa Young 1994).

Contextualizing Women: Dimensions of Difference

Until recently, feminist political scientists have voiced mainly the values of majority culture women of the same race and class and who speak the same language as the majority culture men who dominate official politics. These analysts assumed either that western-style democracy is good for women or that women critical of it would share Marxist-inspired critiques. They also tended to assume that political solidarity built around an undifferentiated concept of sisterhood was both achievable and desirable.

These assumptions have been shaken, however, as international contact among feminists has grown and as racial and ethnic minority women in many countries have begun to challenge the right of majority women to define what women want. Women from countries not of European origin (many of which suffered under European imperialism) often have quite different conceptions of feminism and what women's political goals should be (Mohanty, Russo and Torres 1991). Minority women within states may also have goals different from those of majority women, especially when the communities of which the former are part face racism, oppression or marginalization (Nain 1991). Women who share a country's majority language, race and culture but who are set apart because of age, sexual orientation or disability also may have different needs, goals and values, which must be taken into account in politics and political analysis.

In our attempt to reconstruct political science, we don't want to make the mistake of reifying the experiences of the women of the majority race and cultures in European and anglo-American societies, while ignoring the experiences of differently-located women within those societies and women in the less affluent countries of the world. Thus, our plan must include the crucial principle of **contextualizing** analyses to take into account potential differences in values and activity patterns for differently-located women as a basic part of its methodology. That is, we may not assume all women have common interests, goals and values, as so often happens when political analysis compares 'women' with 'men' as though each were undifferentiated categories. Instead, we must assume that women who are *differently-located* —because of *geography, class, communal affiliation* (race, ethnicity, religion, nationality, language) or *personal status* (age, sexual orientation, disability)—may not have

> Contextualizing: Taking into account ways in which women's (or men's) values and activity patterns differ because of differences in geographical location, class, communal affiliation (race, ethnicity, religion, nationality, language) and personal status (age, sexual orientation, disability).

values, interests and goals in common with majority women. We must demonstrate, not just assume, the existence of common values, interests and goals. Indeed, it is appropriate to begin by assuming that differently-located women often make different choices about goals and values and how and where to participate politically. In the following paragraphs, I explore each of these dimensions of difference as part of the methodological challenge of creating a feminist political science.

Geographic Location

The first dimension involves potential differences in women's experiences resulting from geographic location. Place matters, or, to quote US feminist Adrienne Rich, "a place on the map is also a place in history" (cited in Mohanty 1992:77). Where women live often profoundly affects how they can be politically active and the consequences of their activism.

Much political analysis, both in the mainstream paradigm and its oppositional traditions, assumes a universal experience of politics. By contrast, the framework developed here uses the idea of spatially-based differences to explore identities such as regionalisms and, where state and nation coincide, nationalisms that affect women's political choices.

Moreover, locale may matter as much within states (especially federal states) as between states. As feminist geographer Doreen Massey argues, "most people still live their lives locally [and] their consciousness is formed in a distinct geographic place"(cited in Agnew 1987:36), a situation especially true for women who are often left at home when men migrate.

Pauline Rankin, a Canadian political scientist, shows that patterns of women's political activism can differ quite significantly between cities, even two such as Calgary and Edmonton, within a single province. She also shows that women's political activism in a large metropolitan area such as Toronto involves a pattern very different than that of women's activism in smaller cities or rural areas (Rankin 1996). Agnew argues that explanations of political activity that theorize place and space can provide links between the "micro-sites" of human activity in which agency can be experienced and the "macro-order" of states and economies that direct, restrict and obscure agency (1987:230). Since the issue of how much agency (capacity to choose among courses of action) women have in politics is a controversial topic in feminist political science, exploring women's spatially-based differences is an important task.

Class

The issue of *class,* which is central to the left critique of the political science paradigm, is also important in our analysis. In some countries, class divisions are marked, and class consciousness is strong enough to overpower other affiliations. Where this occurs, women's political activism is sharply divided between the dominant classes, and there is little capacity for cross-class solidarity among women. In other countries, class consciousness is less pro-nounced and may be overpowered by geographic divisions and sympathies or communal affiliations based on race, language, religion or ethnicity. We cannot assume on the basis of theory that one force or another predominates. Instead, we must identify the actual interplay among them and, by contextualizing the analysis, identify the patterns with which differently-located women must contend in particular countries.

Let us take a moment to consider what I am talking about. Theories of class as developed by the left and mainstream political science (and economics) have always been difficult to apply to women, despite the great importance of class as a political phenomenon. Class originally referred to a categorical division in society between those who owned the means of production (such as land or capital) and those who did not. Women have always been hard to fit into this analysis because they are usually part of a class only indirectly; that is, as daughters, wives or widows, they can be part of the dominant class without owning anything themselves, or they can be part of the working class while never going near a factory where work, as defined by the theory, is performed. Marxist and socialist feminists have developed the left-wing critique to provide tools for analyzing society's sexual division of labour. But this analysis gives little guidance as to how the class affects women's politics in non-revolutionary contexts. Despite the problems with existing formulations, however, the impact of class on women's political choices and opportunities is too significant to discard the category. One of the tasks of feminist political science, therefore, is to redevelop the concept to reflect women's actual experiences of class, class consciousness and class politics in different countries.

For the purposes of the framework here, I conceptualize class and its effects on women quite simply. First, I assume that women's political choices are significantly affected by their access to economic resources, whether or not class and class conflict are salient in their society at any particular time. Second, women's ability to identify with other women (gender identity) or with their class, race, ethnic, language, religion or national community depends on how much their political activism involves a basic struggle for survival. For women whose political actions revolve around the survival or security of their families, their class location may overwhelm all other identities. Class frequently overlaps with race and ethnic identity, however, since they are characteristics societies use to 'justify' exploitation and oppression. For many women, therefore, the experience of class and of race or ethnicity may be inseparable. Third, where state power is organized primarily for the benefit of an owning class and the state employs coercion to repress challenges to the position of that class, other possible political identities for women are muted and may even be suppressed by actors for whom the class struggle takes precedence.

Communal Affiliation
The third important area of difference I use to locate minority women is their collective or communal affiliations based on shared race, ethnicity, language or in some cases religion. Of course, majority women who are part of the racial and cultural majority also have a race, ethnicity, religion and language, but only minorities constructed as "others" by those in power are usually thought of as having such characteristics.

Societal majorities use apparent differences in skin colour, language and culture to racialize people who are different or to assign them an ethnicity. These assignments of identity are culturally constructed, as can be seen from the contradictions in how they are created from country to country. In the US, for example, Hispanic women from Mexico, Central America or Puerto Rico are considered 'women of colour', whereas in Canada they are usually thought of as 'white'. 'Black' in the UK is a political designation adopted by 'women of colour' including women of Asian and African descent. In North America, by contrast, 'black' refers to people of African ancestry only.

When a national group exists within a state but does not control its instruments, nationality may join race, ethnicity, religion and language as a communal affiliation that organizes political identity. Communities that consider themselves to be nations but believe themselves ruled by another people may fight to gain self-determination—that is, to gain a state that coincides with their national collectivity. Thus, relationships between sex/gender mobilization and nationalist mobilization of women also need to be explored, and it is important for our framework to conceptualize how sex/gender and national identity are linked (Vickers 1994a).

In short, our analysis requires understanding that women who are part of minority communities often experience politics differently than majority women, who can rely on state instruments to transmit and protect their culture and language. This dimension of difference is collectively experienced and shared with men. Consequently, in negotiating the effects of this aspect of difference, minority women face conflicting pressures from their sex/gender identity, their communal identity and often their class identity.

US feminist philosopher Iris Marion Young (1990) notes that when people are oppressed because of their communal identity, they often make that identity into a badge of pride, initially to encourage collective solidarity in protest against their oppression. Just as class may overwhelm other identities when individual or family survival is at stake and class struggle is intense, so too racial, ethnic, language, religious or national identity may overwhelm sex/gender or class identity. Consequently, different women may have quite different takes on central feminist issues. For example, *majority*[8] women who have no reason to fear the disappearance of their identity group may consider access to birth control and safe abortion bottom line feminist issues. By contrast, women who are part of minority populations concerned about the very survival of their culture and identity may consider such access a threat to the survival of their group.

Personal Status

The final aspect of difference important for our framework is personal status, which involves characteristics, such as age, size, sexual orientation and disability, that result in discrimination against individuals and marginalization or oppression. Reproductive communities do not experience these aspects of difference, but individuals affected may form their own communities, develop distinctive identities and use the language claims of communal groups to assert their rights. For example, some gay men and lesbians have joined together in a group called Queer Nation through which they assert a distinctive culture and claim rights of self-determination like other nations. The kind of analysis employed by those experiencing disadvantage because of their personal status may vary from individual human rights claims to the separatism implied by Queer Nation. Our framework must help us locate this aspect of difference in our analysis of women's political choices.

Common Cause and Solidarity

These four aspects of difference — geographic location, class location, communal affiliation and personal status — will have different effects on women's political activism in different countries. It is important to realize, however, that the identification of difference as an important element in the framework for a reinvented political science does not mean that women share no common causes or are incapable of solidarity. Indeed, my analysis of women's political activism, especially in the international arena, demonstrates that women worldwide share many political concerns and are capable of great solidarity.

The basic methodological point you should retain from this discussion is that you should not assume women share political values, goals or interests simply because they are women. You should always contextualize by locating the effects of women's differences in your analysis. Assertions of a common interest or shared values among women always must be demonstrated with empirical evidence. Every time you state "women want", you need to ask yourself "which women am I talking about" and "can I back up this claim with concrete evidence".

Major Arenas of Women's Political Activity

Drawing on many studies by feminist political scientists, geographers, sociologists and historians, we can identify four major sectors in which women are active. Exhibit 5 presents these four sectors visually. Women's political activism occurs

1. In the *institutions of official politics* at all levels — local, provincial or state, and national or federal — and is aimed at all state institutions — the legislature, the bureaucracy, the judiciary and the coercive arm including the police and military. This sector includes the institutions of the official politics of the international sphere — for example the United Nations and the World Court.
2. In the *institutions of civil society,* including churches, unions, universities,

Exhibit 5.
Four Arenas in Which Women Engage in Political Activity.

1. Institutions of Official Politics	2. Institutions of Civil Society
• Legislatures, courts, etc. • International institutions, such as the UN, the World Court, etc.	• Unions, media, churches, etc. • International civil society structures, such as World Council of Churches, etc.
3. Institutions and Organizations of Autonomous Women's Movements	4. Pressure Groups and Movements
• National women's groups, etc. • International groups, such as Women's International League for Peace and Freedom (WILPF), etc.	• Consumer lobbies, environmental movements, civic associations, etc. • International movements, such as the World Anti-Slavery Association, etc.

the media, and communal and ethnic associations. The institutions of civil society are defined as those that are not under the direct control of government and are not in the domestic (familial or household) sphere. Be aware that the line between the state and civil society changes according to regime type and the society's history. It is also useful to conceptualize an international version of civil society with international churches, unions, movements and NGOs.

3. In the institutions and organizations of *autonomous women's groups and movements*. The defining characteristic is that these groups and movements are all or mostly female in membership and are female-led. Again, many international organizations and movements fall into this category.

4. In *pressure groups and social movements,* including movements for change, those aimed at maintaining the status quo and reactive movements aimed at restoring a previous situation. From a women-centred perspective, the main characteristic of most of these groups and movements is that they are mixed-sex or mostly male-led.

Competing Definitions of Politics

This model of women's political activism is based on the broader conception of **politics** I have already described. From a women-centred perspective, politics involves activity aimed at changing, maintaining or restoring power relationships in society and internationally, usually involving collective (group-based) activity. This definition challenges the definitions used by mainstream political scientists, in part because it categorizes as political all activity aimed at change within the institutions of **civil society** and all collectively undertaken activity aimed at changes in the domestic sphere. In the model presented here, efforts to change power relationships in churches or unions, to support the status quo through use of the media or control of the university curricula, and to achieve change in communal or ethnic associations are as political as running for election or lobbying for new legislation. Because the political science paradigm accepts institutionalized male dominance as more or less natural, it does not theorize about how patriarchy is maintained; feminist analysis, by contrast, identifies the importance of the institutions of civil society in maintaining and replicating institutionalized male dominance. Similarly, political science naturalizes domestic relationships and defines the division of labour between the sexes as non-political; feminist political science, however, considers collective efforts to change domestic relationships and the sexual division of labour to be central to women's politics.

Historian Gerda Lerner (1986) and anthropologists Peggy Sanday (1981) and Sherry Ortner (1974, 1978) demonstrate the importance of symbol systems, including religion, philosophy, literature and popular culture, in maintaining and replicating the power relationships that make up political systems of male dominance and the broader social systems that sustain them. In order to understand women's activism, therefore, we must conceptualize as political their efforts to become priests or to introduce more gender-inclusive language to liturgies, even while we accept the desirability of leaving the basic activities of the institutions of civil society free from state direction. Our broader understanding of the nature of politics also allows us to recognize as political such things as the struggles of students to be taught from a curriculum that is inclusive of difference, and the efforts of racial and ethnic minority women to shape their communities' cultural practices so that both their heritage and their rights and dignity as women are sustained. Because our framework sees political change as involving far more that state action or coercion, we can focus on cultural contestations as essential parts of politics.

Perhaps most important is that this broader conception of politics allows us to reinstate as political the many contributions to community-building and nation-building our mothers and foremothers performed, activities that were discarded as women's "good works" when the mainstream political science paradigm was developed in the 1950s.

This pattern of women's activism is of great antiquity and appears in many countries around the world. We know that in pre-state societies, from the Igbo village democracies in Africa to the Iroquoian longhouse communities in North America, women exercised a strong **counterpower** to men's political and military activities and participated effectively in political decision-making and community-building. As the specialized institutions of the state grew more powerful and complex, these older arenas of women's activism were marginalized. They reappear in times of crisis, however. For example, when people move to new countries as forced or willing emigrants, women's roles in building and sustaining communities have often become especially important.

> Counterpower: The power women exercise by contesting male dominance through protests or longer-term actions conducted mainly through associations within civil society.

To some feminist political scientists, such as British scholar Joni Lovenduski (1986), women are active in marginalized political activities mainly because they have been excluded from official politics. Quebec historian Yolande Cohen, on the other hand, distinguishes between the power of formal politics and the *counterpower* women create through their activism and their associations[9] (1989). To Cohen, counterpower includes all efforts to contest male dominance, including the power of protest, the power of non-cooperation and the organized power of associations. Cohen's point is that women already have power, acknowledged or not; that is, women's activism in associations in civil society can be the counterpower through which the society can be radically transformed.

Notice that the visions underlying Lovenduski's and Cohen's analyses are quite different. What they have in common is the insistence that women's activism in civil society in both mixed-sex and autonomous women's groups and movements, as well as in more spontaneous protests and contestations of male dominance, must be considered political.

The Attraction of Various Arenas

To date, official politics is the sector that has received the most attention from feminist political scientists. Much attention has been devoted to **electoral projects** — the systematic efforts of women in a jurisdiction to get more women elected to its legislatures. Women's voting behaviour and distinctive political attitudes have also been heavily studied as the concept of the **gender gap** has gained popularity. As noted earlier, however, the main work of feminist political science has been focused on barriers research, which has resulted in some useful findings about aspects of existing political systems that impede women's election to legislative office. (I discuss some of these findings in Chapter 5).

Electoral project: Systematic efforts by women in a country, state or province to get more women elected to its legislature.

More important, however, have been the insights into the attractions and impediments to women's activism in each sector of political activity. Exhibit 6 is a preliminary map of these findings, indicating the main poles of political attraction for women in a country such as Canada. That is, the exhibit shows from the perspective of majority women the costs and benefits of being politically active in five arenas mapped by feminist researchers. (Keep in mind, however, that the picture may be different for minority women and women in other countries.)

Moving beyond barriers research to consider both the attractions and the impediments to women's activism in a particular sector avoids the trap of considering male patterns of activism as the norm. For example, an arena's location of activity — close to or far from home — affects its attractiveness more for women rearing children than for other women, as long as the current sexual division of labour, which assigns most childrearing to women, continues and as long as most official politics involves face-to-face activity in a central location. Such things as the size of the country (distance to the political centre) and women's class affect their estimation of what it will cost them to be active in a particular arena.

Further, the way an arena's political structures are organized — in a power hierarchy or in a flatter arrangement with more power-sharing — affects whether women face a low, moderate or high opportunity for leadership and low, moderate or high competition for achieving political influence. In Canada, for example, only a tiny fraction (about 5 percent) of men and women active in federal or provincial political parties ever get a leadership opportunity within their party, let alone within the legislature, and far more men than women get the actual chance to lead. By contrast, my investigation of movements for

Exhibit 6. A Model of Competing Poles of Political Attraction for Women.

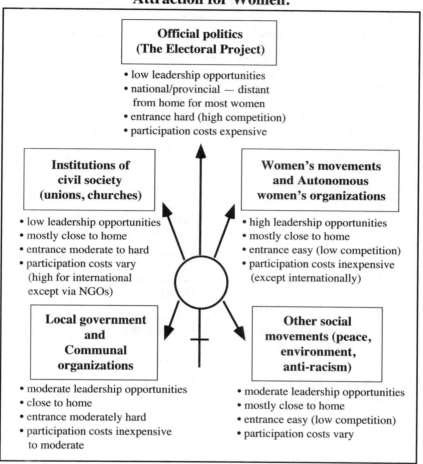

change in Ontario shows that about a third of the men and women active in them had been or were group leaders, and that an equal number of men and women got the chance to lead (Vickers 1992). If the chance for leadership were the only factor involved and if the various arenas offered the same power to influence political outcomes, women would have a clear and obvious choice.

Opportunities for leadership or lack thereof, however, are only one thing that may attract women to or deter them from entering particular arenas. Indeed, for many women, what is important is opportunities not for leadership but for influencing public policy. Exhibit 7 illustrates women's relative opportunities to influence public policy by their political activity in the four sectors. (The base is again Canadian research.) Notice the implicit distinction between the ability

Exhibit 7. Women's Opportunity
to Influence Public Policy: Canada

Institutions of Official Politics	Institutions of Civil Society
• Leadership and important bureaucratic positions remain male-dominated (especially marked in international politics)	• Leadership and bureaucratic positions are hard to gain and mostly held by men
• Academic disciplines and media that shape public policy discourse remain male-dominated	• If women can gain leadership, they can influence policy positions as individuals
• Power of the sector to set political agendas is high	• Policy is difficult to influence from rank and file positions
• Power of the sector to shape policy is high	• Power of the sector to set political agendas is medium
	• Power of the sector to shape policy is medium
Autonomous Women's Movement/Organizations	**Other 'Social' Movements**
• All leadership and bureaucratic positions held by women	• Women may have significant opportunities to gain leadership and high bureaucratic positions
• Women can shape policy as individuals and collectively	• Some opportunities to influence policy are available to the rank and file
• Some groups are less hierarchical	• Power of the sector to set political agendas is medium
• Power of the sector to set political agendas is medium	• Power of the sector to shape policy is low
• Power of the sector to shape policy is low	

to influence political agendas and to actually shape public policy. Activities involved in what Cohen calls women's counterpower can get things on political agendas. Mass protests and contestations of male dominance, for example, can force those holding political power to recognize that they have to do something about an issue women have raised. By contrast, the activities that make up counterpower are less successful in shaping the nature of the public policy used to respond to the new agenda item. Here, the men who hold senior political, judicial and bureaucratic office have more influence, as do those who are powerful in the media and the academic disciplines that shape public policy discourse.

The International Dimension

The mainstream paradigm of political science is based on a model of a nation-state in which a cultural entity (a nation) and a political entity (a state) coincide. The "American science of politics" also has a model of the international realm that flows quite directly from the cold-war environment I described earlier and that also underlies what is called the 'realist approach' to international politics. Developed in the 1950s and 1960s, the realist approach views the international arena as dominated by hard-shelled states that, like billiard balls on a table, interact with each other in conflicts of interest (some violent) and much less often in cooperation.

I was taught international politics in the early 1960s from one of the classic texts of that realist tradition: Hans J. Morganthau's *Politics among Nations: The Struggle for Power and Peace* (Third edition 1960, First edition 1945). In it, the author demonstrates the high degree of convergence between the framework of realist theory and the mainstream political science paradigm. His first principle is "Political realism believes that politics . . . is governed by objective laws that have their root in human nature" (1960:4). The drive to power and the roots of war and imperialism are also assumed to be rooted in an universal (and relatively unchangeable) human nature, which can be understood scientifically. The basic motivation in international politics is "interest defined in terms of power"; neither altruism nor ideas "direct the actions of men" and "universal moral principles cannot be applied to the actions of states". Finally, political realism insists on the autonomy of the political sphere and defends it against reduction to other causes, whether moral, historical, cultural or economic.

Ironically, Morganthau himself believes in the "obsolescence of the nation state and the need to merge it into supranational institutions of a functional nature" (preface to the third edition). Realism, however, emphasizes the power conflicts among nation-states and empires, rather than focusing on the building of international institutions to regulate conflict. Nor does it place emphasis on the role of international civil society, international NGOs or movements in international politics. In fact, although Morganthau argues for such institutions as necessary to avoid the threat of nuclear war, his analysis ignores totally the many contemporary NGOs that were actively pursuing peace and fostering development and reconstruction in war-torn Europe and the newly-liberated former colonies of the European empires.

Not surprisingly, the "human nature" realism portrayed shows no sign of female characteristics. The title of another text, Waltz's *Man, The State and War* (1959), makes the point clearly. If domestic political science is mainly about political man acting in governmental institutions, international politics is even more a male realm. Women's extensive international activism in the nineteenth and twentieth centuries, in anti-slavery and anti-war organizations, for example, is completely ignored, as are women's efforts to support reconstruction and development through NGOs. Certainly, the institutions of the autonomous international women's movement are never seen as part of international politics in this tradition.

Today, despite the radical changes that have occurred in international politics, "neorealist international relations theory [still] begins with the sovereign state as a given" (Tichner in Peterson 1992). It assumes the essential similarity of states despite their profound internal differences. States are set up as the actors in international politics, with very little attention paid to how their international policies are shaped. Some forty years later, despite now-competing traditions, the dominant formulation of the field remains largely unchanged. Political science students are still taught that the field is about men, states and conflict.

Feminist Work in International Affairs
Only recently have feminist analysts of international relations begun the process of opening up space for a reframing of the field's key concepts and theories from a women-centred perspective. The delay is not because of any lack of energy on the part of women in the field (although they are few). The problem is simply that international relations remained an exclusive preserve of men far later than domestic politics. Women in official international organizations are even scarcer than women in domestic legislatures and cabinets. At the UN, for example, less than 5 percent of senior professional staff are women, a proportion that has grown little in the past decade (Karl 1995).

Because feminist work in international politics began later than the study of domestic politics, most research is in the form of critiques revealing the profoundly gendered character of the field's concepts, theories and assumptions. V. Spike Peterson identifies two kinds of feminist projects now underway: projects of deconstruction, which reveal "invisible" gender characteristics in the field and which identify and correct distortions resulting from the field's **androcentrism** (male-centred bias); and projects of reconstruction, which explore the "theoretical implications of taking gender seriously" (1992:2). Reconstructing a field from a women-centred perspective is a far more difficult and lengthy task than critiquing its biases.

In Chapter 6, I explore some of feminist scholars' approaches to public policy issues in the international field. In integrating the international dimension into the framework I am presenting, I proceed in the same way as I have with domestic politics, pointing out the main forms of women's existing political activism. Following the typology of Exhibit 5, I locate the major areas of women's activism in international politics:
1. Official international political institutions, such as the UN.

2. The institutions of international civil society. Women are very active in some of these institutions, and some of that activism is political because it involves attempts to change the institution or international politics through the institution.[10]

3. International pressure groups and movements for and against change. Since women's involvement in the world's anti-slavery movement, they have been consistently active in mixed-sex movements and pressure groups.

4. The institutions and organizations of autonomous international women's movements, some of which are now more than a century old. These organizations include women of all perspectives from the most traditional (Associated Country Women of the World, for example) to the most radical (Feminist International Network of Resistance to Reproductive and Genetic Engineering, for example).

This approach to integrating women's political activism into our framework for developing a feminist political science must not hide the fact that a major aspect of politics in the international realm involves violence—whether in the form of terrorism, police actions or war. As we've already seen, the fact that all states are patriarchal has meant that women have usually been excluded from the use of weapons and discouraged from developing the physical capacity for combat. Ultimately then, we must explore the continuum of violence and the threat of violence that lie behind all politics and government—domestic or international. I begin this task in the next chapter as I explore the basic concepts that underlie mainstream political science and feminist reconstructions.

Consider, however, that the next chapter may not be what you want to read next. If your interest is less in ideas than in what has and is happening to women's activism within a single country or in terms of comparative politics, you may turn to Chapter 5. And if your focus is on public policy, you can go to Chapter 6 for views from both the affluent 'western' democracies and those from poorer countries. Nonetheless, I recommend you proceed with a straight read-through.

Further Reading

Cohen, Yolande. 1989. "The Role of Associations in Democracy." In Yolande Cohen (ed.), *Women and Counter-Power.* Montreal: Black Rose.

Karl, Marlee. 1995. *Women and Empowerment: Participation and Decision Making.* London: Zed.

Mies, Maria. 1991. "Women's Research or Feminist Research? The Debate Surrounding Feminist Science and Methodology." In Judith Cook and Mary Margaret Fonow (eds.), *Beyond Methodology: Feminist Scholarship as Lived Research.* Bloomington and Indianapolis: Indiana University Press.

_____. 1983. "Towards a Methodology for Feminist Research." In Gloria

Bowles and Renate Klein (eds.), *Theories of Women's Studies.* London: Routledge.

Vickers, Jill. 1983. "Memoirs of an Ontological Exile: The Methodological Rebellions of Feminist Research." In Angela Miles and Geraldine Finn (eds.), *Feminism in Canada: From Pressure to Politics.* Reprinted 1989, Second edition. Montreal: Black Rose.

Young, Iris Marion. 1990. "Five Faces of Oppression." In Iris Marion Young, *Justice and the Politics of Difference.* Princeton, N.J.: Princeton University Press.

Questions for Discussion

1. What are the six ways in which feminism challenges mainstream political science?

2. In what ways are women and men differently related to states?

3. What are four ways in which feminist methodology differs from the methodology of mainstream political science?

4. In what ways are women differently-located? How does each aspect of difference potentially affect their experiences of politics?

5. What are the four main sectors in which women's political activism occurs? Does this model apply to women's activism in the realm of international politics?

Notes

1. More complex regime **typologies** exist. Nelson and Chowdhury (1994), however, make a very good case that this simple schema works effectively for a women-centred analysis. In their analysis of women's politics in forty-three countries, they add a partly democratic category to cover the many regimes that are transitional.

2. Whether state-socialist or democratic regimes are "better" from a women-centred perspective is a much tougher question to answer. I won't try to deal with it here. You can consult Nelson and Chowdhury (1994) for an analysis of the question.

3. My own work explores this issue in an attempt to understand why franco-Quebec feminists are eager to see power decentralized to Quebec while anglophone feminists want the federal state to have power over key areas (Vickers 1991 1994b).

4. Women have been active in anti-violence campaigns at all levels along this continuum, from establishing safe houses and shelters for the victims of family violence to anti-war activism at the level of state and global politics.

5. I focus on democratic states here to keep the discussion simple. The pattern for affluent, western states, however, is not replicated in less affluent democracies with less extensive welfare systems. The pattern I describe is, however, replicated more extremely in authoritarian regimes and in a different way in state-socialist regimes (Nelson and Chowdhury 1994). A major new field for feminist political science is the exploration of how women are related to their states in different

kinds of regimes and in countries with different levels of affluence.

6. Two children are allowed in the countryside, and some minorities are exempted.

7. Nevertheless, the experiences of men, like those of women, need to be contextualized to take into account the experiences of members of racial and ethnic minorities and other marginalized individuals. Although mainstream political science does not treat men as sexed and gendered beings, feminist political analysis considers important the differences experienced by racial and ethnic minority and other marginalized men in their relationships to the state, especially in terms of relative power. For example, Canadian prisons hold far more aboriginal men than their proportion of the population accounts for, and far more US black men died in the Vietnam War than their proportion of the population warranted.

8. *Majority* refers to the racial, cultural and sometimes religious group that controls most of a polity's institutions of political power. It is usually but not always a numerical majority. In apartheid South Africa, for example, whites were dominant but made up only a small proportion of the population.

9. Which, she argues, must be located in civil society.

10. Women's ability to take part in international relationships is limited because women are everywhere poorer than men. They have been willing to do everything from holding bake sales to selling their possessions to participate in international meetings and contribute to development and reconstruction projects. This tradition of women's international activism goes back at least to the early nineteenth century.

Chapter 4

THINKING BEYOND MALE DOMINANCE: REVISING CONCEPTS AND REINVENTING THEORIES

Having set out some basic ideas and history for you to think about, I now examine the concepts necessary for developing a feminist political science, one that understands politics from a women-centred perspective.[1] Some repetition from Chapters 2 and 3 is inevitable, but here I go into more detail.

The chapter has three parts. In the first, I explore some of mainstream political science's basic concepts such as *order* and *justice, authority* and *contract,* and *freedom* and *obligation.* These concepts have been considered over many centuries in western political thought, and they are contested, with different traditions giving them different meanings. I map the basic issues in dispute and, where necessary, provide alternate definitions for you to consider. I also present some other concepts of today's mainstream political science drawn from more modern social and political theory, including *power* and *rationality, class* and *exploitation, quality* and *representation.* The objective is to orient you to the core ideas about politics that currently structure the field and that a feminist political science must assess for their ability (or lack of ability) to explain women's political experiences.

In the second section, I provide an overview of the core ideas that shape today's feminisms.[2] I already have introduced some, such as *patriarchy, the public/private split, consciousness-raising* and *consensus,* the *ethic of care* and the *sexual division of labour.* Other key ideas to be explored include *autonomy* and *choice,* the *continuum of violence, dominance* and *oppression, equality* and *liberation, systemic discrimination* and *affirmative action, needs* and *rights.* Again, these concepts rarely have single definitions since different strands of feminism give them different meanings; differently-located women also may have different understandings of them. My goal is to provide a mapping of the conceptual landscape so that you can understand the ideas and the conceptual debates that shape feminist approaches to politics.

All these ideas reflect the experiences, values and intellectual discourses of European and North American women who are secure and affluent. Too often they have assumed their concerns about legal equality with men and freedom from reproduction are shared or given the same priority by minority and 'third world' women who are often forced to be more concerned with the security and economic well-being of them-

> Patriarchy is A HISTORICAL CREATION formed by men and women in a process which took nearly 2500 years to its completion.
> Gerda Lerner, 1986

selves and their families. Nonetheless, in Asia, Africa and Latin America, indigenous women's movements in the nineteenth and twentieth centuries also developed feminist ideas that reflect women's experiences in countries suffering under colonialism, cultural imperialism and economic exploitation. Thus, I also present some present-day feminist ideas articulated by these differently-located women.

In the third section of the chapter, I explore six sets of concepts that illustrate the basic theoretical differences between feminism and political science. Through this discussion, I explore the possibility of building conceptual bridges between the two sets of ideas, bridges upon which feminist political science can be constructed. While this discussion does not pretend to be a complete reinvention of political theory, it provides a scaffolding you can use to work in political theory from a women-centred perspective, one that will allow you to communicate with those working within the two worldviews.

I also give you an overview of feminist political thought, which you can explore more deeply on your own. My basic purpose, however, is to provide you with an understanding of the ideas on which feminist political science is being built (see Exhibit 8).

Exhibit 8. The Core Concepts of Feminist Political Science.

The ideas on which feminist political science is being built are:

- Patriarchy, power/empowerment, authority
- Equality/equity, democracy, consensus
- Citizenship, participation, representation
- Discrimination, oppression, marginalization
- Interests, needs, rights
- Freedom, diversity, identity

Central Concepts of the Mainstream Discipline

The conceptual framework of modern political science is gender-blind in a way that would have been inconceivable to the thinkers who shaped western political thought.[3] Major philosophers, from Plato and Aristotle, writing about politics in the Greek city-states four centuries before the birth of Christ, to Hobbes and Locke, writing in seventeenth century England at the beginning of the emergence of the liberal state, "reflected an acute sense of the centrality of gender to the rationalization of political life" in their writings (Jones 1988:11).

Underlying these writers' theories are conceptions of politics as an activity from which women were excluded on the belief that their 'nature' and reproductive activities made them unfit to be either rulers or citizens[4] or on the idea that the state was founded as an agreement among men to which women were deemed to have agreed by consenting to marriage.

A division between the private and the public sphere is evident in the early archaic states of Mesopotamia, thousands of years before Plato and Aristotle (Lerner 1986). The ideas that first **legitimized** male rule in the earliest western political thought came from religious teachings and from the era of Plato and Aristotle when the consolidation of male rule in the Greek city-states was still quite recent (O'Brien 1981).

Legitimizing Unequal Rule

During the fifteen years I taught a course in the history of western political thought, every year students asked me two questions: why some theorists were included in the parade of great thinkers while others were not, and why the history being taught began with the political philosophers of classical Athens.

Histories that begin with Plato and Aristotle begin with two of the strongest arguments to legitimize unequal rule—the rule of the many by the few. Indeed, much of the tradition of western political thought as it is usually taught in today's political science classes involves various justifications for inequality in the structuring of political systems, so the question of which theorists get included is important. In every period, some groups and individuals have challenged the dominant view. Classical Athens, for example, had advocates of ancient Greek democracy,[5] although both Plato and Aristotle wrote explicitly against it as it embodied political equality. When the liberal states were emerging in Europe in the sixteenth and seventeenth century, groups such as the Levellers, the Diggers and the Quakers argued for political,

> **Democracy:** In theory, government or rule by the people. At a minimum, it is exercised through representatives who are chosen in periodic, open, competitive elections and who make decisions for the society as a whole after being chosen in such elections. The word is derived from Greek *demos*, "the people".

economic or spiritual equality. But it is those who relegitimized unequal rule on a new basis who are usually taught.[6]

Once unequal rule is legitimized as a principle, women's exclusion becomes part of the map of politics. It is naturalized (made to seem natural) and the vocabulary of politics is all about political man.

Examining the historical origins of states makes it easy to understand why the legitimizing of unequal rule is the major theme of western political thought. In fact, were the histories of Chinese or Indian Mesoamerican political thought taught in North American courses, the same theme would be equally important. Wherever archaic states developed (a process that took a thousand years), a complex political form emerged, characterized by

> the emergence of property classes and hierarchies, commodity produc-
> tion with a high degree of specialization and organized trade over
> distant regions; urbanism; the emergence and consolidation of military
> elites; kingship; the institution of slavery; [and] a transition from kin
> dominance to patriarchal families as the chief mode of distributing
> goods and power (Lerner 1986:54).

Associated with the invention of the state, as part of the new technology of political rule, were the invention of symbol systems in the form of writing and numbers and the formalization of learning. Most women and many men were denied access to these skills and thus excluded from influence on the ideas (including laws) now used to support unequal rule (Sanday 1981). Anything written down became much more authoritative because it was written down, and whoever controlled that process could control what people thought about unequal rule. This control of symbol systems was as important to states' political technology of unequal rule as the coercive forces exercised by their first institutionalized military forces.

The archaic state in the Ancient Near East emerged in the second millennium B.C. from the twin roots of men's sexual dominance over women and the exploitation by some men of others . . . . The control of male family heads over their female kin and minor sons was as important to the existence of the state as was the control of the king over his soldiers. Gerda Lerner, 1986

Concepts Justifying Unequal Political Rule

Western political thought was, until quite recently, part of the system of ideas that legitimized the unequal rule states created and maintained. For a long time, the question of institutionalized male dominance wasn't even on the agenda since women's invisibility in political thought seemed as 'natural' as their exclusion from citizenship and political rule.

How did the main preoccupations of western political thought support unequal rule? Traditional political thought has been seen as the search for justice, the attempt to understand political authority and why people ought to obey those who hold it, and a search for order and security in a world too often marked by conflict, violence and insecurity. Thus, political theory, Thomas Spragens writes, "tries to make the world of politics intelligible to us . . . . It sketches for us the geography of politics; and this kind of map tells us where we stand and what routes will tell us where we need to go" (1976:5).

This 'neutrality' is deceptive, however, since most political theories are written from the perspective of the powerful (although few political theorists themselves actually governed). Not surprisingly, then, the great issues rarely involved questioning authority or unequal rule.[7]

Contract Theories

The idea that unequal rule achieves the common good and, therefore, is in the interests of the many is at the core of traditional political thought. Indeed, the existence of states is often explained by theorizing the endemic existence of conflict and violence that can be avoided only if the many have a government to protect them.

The powerful liberal thinker Hobbes, for example, argued that fear of conflict, violence and death was 'man's'[8] strongest instinct. He contended that men consented through a contract—a binding agreement among themselves—to establish and obey an all-powerful authority or sovereign power; otherwise, "in the state of nature", life was "nasty, brutish and short" as a consequence of 'man's' drive to best others in order to protect himself. To Hobbes, the self-interest of the many demanded rule by as powerful a **sovereign** as possible, whom he believed should be a single ruler.

Sovereign: Supreme authority to rule; the individual or body who holds such authority.

As Australian political theorist Carole Pateman demonstrates, the hypothetical social contracts such thinkers used to relegitimize unequal rule in the seventeenth and eighteenth centuries always excluded women and reconstructed the state and government only in the interests of men, whose rule over women was to be maintained and defended by states and governments (1988).

The Presumed Superiority of the Few

Much older than the contract theories are theories that justify unequal rule by appealing to the supposed *superiority of the few who rule* and the *inferiority of the many who are ruled*. Plato, for example, argued that justice could be achieved only when 'the best' or the wisest ruled.[9] True justice required rule by the wisest—by a philosopher-king who knew 'the good'. In the final analysis, however, he believed that the best approximation his contemporaries could hope for was impartial rule according to a code of laws devised by the wise and administered by men who were not easily corrupted.[10] Plato's student, Aristotle, thought that justice was "to give to each his due", which ultimately also meant letting those who were wise or strong rule.

What both of these theorists believed firmly was that rule by the many would always be unjust because they lacked the intellectual capacity to rule wisely and would instead always act in their own self-interest.[11] Aristotle attributed the intellectual inferiority of the many to the fact that the lives of most men and all women were dominated by the forces of necessity—that is, by the need to do 'menial' labour to extract food and shelter from the environment and to labour to produce and nurture children. Only those who did not need to engage in the activities of necessity had the intellectual capacity to make 'rational' political choices.

Out of this analysis came the long-standing conception of the citizen as a male person who enjoyed freedom, and thus became the attribute of a man who could transcend necessity and was not dependent on the will of another. This definition was used to justify excluding all women and most men from citizenship and political rule.

Authority

Closely connected to theories that justified rule by the few was a theory of **authority,** which distinguished between legitimate rule and regimes in which power was usurped or made illegitimate because the actions of the ruler were extremely unjust. A central problem these theorists explored was the source of the authority (as opposed to the capacity or power) to rule.

> Authority: The recognized and legitimate right to give orders (make decisions) and make others obey them.

To Hobbes, the simple fact that someone had the power to compel people to obey might be more important than the matter of whether that power was legitimate. Most traditional political theorists, however, argued that power became legitimate (that is, became authority) when its holders received their office properly or, if they usurped power, if their rule was not unjust.

Theorists differed on the question of how rule must be transmitted to be legitimate. To theorists influenced by religious ideas, those who legitimately held power did so because God had willed it. Theories such as the divine right of kings, therefore, gave authority to the rule of all kings and their legitimate heirs.

Consent theorists argued, in contrast, that legitimate political authority could be conferred only through the people's consent, which was symbolized by the hypothetical social contract. Few consent theorists supported democracy, and those who did, such as Rousseau didn't include women among "the people" who consent. Some consent theorists justified rebellion against rulers considered illegitimate because they did not rule in the interests "of the people"; a convenient belief for a rising class of propertied men to use against the defenders of the divine right of kings and aristocratic privilege. Hobbes concluded, however, that people were obligated to obey anyone with the power to protect them and compel their obedience (although he also asserted they had the right to resist any authority that tried to take away their lives, even as punishment for crimes they had committed).

The idea that people are under an **obligation** to obey legitimately established rulers was very powerful because it made obedience more than a matter of prudence or compulsion. It became a matter of moral and even religious obligation. Theories of political obligation based on the concept of consent, however, began to include the idea that this obligation had limits: there were circumstances in which disobeying even the commands of legitimate authorities could be justified by reference to moral principles or religious authorities. As the founders of the United States affirmed in their *Declaration of Independence*, the obligation to be true to a higher power or principle made it possible to justify even revolution.

> Obligation: What one must do because of a law, contract (binding promise) or moral precept; one's duty.

Women Vanish

From the sixteenth to the nineteenth centuries, **liberalism** emerged as Europe's dominant political philosophy and capitalism as its mode of economic organization. The consolidation and centralization of the European nation-states also occurred in this period, resulting in the suppression of minority cultures and languages. Colonialism and imperialism also marked these centuries as European empires covered the globe and white Europeans established 'new nations' based on the domination of peoples with black, yellow and red skins.

The many in the European nations increasingly challenged unequal rule through rebellions, revolutions, strikes and demonstrations. Others chose (or were forced) to populate the 'new nations'. The new affluence of Europe, which ultimately underwrote the development of liberal democracies in which the many now play a role in choosing those who will govern them, came from the exploitative relationships established with their colonies. And women almost vanished from most thinkers' minds.

The Coming of Modernity
Historians mark the beginning of modern western political thought with the rise of the European nation-state, capitalism and liberalism (Germino 1972). From a male-centred perspective, this statement makes sense since the cultural movement of the Renaissance, in which ancient learning was rediscovered by Europe, and the religious movement of the Reformation, which transformed

Christianity and ended the dominance of the Roman Catholic Church, were great watersheds that stimulated political developments. Yet, as many feminist historians[12] assert, these movements were male-led and they reshaped male-dominated institutions, although women were profoundly influenced by them and some women played significant roles in them.

By contrast, many negative changes occurred for women in the creation of this modern era. Social and political theories increasingly were influenced by ideas that obscured even further women's activities and political interests. Concepts such as *power* and *rationality* were built on male experiences in increasingly formal, centralized institutions from which women were excluded. (For example, universities now existed in many European cities, but most denied women any access to formal learning.) Formal government institutions, such as legislatures, reemerged in Europe, and bureaucracies and courts took new forms with little space for women's participation, except in rare cases when hereditary rule compelled it. The increasing privatization of 'good' women in affluent families was paralleled by the increasing destitution and exploitation of poor women (and their children) on the streets, in the new factories and mines and in the colonies. Not surprisingly, women virtually disappeared from the social and political ideas allowed to march in the parade. Ironically, as the first women began to write about women's experiences of exclusion, as Mary Wollstonecraft did in *A Vindication of the Rights of Women* first published in 1792, women all but disappeared from the dominant texts dealing with politics and government.

Two new intellectual forces contributed to the invisibility of women. First the increasing prominence of science began to influence the study of social and political phenomena. By the nineteenth century, the liberal Utilitarians, the conservative Social Darwinists and the new 'social scientists', such as Comte de Saint-Simon and Auguste Comte (the inventor of sociology), were all impressed by the authority of science and tried to formulate their ideas in ways that imitated the universal claims of the physical sciences. Also by the nineteenth century, a second and not unrelated force emerged: Marxism or 'scientific socialism', which also cast its arguments in terms of universal forces and causes.

These competing schools of social and political thought attempted to explain the same phenomena: the terrible conditions produced in Europe by largely unregulated capitalism in political systems dominated by the owning elites. Their explanations — whether justifying inequality so only the fit would survive (Social Darwinism) or critical and apocalyptic (revolutionary Marxism) — were cast in terms of universal historical or scientific forces. They made no appeal to women's different nature or special function. Instead, the forces of power, exploitation and class conflict were described as rolling over men and women without distinction and, it was assumed incorrectly, in the same way.

The legal disabilities of women were questioned by a few, including utilitarian John Stuart Mill and his partner Harriet Taylor in their work "On The

Enfranchisement of Women", and by Mill in *On the Subjection of Women* (first published in 1869). That women may be doubly exploited by those who own the means of production and by their husbands was recognized by Marxism, at least in the works of Engles. Yet, even these accounts, critical of the forces subjecting and oppressing women, accepted the unequal division of labour between the sexes and, therefore, the dominance of men in both the family and the public realm as part of the universal and 'natural' fabric. The idea of *rationality*, important to the methods of the social 'sciences', assumed a single intellectual standard was at work in these impersonal forces. The content of the idea of rationality, however, was derived only from men's experiences of the world and thus perpetuated a male norm in the guise of universally applicable scientific or historical forces.

The Reemergence of Democracy

The consequences of unequal rule had revived democratic ideas, and new forms of the state that emerged in the nineteenth and twentieth centuries combined aspects of liberalism with aspects of democracy. At the core of both the **liberal democracies** and the **social democracies** that developed in Europe, North America and other Europeanized parts of the world were the concepts of *equality* and *representation*.

The democracies established in the twentieth century have all been **representative democracies,** in which the many choose the few who will rule them. None are **direct democracies,** in which politics is organized in units small enough for people to participate directly in making political decisions about their lives and communities (although many commu-

The concept of representation . . . contradicts some principles of feminism. The very idea of representation implies a delegation of power, resulting in a legitimate concentration, which seems to be irreconcilable with the participatory and decentralized view of power held by many feminists. The problem, then, is that representation as currently understood by powerholders implies a sort of inequality between the representative and the one who is represented. Chantal Maillé, 1997

nities in the 'new world' countries enjoyed periods of autonomy or self-rule).

The dominance of representative democracies conflicts with the vision of self-rule central to the challenge modern feminism poses to existing political systems. Indeed, some feminists argue that equality cannot be achieved through representative democracies, although others believe this form of government can be made more responsive to the views and participation of women.

The debate is an important one. Canadian political scientist H.B. Mayo says

> [v]irtually every democracy has rejected in practice (if not in theory) [the idea] that the representatives should collectively be a kind of mirror-image or, better, a 'map to scale' of interests and opinions in the country as a whole (1960:101).

Mayo's defence of this rejection reveals the reasoning that has permitted representative democracy to co-exist with various forms of unequal rule. First, he argues that virtually every democracy has worked out some method of ensuring the representation of minorities, neglecting the fact that women, as a numerical majority, remain largely unrepresented in governments everywhere (unless one accepts the outmoded theory of *virtual representation,* which held that women's interests are contained in the votes of their husbands or other adult male relatives). He also ignores the fact that racial minorities and aboriginal peoples are rarely represented except in a token way.[13] Second, he contends that representatives — that is, politicians — are at least semiprofessional, and citizens are all better off being represented by competent specialists rather than "one of their own kind". Finally, he argues, people's interests are represented through political parties, not through their "representatives" (a term he asserts he would abolish if he could).

This understanding of representation, which is by no means uncommon, confirms Pateman's (1988) assertion that representative democracy, as conceptualized by male-stream political theory and realized in modern states, has been compatible with the virtual exclusion of women from governing. Many of today's feminist critics of politics suspect all forms of representation as thinly disguised structures of unequal rule in which women's exclusion can be attributed to the principle of 'democratic choice' exercised through 'free elections', rather than to structured male privilege.

Others, however, believe it is possible for women to achieve significant changes in the structure and operation of representative government, leading them to support electoral projects to get more women elected to legislative office. The assumption is that women who are elected are more likely to understand politics from a women-centred perspective and to put pressure on representative institutions to achieve their transformation.[14]

Equality
In the concept of *equality,* another idea from this period, political theory purported to provide universal (unisex) explanations. The word equality has many different meanings, ranging from the idea that all citizens should receive equal treatment from the state — that is, be treated identically — to the idea that people should be *treated* as equals and consequently in ways appropriate to their different needs since identical treatment has different consequences for people who begin in different circumstances (Vickers 1983/84, 1986).

Even in the late twentieth century, however, some still believe that even

Formal equality: With formal equality, the state treats women exactly the same as it treats men; also called *legal equality*. The contrast is substantive equality, in which women are treated as equal citizens but also as different when appropriate so that men and women enjoy equal results from their citizenship. Theories of substantive equality mandate the use of devices such as affirmative action, pay equity and party quotas for women candidates.

formal (legal) equality among citizens is undesirable, as is shown by the continued resistance to legal rights for gays and lesbians. The **substantive equality** many feminists demand, which requires the state to undertake positive action to correct inequalities, faces even deeper resistance. The collective equality rights sought by many minority communities, such as indigenous peoples, that require states to surrender some decision-making powers meet even more profound resistance.

All this resistance reflects the fact that the liberal democracies that emerged in most western European and anglo-American countries were shaped more by the values of liberalism than by the democratic value of equality. The social democracies developed in the Nordic countries were influenced more by the value of equality and have been somewhat more accepting of state intervention in order to achieve equality of condition among their citizens (Haavio-Mannila et al. 1985).

Liberalism has taken a different form since its first appearance in European thought. Indeed, a major controversy within feminism is whether it is useful at all in the development of a women-centred vision of politics. Mainstream political thought pays little attention to the conflict between liberal and democratic values (see Exhibit 9) or among different ideas of equality—conflicts that are of particular importance in feminist analysis. As Haavio-Mannila et al. argue, moreover, even "[a] predominant ideology of equal status and equal treatment provides no guarantee of material equality and real equal treatment. On the contrary, this ideology can help sustain oppression, precisely by concealing its existence" (1985:159). Again, the unisex claims of democratic theory often hide the institutionalized male rule and female *oppression, subordination* or *marginalization* behind an ideology of equality and the popular will. By glorifying the tradition of the epic theorists of the western tradition, political science replicates the distrust theorists of unequal power had of the powerless and less powerful. Intellectually, political scientists have aligned themselves with the few who rule, rather than with the many who are ruled. The first break in that practice came from the Marxists and socialist critics, who took the standpoint of the ruled and effectively challenged the myth that unequal rule benefits the many, and from early feminist thinkers, such as Mary Wollstonecraft, who challenged the idea that male rule is always in women's interests.

Since that time, feminists have developed concepts and practices that address unequal rule—ideas and practices that I examine in the next section.

Exhibit 9. Some Contradictions between Liberal and Democratic Values.

Liberalism's Central Value Is Freedom	Democracy's Central Value Is Equality
Freedom to accumulate property	Right to basic sustenance and equality of condition[1]
Freedom of contracts and free markets	Equal pay for work of equal value; consumer protection; etc.
Legal equality; equal opportunity	Substantive equality/equality of results
Freedom from interference	State action to achieve equality
Freedom of speech, expression and the press	Equal dignity of persons may require state intervention in the institutions of civil society; for example, to enforce right to equal access[2]
Freedom of association	Right to collective action in unions; access to male-only, white-only clubs
Freedom of religion; non-interference	Equal dignity of persons may require state intervention in the institutions of civil society; for example, to enforce right to equal access.[3]
Right to self-defence	Right to enjoy equal personal security
Freedom of movement	Equal security of persons may limit the movement of others[4]

1. Leading, for example, to state guarantees of minimum annual incomes or basic health care.
2. Leading, for example, to laws restricting hate propaganda and verbal forms of racial or sexual harassment.
3. Such as affirmative action access to universities.
4. For example, by restraint orders.

Feminist Ideas: An Overview

Just as most media gurus and politicians assume 'women' are a homogeneous group, most political scientists assume that there is only one set of feminist ideas. Too often, moreover, feminist ideas and theories are dismissed as mere grievances, and the challenge they pose to contemporary political systems is rarely seriously examined.

In reality, feminist theories and perspectives differ widely. What they have in common is acceptance as facts:

• That today's societies do not treat women as equals to men.
• That this situation is wrong.
• That this situation can and must be changed.

But feminist theories and perspectives differ on whether male dominance is rooted in the physical nature of the human species or socially constructed. They differ on whether the resulting condition for women should be called *subordination,* **marginalization, oppression** or exploitation.

As I partially explained in Chapters 2 and 3, the main approaches to feminist theory in the 'western' countries are *liberal, left-wing* (Marxist and socialist), *radical/cultural, existential, psychoanalytic and postmodern.15* Minority women in western countries have also developed *lesbian feminism, black feminism, womanism, Latino feminist* and *communitarian feminism.* In the 'third world', although the term *'feminism'* itself may be controversial, especially when it is seen as involving ideas developed by western women, all varieties of feminist thought are found, from the most academic to the most practical.

One reason for the many variations is that differently-located women often have different priorities and goals for their activism. For example, feminism in some countries is associated with struggles against other oppressive systems, such as national struggles for liberation against imperial powers (Jayawardena 1986). In the countries emerging from the break-up of the Soviet empire, feminism is also emerging, despite the bad reputation that the official, Marxist version of feminism had developed among women (because it was associated with the intolerable double burden they were expected to carry by the old regime). In these countries, however, women find the new 'freedom' and 'democracy' often mean losses for them as men use their own new freedom to close child services and displace women from their jobs; men can compete more effectively (and ruthlessly) because of the sexual division of labour that frees them from most domestic and reproductive labour.

In South Africa, women who long subordinated their gender-based needs to the struggle against apartheid are now also demanding change. The South African Commercial, Catering and Allied Worker's Union, for example, fought for and won a contract that pays parental leave to both women and men. *Sharing the Load,* a book in which the union outlines its principles, asserts:

[w]ithout the re-organization of family life in such a way that it is shared between both parents, we cannot talk about freedom for both men and women. For as long as women are seen only as mothers, cooks and cleaners, there can be no equality between men and women in society (cited Karl 1995:52).

It is not my purpose to give you a detailed account of the many varieties of feminist theory. Instead I explore the core ideas that have shaped and are shaping present-day feminism as it relates to the development of feminist political science.[16] I also explain the disputed meanings attributed to those concepts by the different strains of feminism and by differently-located women. Although I often consider first the majoritarian versions of feminism, I also apply the methodological principle of **contextualizing** for difference developed in Chapter 3 to ensure that our understanding of the basic ideas of feminism does not just reflect the experiences of privileged women in a few affluent countries.

The current wave of women's activism has its origins in the 1950s and 1960s. The triggers were politics as diverse as the women's international anti-nuclear movement, the bus boycott of the black civil rights movement in the US, the struggles for self-determination in Africa and on the Indian subcontinent, the 'red power' movement of aboriginal peoples in the Americas and the struggle of Scandinavian women to participate in public decision-making. Because the period was dominated by the cold war between the US and the Soviets, however, women in different parts of the world until the mid-1970s had relatively little interaction. Consequently, the 'western', especially the US, versions of feminism came to predominate in both popular and academic cultures.

Feminisms' Roots

Forms of **liberal feminism** and **left-wing feminism** have existed since the late eighteenth and early nineteenth centuries. For the first time, accounts of unequal rule written by the less powerful appeared in the public discourse. Within liberalism, feminists concentrated on the concept of *equality* and on the goal of equal citizenship. Within socialism, feminists explored women's economic and social subordination to men and advanced cooperation as the basis of a new form of society. Within Marxism, the 'woman question' was understood as something that could be resolved only after capitalism had been transcended. Indeed, feminists within Marxism believed that class best accounted for women's condition (Tong 1989:39).

By the late nineteenth and early twentieth centuries, many North American women struggling to achieve the right to vote advanced what has been called **maternal feminism,** arguing that their experience as mothers would bring a new quality to politics and that they should be granted the vote because of that experience and quality. The contemporary **equal rights feminists** also fought for the vote but on the grounds that female citizens were due the same treatment

> **Maternal feminism:** A late nineteenth- and early twentieth-century theory that women should be given the vote because they were mothers with a unique perspective on public policy. By contrast, equal rights feminists of the same period argued for the vote as part of the equality owed to all citizens.

as male citizens.

After the Second World War a new form of feminist activism emerged that is still influential today. Its difference lay in being mobilized by a radical form of feminist thought that asserted that gender and sexuality were at the core of women's oppression. **Radical feminists** saw women being oppressed by men, not just by neutral forces or society, a perception that personalized oppression in a new and unique way. They also identified men as privileged by systems of *institutionalized male dominance,* which they called **patriarchy.** And their analysis of the nature of patriarchy included sexuality; the sexual division of labour; the cultural assignment of women to the domestic sphere through the ideologies of femininity, heterosexuality and mothering; and the existence of violence in the intimate relations between men and women—all concepts that made this body of thought distinct from other, earlier forms.

Radical feminists challenged all other explanations of inequality, arguing that the oppression of women was the first, the deepest, the hardest to eradicate and the most painful form of oppression because it afflicted more than half of humanity (Jaggar and Rothenberg 1984:186). This assertion, made originally to claim space to explore women's experiences in other movements that rejected the idea of women's oppression, would ultimately divide feminists over who was the most oppressed and whether by racism, sexism or homophobia.

An example of the effects of this conflict can be seen in debates concerning women's autonomy and reproductive choice. From the perspective of relatively affluent majority women, whose cultural identities were secure, women's autonomy seemed the right goal, and the concept of freedom came to mean individual self-government. Women were to be 'free' as they believed men were free—not subject to the will of another. Nor were they to be subject to the will of the wider community. This understanding of freedom was drawn from observing the behaviour of affluent, majority men, especially in the US. It also reflected the profoundly individualist conceptions of freedom that are part of white US culture.

Although radical feminism did not explicitly explore this concept of autonomy, it is the basis for the central ideas of *reproductive freedom* and *reproductive choice,* which became understood as freedom *from* reproduction and the freedom to choose *not* to reproduce.

In contrast, many minority, aboriginal and 'third world' women facing racism, economic exploitation and threats to their communities and cultural identities have rejected the concepts embodied in the terms *reproductive freedom* and *choice.* Instead of freedom *from* reproduction, they seek the genuine ability to choose, which must involve economic well-being and the security to have babies and raise them to adulthood sharing their parents' identity. Those women have also rejected the priority most western, majoritarian feminists give to reproductive freedom—understood as access to contraception, abortion and child care; poverty, access to employment and basic services, and racism are often a higher priority (Nain 1991). For women with disabilities and many lesbian women, reproductive freedom means having access to reproductive technologies and changing laws so as to have the right to reproduce.

Many minority and 'third world' women also challenge the individualistic basis of the radical feminists' concepts of autonomy and reproductive freedom. To majority women, autonomy and self-determination can be attributes of free and equal persons because their cultural community lives more or less securely within their nation-state. To many 'third world' and minority women, autonomy and self-determination are first the much sought-after attributes of nations and communities on which individual freedom can rest.

Women's 'Liberation'

In addition to the goal of autonomy expressed in the struggle for reproductive freedom, the concrete political agenda of majority, western feminists centred on issues of sexuality, male violence against women and the cultural debasement of women.

This strong political agenda was created by women out of their direct experiences, which they discussed collectively. Influenced by the ideas of the **New Left** movement, majority women engaged in the radical process of **consciousness-raising** (CR), in which groups of women (no more than about fifteen) would meet for six months to a year. Each woman described the circumstances of her own life; these insights were shared, and the group then developed an analysis of the causes and forms of women's oppression. This process produced radical results as ideas emerged that focused, for the first time, on the domestic sphere, women's relationships with men and experiences of mothering. As French observer Ginette Castro concludes in her book about US feminism, the key difference was that "[w]hile the militants of the earlier Women's Rights Movement had only talked about sexual discrimination, those of the Women's Liberation movement dared to speak of sexual oppression" (1990:22).

In their analyses, radical feminists deliberately drew comparisons between women's experiences and those of people oppressed because of race, class or nationality. Recall that this period was one in which movements of national liberation were challenging European imperialism worldwide. Everywhere, aspiring nations used the language of oppression and liberation. US blacks used the concepts of civil rights to mobilize against a vicious system of racism and segregation that privileged whites. Leftists used the concepts of class conflict, exploitation and the inevitability of revolution to mobilize against capitalism.

Radical feminism drew from all of these discourses and presumed to apply them to all women everywhere, who were seen as oppressed by men in their sexual and reproductive relationships and discriminated against in the public realm. Having broken the silence about the sexual division of labour (who cleans the toilet), sexual relationships and violence in those relationships, they considered a revolution in the domestic sphere necessary and possible.

The radical women's movement was called the **women's liberation movement** and, in the US and some European countries, it was sharply differentiated from older, reform-minded women's rights movements. Equality with men was not this movement's goal. Women sought *liberation* from male *oppression*; many worked in separate women's organizations and rejected compulsory heterosexuality by choosing lesbian relationships.

The key structure in this movement was the small group within which consciousness-raising had occurred when that phase was over, these groups became *collectives*, which undertook many projects at the grassroots level. Equality among members was the central principle and each group operated on a process of **consensus** in which votes were not taken; instead, discussion continued until all members agreed on (or were willing to accept) a position, as the concept of individual self-determination required. The groups had no formal leaders and, in the tradition of direct democracy, all specialized tasks were assigned by lot. Conventional politics and cooperation with traditional institutions were suspect; co-optation was feared as the likely consequence.

An Emerging Political Agenda
Both the radical political analysis and its challenge to traditional modes of political organizing spread from the US to other western countries. The consciousness-raising (CR) process, which produced the political agenda, was the source both of the movement's strength and its weakness — its inability to contextualize difference. CR groups drew together women who shared characteristics and believed the analysis that they developed constituted a general account of women's experiences.

Nonetheless, this dynamic process of the less powerful exploring their common experiences of subordination or oppression produced a remarkable political agenda that mobilized millions. Women exposed the violence that existed in some domestic and sexual relationships, including the casual violence to which many girls and women are subjected. Some women explored alternatives to heterosexual relationships. Some organized to resist the exploitation of women in pornography. Most profoundly, they began to challenge the division of labour between the sexes, which allocated domestic and nurturing tasks to women while reserving decision-making for men.

This emerging political agenda also produced concepts that made possible analysis of patriarchal governance from a women-centred perspective.

Gendered Visions

One set of new concepts emerged when feminists began to conceptualize the work of domestic reproduction, including 'mother work' and other nurturing activities assigned to women in the sexual division of labour, as producing an ethic of care. Feminist psychologists such as Carol Gilligan (1982) assert that women's ethical understanding of the world differs from men's because women and men experience it differently. While men work from abstract principles like justice, Gilligan postulates, women are moved by an ethical system that looks at the actual harms or benefits of actions to individuals.

Feminists debate whether or not differences in the ethical systems of women and men are inherent because of women's actual or potential reproductive roles as mothers and their experiences as daughters instead of sons. **Cultural feminists** believe women have an inherent attachment to different values. Other feminists argue that such differences are situational and would change if childrearing and care of the sick and elderly were shared more between the sexes. Regardless of their position in this debate, however, feminists have increasingly asserted that 'women's values' —the values of the ethic of care— ought to play a role in political decision-making, which is currently dominated by abstract, largely economic concepts of rationality and efficiency.

This idea has supported concepts of feminist political analysis such as the **gender gap.**

The Continuum of Violence

Another important concept transferred from consciousness-raising groups into feminist political analysis has been the *continuum of violence* (see Exhibit 10).[17] This idea rests on the observation that violence against women exists in varying degrees in all patriarchies in the form of rape and battering, child abuse and incest, gang rape and rape in war. The concept links these and other manifestations of violence against women together, positing violence as part of a process that limits women's choices and mobility and that men use, collectively and individually, to control women, especially when other mechanisms of control break down. The identification of such *structural violence* permits identification of the limits imposed on women (including those which are self-imposed): fear of and threats of male violence keep women out of many occupations, places and activities, reducing their opportunities for autonomy, income and leadership. Feminists also call attention to the cultural manifestations of violence against women in pornography, popular and high culture.

This analysis has led directly to political actions and demands that have rocked contemporary politics, as in the 1991 Clarence Thomas/Anita Hill case in which the alleged sexual harassment of a colleague by a prospective US Supreme Court justice was aired on international television.[18]

This kind of analysis is controversial, as feminists discover when they make these links in public discourse. For example, when they linked the Montreal

Exhibit 10.
The Continuum of Violence and Women's Responses.

Type of Violence	Responses
• War	• Anti-war activism
• Ethnic cleansing	• Campaigns to include sex oppression in definitions of refugee status
• World trade in sex slaves	• Campaigns of rescue and attempts to get UN action
• Massacres of women	• Campaigns for gun control
• Gang rape, stranger rape, partner rape	• Establishment of safe houses and shelters;
	• Campaigns to protect rape victims against legal harassment and judicial blame
	• Campaigns for legislative changes to make rape in marriage illegal
• Date rape	• "No means no" campaign
• Wife battering	• Establishment of shelters; campaigns for legal changes
• Child assault/incest	• Establishment of support groups; legal action
• Cultural violence	• Anti-pornography campaigns
	• Campaigns against violence on TV and war toys
	• Creation of positive counter images
• Structural violence	• Self-defence training for women; CR
• Sexual harassment	• Campaigns for anti-harassment codes

'massacre', in which fourteen women engineering students were shot because their killer saw them as feminists, to other forms of violence against women, such as wife battering and rape, Canadian feminists were confronted by a firestorm of public and media opposition. The popular (and far safer) explanation was that the slaughter was shocking but the work of a lone madman. Women who demanded the right to commemorate this event in women-only groups were themselves subject to extensive abuse, especially by the media. Anita Hill was abused by the US senate committee and the media for insisting on a connection between Justice Thomas' alleged harassment of her and his fitness to hold judicial office.

The radical consequence of this kind of analysis is that it breaks down long-standing divisions between men's private, domestic and sexual conduct and their conduct of public affairs. Many Canadian men resisted any implication of shared gender guilt in the Montreal event. Other men, however, began what they called a White Ribbon Campaign in which groups began to explore the implications of the continuum of violence for their experience of masculinity. Men and women, led by female relatives of the fourteen murdered women, worked together to enhance gun control, though gender gaps concerning gun-control legislation are common.

Majority and minority women, while equally concerned about the many manifestations of violence against women, often differ about how violent men should be treated. Some minority and aboriginal women argue that men from racial minorities are too often victims of police violence and are more often imprisoned than majority men. They argue that the need for solidarity with men in the struggle against racism and poverty makes community healing or collective female actions against perpetrators a better strategy than legal action.[19] Some black women also point to the lynch-mob overtones that can mark feminist political actions against male violence, such as Take Back the Night marches—impressions that arise because white women were for so long controlled by images of the rapist as a stranger rather than as a partner, boyfriend or next-door neighbour (as is more often the case).

Discrimination and Oppression

Systemic discrimination is another concept that radical feminists have developed into a framework of analysis with significant impact in mainstream politics in the liberal and social democracies. Traditional liberalism used the weak concept of **discrimination** to describe circumstances in which individuals were unfairly denied the rights of equal citizenship because of conscious *prejudice.* While contemporary feminists use the language of rights basic to individualistic liberalism, they also use the concept of *oppression,* which names something both more serious and more systematic. As a bridge between liberalism and this more radical concept, many of today's feminists have adopted the concept of **systemic discrimination.** The idea is that the equality of women as a group

Systemic discrimination: A complex system of laws, policies and practices that are seemingly neutral in their impact but that, overall, have a disparate impact on an individual or group. Such discrimination does not rely on conscious prejudice and cannot be changed simply by people's becoming less prejudiced.

faces barriers from which men benefit as a group and that these barriers are built into the structures of society, especially into its system of opportunity and its division of labour between the sexes. This idea is far more powerful than the idea that prejudiced individuals have discriminated against other individuals by denying them rights.

The same analysis was developed, especially in the US, around racial discrimination and the two analyses together support the theory and practices of **affirmative action.** Barriers that are systematic and structural require positive action by the state and institutions to remedy the problem, not just rectify it by providing the rights denied to individuals. Nor has the analysis of systemic discrimination focused only on individual rights. Thus, the *Canadian Charter of Rights and Freedoms,* enacted in 1982 as part of the Canadian constitution, explicitly defines affirmative action programs as part of a process of achieving the equality rights of members of groups disadvantaged and, consequently, constitutionally protected. The Supreme Court of Canada, for example, described *systemic discrimination,* using the words of Justice Rosalie Abella, as "imposing burdens, obligations or disadvantages" and "withholding or limiting access to opportunities, belief and advantages available to other members of society" (*Andrews* v. *Law Society of British Columbia* 1989). Thus, the ruling recognized explicitly that individuals may experience disadvantage *because* they are members of a group.

Despite the current backlash, the concepts of *systemic discrimination* and *affirmative action* are part of an equality-seeking process that is changing the nature of politics (Vickers 1986).

Core Concepts of Feminist Political Science

In the final section of this chapter, I present the basic conceptual structure that feminist political scientists have derived from women's political activism and modern feminist movements. It can act as a bridge between feminism and mainstream political science. I outline six sets of concepts with a working definition of each and a discussion of the issues surrounding its use. Where disagreement exists about the meaning of a concept, I explore that disagreement. I also explain how feminist politics uses each concept and how that usage relates to mainstream political science.

Patriarchy, Power/Empowerment, 'Authority'

Patriarchy, as used in feminist political science, means a political system in which men enjoy a monopoly on decision-making positions in the key institutions of the state and where the balance of power in other institutions tends to favour men.[20] It does not mean that men have all the power and women none; indeed, the work of feminist anthropologists demonstrates that female power has often existed with overall male dominance — that is, female power and male dominance can and do co-exist. Nor does the definition mean that male rule takes the same form everywhere or in every period; feminist political science analyses how male rule has changed over time and how it reflects different cultures. Finally, it does not mean that male rule is universal or inevitable; patriarchy or institutionalized male rule is an historical phenomenon created by human beings, not by nature.

The very word *patriarchy* has created debate. Carole Pateman points out important distinctions between patriarchal male dominance in the form of rule by fathers, which prevailed in earlier centuries, and contemporary male dominance in the form of fraternal rule, based on an agreement among men as "brothers", "mates" or "chaps", which emerged under liberalism. Believing that most observers think *patriarchy* refers to an ancient system long ago discarded for democracy, she maintains:

> A very nice conjuring trick has been performed so that one kinship term, fraternity, is held to be merely a metaphor for the universal bonds of humankind, . . . while another kinship term, patriarchy, is held to stand for the rule of fathers which has passed away long ago. The modern civil order can then be presented as universal ('fraternal') not patriarchal. Almost no one — except some feminists — is willing to admit that fraternity means what it says: the brotherhood of *men* (1988:78).

Seeking to avoid this trap, feminist anthropologist Gayle Rubin (1975) coined the term *sex/gender system* to refer to an institutionalized system that allocates status, privileges, property and other resources to people on the basis of their sex and their culturally-determined gender role. The concept of **sex/gender** is useful because it captures the impact both of biological sex (that women, not men, bear and nourish children from their bodies) and culturally-assigned gender (that women, not men, rear children after they are born). The concept of a sex/gender *system*, which Rubin intended as a substitute for patriarchy, is less useful because it captures all aspects of a society. That inclusiveness presents a problem for political science, which needs a term that can be applied specifically to political systems.

Connell (1987) uses the concept of a *gender regime,* which permits exploration of the extent to which state institutions and processes are masculinized, and how relationships between the genders are configured. His model, however, deals with all institutions, making it less useful than an approach that deals explicitly with the political system and in which the political consequences of sex (that women can physically reproduce identity groups, while men cannot) as well as gender can be acknowledged and explored.

Despite the persuasiveness of some of these arguments, I retain *patriarchy,* carefully defined, because my purpose is to *bridge* between feminism, as it is practised in present-day politics, and mainstream political science. Patriarchy is the most powerful concept developed by contemporary feminists. Discarding it would be like the linguistic cleanups that substitute *spousal abuse* for *wife battering,* thereby hiding the reality of the phenomenon.

Power

The concepts of *power* and *authority* have been especially difficult for feminists to encompass. Most give power a negative meaning because they experience the exercise of power over them negatively. Nancy Hartsock (1983) conceptualizes power as involving coercion and will—that is, the ability to make others do that which they otherwise wouldn't do. She demonstrates that traditional political science understands power as quantifiable, a currency that represents the relative capacity of individuals, groups and countries to express their will and gain what they want. For example, Lasswell and Kaplan, 1950s political scientists, asserted that: "It is the threat of sanctions which differentiates power from influence. . . . Power . . . is the process of affecting [the] policies of others with the help of (actual or threatened) severe deprivations for non-conformity with the policies intended" (1950:76).

Because few women have exercised power of this kind, feminist reactions to power, understood as power over, have often been hostile. And because women experienced such power exercised over them as less powerful or powerless people, they have a different take on power than men who write from the perspective of the powerful. While few men acknowledge or even recognize the fact, women increasingly understand that sexuality is a major instrument by which power over women is maintained. For women, then, power is something woven through both the public and the domestic realms and is present even within their most intimate relationships.

Although women are ambivalent about exercising **power over,** also called *domination,* many advance the idea that power has two faces: the familiar face of dominance and the less understood face of **power to** or capacity. To understand this aspect of power, women have looked to the capacity of the weak, to relationships among equals and to relationships between mothers and their children (Vickers 1980). As Janeway (1981) shows, even weak individuals can have power collectively by disbelieving the powerful and organizing together to achieve their own ends. Hartsock (1983) notes that women's writings emphasize the idea of power as capacity, energy and potential, which recasts women as active participants in the power order rather than as passive victims of domination or oppression.

In a recent collection of essays, Radtke and Stam (1994) show that the concept of power becomes a far more complex and subtle concept when women's experiences of the two faces of power are explored. Earlier social and political theorists knew about some aspects of

> Power: Two Faces: Power over, or domination, means having the capacity (ultimately based on coercion) to make others do what one wants them to do and that which they otherwise wouldn't do. Power to, or capacity, is based on ability, energy, skill, leadership, affection or collective action in which coercion (or threat thereof) is not involved and in which exploitation or oppression does not result.

this richer understanding of power. Max Weber, for example, advanced the concept of charismatic power to identify men (in Weber's account) able to command people because of the force of their personality or their followers' enthusiasm of their leadership. Weber considered charismatic leadership unusual, however, and thought most power relationships were routinized.

Some feminist analysts have borrowed the term *empowerment* to describe the assumption of capacity or energy (power to) by an individual or group. This concept is used extensively to describe the process of collective self-assertion central to women's political activism.

Authority

The concept of *authority* has been the subject of extensive reconstruction by Kathleen Jones, a feminist political theorist. In her book *Compassionate Authority* (1994), she asserts that traditional conceptions of authority conflate the idea with male practices of command; that is, authority came to be understood as the right of the dominant to coerce obedience from those they can subordinate. Jones maintains this conception of authority as "commanding sovereignty" represents the masculine practice of authority over a number of centuries, which eventually became normative. Domination involves only power over—being able to make others act against their wishes or interests— because subordinates cannot pursue their own choices without risking harm. Jones argues that feminists have often accepted this conflation of the concept of authority with the male practice of command. They have then argued that women should either be included as commanders or not become involved in such distasteful actions.

Jones concludes feminists must reconstruct the concept of authority. Instead of looking only to male practices, they should also look at actual and potential female practices of power.

This insight leads her to consider a compassionate form of authority exercised with the goal of achieving the needs and interests of those led, and she suggests looking at authority relationships other than those of command/coercion to find new understandings of what that new authority would be like. Her renovation of the concept of authority opens up the possibility of looking at nurturant authority relationships between parents and children, teachers and students, or care-givers and patients for other images.

In brief, feminist analysis reveals both complete powerlessness and all-powerfulness as myths needing reassessment. The symbols supporting traditional and limited conceptions of authority also require redevelopment by examining more situations of authority. In particular, the role of nurturing, love, sexuality, admiration, empathy and friendship in authority relationships need to be examined.

Equality and Equity, Democracy and Consensus

Another core group of concepts revolves around equality—what it means and how to achieve it for all individuals.

Equality and Equity

Equality is the central value of modern feminist thought, but there have been few attempts to explore its implication in terms of theories of democracy. As late as the 1970s, the main goal underlying much feminist work was *legal* or *formal equality* with men, an approach that rejected the idea of different treatment for women and men.

The consequences of the campaign to have women treated exactly the same as men were considerable, including increased pressure from men for custody of children, a decline in the incidence of alimony on divorce and the prospect of subjecting women to the military draft.

Some aspects of women's inequality cannot, however, be corrected by their attaining formal equality. Identical treatment creates problems when 'real differences' between the sexes matter, especially in circumstances involving physical reproduction and physiological differences.

The thesis that women need identical treatment to be equal also ignores the fact that most women's lives are marked by centuries of educational deprivation and economic disadvantage. To take a simple case, in many countries, women earn about a third less than men. Suppose the matter at hand is a wage supplement set at 10 cents. If a women's wage is 66 cents, the supplement results in a wage of 76 cents, while the same 10 cent supplement to the male wage of $1.00 results in a male wage of $1.10. Although this identical treatment improves women's economic well being, it results in no change in the wage inequality.[21]

Women in some countries have questioned the value of equality understood as identical treatment, while others have supported it. US women have relied on legislation mandating affirmative action to correct male-female wage and employment inequities. Yet they also pursued (unsuccessfully) the **Equal Rights Amendment,** which was based on the principle of complete formal equality. The *Canadian Charter of Rights and Freedoms,* on the other hand, covers both identical treatment and appropriately different treatment, including constitutional sanction for affirmative action programs. Canadian feminists supported this approach because they had discovered, through cases brought under the old Bill of Rights, that identical treatment is often not enough.

Yet women differ in how they believe 'real differences' between men and women should be treated. Does substantive equality mean always treating men and women differently in some respects because they always will *be* different (for example, with regard to reproduction)? Or should it be achieved by providing programs to make women and men as similar as possible so that in fact as well as in theory a unisex citizen exists?

This issue is approached differently by three kinds of feminisms: feminisms of equality, feminisms of difference and feminisms of androgyny (see Exhibit 11).[22] Each offers a different vision of what equality should mean for men and women and whether women should work primarily in the arena of official politics to achieve their vision of equality. Most Nordic women, for example, have chosen the path of **state feminism** —a primarily androgynous feminism. It requires state programs to support both women's greater responsibilities in the public realm and men's greater responsibilities in the domestic sphere. Notice that this androgynous goal does not assume that women must become more like men; rather, it implies that both men and women must be helped to become more like each another.

Many racial and ethnic minority women suspect the concept of equality as a goal, largely because the emphasis has been on achieving equality between majority women and men with little focus on equality among women or among men. They also point out that affirmative action programs such as pay equity and employment equity favour well-educated, majority women. They propose instead the concept of equity (as in *pay equity* and *employment equity*) meaning to treat people fairly by treating them appropriately rather than identically. Ironically, the term has its origins in Aristotle's theory of *in*equality, where *equity* meant to give to each his due—in this usage, a code word for unequal results, justifying the exclusion of women from public life and justifying slavery, provided the person was a "slave by nature".[23] I find the distinction between formal and substantive equality more useful, provided analysts contextualize for differences among women, rather than focus exclusively on inequalities between women and men as majority feminisms have done.

Democracy

That feminists have not yet developed a systematic theory of **democracy** is not surprising since women were denied even the legal rights to citizenship everywhere in the world until this century and are still denied that right in some countries today. Theorists such as Pateman (1988) have developed critiques of existing forms democracy, which are the basis for my conclusion that *repre-*

Exhibit 11. Three Types of Feminism.

	Ordering principle	Source of standard	Causes of attitudes, values, inequality	Approach to inequality
Feminisms of equality	Women equal to men	Established by men, adopted by women (male is norm)	Sociocultural norms	Absolute equality; sex- and gender-blind
Feminisms of difference	Women different or separate from men	Arrived at by women (female is norm)	Men; the family; economic status; biology (some)	Gender-specific, recognizing meaningful differences between men and women
Feminisms of androgny	Women and men equal to each other	Arrived at by men and women together	Institutional capitalism; anti-feminist structures	Sex-specific but gender-neutral, recognizing only sex-based differences

Sources: Vickers, Rankin and Appelle 1994:250; Dumont 1986; Yates 1975.

sentative democracies, as currently structured, do not admit women as sexed and gendered people into the polity, except to cast their votes. This work is continuing, however, and I do not explore it here. Instead, I examine several attempts to reconceptualize democracy from a women-centred perspective and women's political practices concerning democracy in the autonomous organizations they have created.

Zillah Eisenstein, a US feminist political theorist, writes: "Given recent developments throughout the world, any discussion of democracy must begin with what is missing in both socialism and liberalism" (1994:11). Because both liberal and socialist systems rest on patriarchal foundations, neither provides the basis for a democracy within which women, especially differently-located women, can operate as political equals.

Feminists have seized on liberalism's rights discourse as a lever for practical political actions and on socialism's promise of more substantive equality. Eisenstein asks, however, when the limits are reached:

> The struggle toward democracy is a struggle, in some sense, over just how democratic liberalism and its discourse of rights can become. Just how much of the socialist promise of equality can liberalism incorporate without losing its commitment to individual freedom? (1994:11)

Eisenstein emphasizes practice over theory as the guide to what kind of democracy would best help women achieve their goals. This approach leads her to examine women's struggle for democracy in settings as diverse as the new Eastern European "male democracies" and the US, where racism, violence and backlash make the struggle to incorporate women's equality goals particularly difficult. Her analysis looks beyond these crises to a form of democracy in which *bureaucratic statism* is replaced by more decentralized and responsive structures that women can shape to meet their needs.

Viewing women faced with such difficult struggles, however, Eisenstein reasserts the centrality of their bodies to the process of rethinking democracy: "Feminists can insist on using our bodies to push out the boundaries of democratic theory" (1994:171). In her earlier work, Eisenstein has always argued that obscuring women's power to reproduce identity groups, from families to races and nations, is a central strategy of patriarchies (1981). Mary O'Brien (1981), too, considers women's power to reproduce a central fact of democracy, both in political theories and existing democracies. Feminist political scientists have followed this insight by insisting that reproduction and sexuality are essential aspects of politics. Democratic theory and practice must be reconstructed to reflect the fact that citizens are sexed and gendered.

Is a reconciliation of liberalism and equality for women even possible? In their assessment of the relative success of the Scandinavian social democracies, Haavio-Mannila and her colleagues conclude that they fail to achieve equality for women even with extensive efforts to 'socialize' and 'feminize' liberalism (1985). Observers from outside the Nordic countries consider social democracies to be far better than liberal democracies in achieving *substantive equality* for women, especially in terms of recognizing the relationship between their political lives and reproduction and sexuality. In a 1991 study of women's status in twelve countries in Western Europe and North America, Canadian feminist leader and journalist Doris Anderson concludes that social democracies produce more substantive equality for women and that the presence of women in political decision-making facilitates these results.

By contrast, US feminist political scientist Joyce Gelb, in her study (1989) comparing the US, the UK and Sweden, says that the absence of a strong women's movement outside of Sweden's *state feminism* weakens women's capacity to influence politics independently. She argues that a strong, autonomous women's movement that can lobby governments produces better results for women. The authors of a recent study of women's politics in forty-three countries (Nelson and Chowdhury 1994) found that democracies, even when partial, produce significantly better results for women than do authoritarian regimes. (Their project also provides evidence for women to continue the debate concerning the relative advantages of different kinds of regimes to the achievement of women's goals.)

In brief, women's struggle for democracy, *substantive equality,* equal rights as citizens and equal access to decision-making opportunities, then, is of great importance even though their efforts to push out the boundaries of theory have not yet produced systematic feminist theories of democracy. Their goals for democracy must include incorporating women as sexed and gendered people whose political concerns involve some issues that result from their being women. Feminists are also now actively debating what kind of democracy is best for women—liberal democracy with a strong market, or social democracy with significant state activism to support women's citizenship activities.

Direct Democracy
Women's practice of politics in autonomous women's organizations also contributes to understanding a women-centred approach to democracy. Radical/cultural feminists argue that only *direct democracy* in small groups working through *consensus* permits each woman autonomy and self-government. This position is criticized by many people as unrealistic in large-scale, mass democracies. It is also criticized by some feminists as potentially undemocratic: women with forceful personalities can dominate a small group, and a structureless, consensus-based practice offers no way to hold dominant individuals responsible or remove them from their positions of de facto leadership.

Despite these criticisms, the idea of a politics in which all individuals can have an authentic voice is very powerful in feminism. Indeed, the success everywhere of political movements reflects the increasing desire of women and men to experience genuine democracy, if only in a small-scale, grassroots group. The experience of direct democracy in small groups, however, leads today's feminists to challenge deviations from it in larger organizations based on elected leadership and representation (Vickers, Rankin and Appelle 1994).

The conflict between the experience of direct democracy in grassroots groups and the practice common in large-scale organizations is a problem for feminism. But it is also an opportunity to develop further insights about democracy itself. Modern technology is eliminating many of the practical barriers to all citizens' having more involvement in political decision-making. So the relevant question involves Mayo's argument (1960) that political decision-makers ought to be professionals. Clearly feminist theorists of democracy must decide if they agree with that view and should, therefore, advocate the training of more women for professional politics, or if they should pull back from professionalization, advocating more and more extensive involvement of citizens in decision-making. Kathy Ferguson (1984) urges rejection of the bureaucratic statism that professionalizes and centralizes power into unequal rule, despite the myth of democratic control. Australian **femocrats** see this perspective as naive, arguing that women must be where decision-making power is if they are to have influence. Many Quebec feminists argue that the best model on which to build a new vision of democracy is a radical decentralization of state structures so that women and men can participate in decision-making close to home.

Citizenship, Participation and Representation

The answers to the questions that ended the previous subsection lie, in part, in what feminists political scientists have begun to understand about *citizenship, participation* and *representation* when viewed from a women-centred perspective.

One way to understand different kinds of democracies from the perspective of women is to explore what citizenship means and doesn't mean. Historically, western women's demand was for *equal* citizenship in which their differences from men would not be held against them. In the feminisms of strict equality, the goal was a state that would be impartial and in which citizens would all receive the same treatment. As Pateman (1988) argues, however, once women are included, citizenship can be defined in a common, universal way only if the resulting universal citizen is disembodied. But that disembodied citizen is not, in fact, unisex or asexual since every assumption underlying how citizens act assumes they are male or act as men have acted. Moreover, as Iris Marion Young observes, "The universal citizen is also white and bourgeois. Women have not been the only persons excluded from participation in the modern civic public" (1990:110).

The idea of a common, universal citizenship had emancipatory consequences in the past when class or ancestry privileged some over others in terms of legal rights. Now, however, Young (1989) argues that a differentiated citizenship, which achieves the representation of people's collective or group identities as well as their individual identities, would better serve women's needs and the needs of other marginalized or oppressed groups. Liberalism, however, offers little recognition of the role of identity groups and communities because it conceptualizes rights as rights of individuals. Disadvantaged individuals find it far harder to express their rights as citizens (Gutman 1980). Indeed, Young (1989) argues that communities of disadvantaged individuals are far better able to represent themselves and advance their needs by pooling their powers (the powers of the weak). Her idea of a "differentiated citizenship" reflects the feminist goal of achieving both substantive and formal equality. Citizens must be treated as equals in relation to rights but appropriately to their circumstances in relation to their entitlements. This consideration justifies the idea of state action (affirmative action) to achieve substantive equality for those denied it.

Social-democratic conceptions of citizenship provide more space for group representation than liberal-democratic conceptions. Scandinavian feminists have advanced the idea of *welfare state citizenship* to assert that the state should actively facilitate women's integration into the public sphere (and men's greater presence in the private sphere) through a network of the social services women need if they are to be citizens in fact as well as in law and theory.

This idea, like Young's concept of differentiated citizenship, reflects feminist political scientists' growing understanding that politics is not an equal opportunity activity. Women must compete with men as individuals to express themselves politically as citizens. But men will usually win such a competition as long as the division of labour between the sexes continues to free them from most reproductive and nurturing work and as long as cultures sanction male dominance in heterosexual relationships while oppressing people who choose same-sex relationships.

Citizenship is a matter of being treated equally before the law and receiving equal dignity as a person. For most women, however, it is also about the need to gain strength from communities and groups within which their identity is confirmed, often more so than from equal individual citizenship. Most women find little actual activity as citizens beyond voting impossible without group involvement and a network of supportive social services. Most also need their male partners to provide more support, and those who choose female partners need acceptance of their choice.

Participation

Barriers research—the study of the barriers that limit women's participation at the elite levels of **official politics,** especially in elected office—is the oldest and largest branch of feminist political science. One aspect explores the biases within traditional political science models that claim to explain citizen participation. Because of the dominance of the "American science of politics", these models have mostly been based on observations of the US political system, which has low levels of citizen participation, even in voting, especially by disadvantaged groups. In these models (for example, Milbrath 1965; Verba and Nie 1972), the assumption is that participation rests on personal choice: if someone doesn't participate, that's his or her decision. The fault is in the individual, not in the system.

This victim-blaming is summed up in the use of the word *apathetic* to describe people who don't get involved in official politics. Yet, these models assume all citizens have equal access to all types of political participation. They also assume that activism at lower levels—described by Milbrath (1965) as "spectator activities"—is not essentially different from elite-level activism ("gladiator activities"), such as holding office. And they assume the existence of a free market in opportunity for political action, reflecting the myth that any poor boy can become president of the United States if only he tries hard enough.

These models are misleading for most male citizens, and they are completely unable to explain patterns of women's political activ-

Political opportunity structure: The alignment of political forces, structures and ideas that characterize official political systems and that enhance or deter women's political participation. For example, most proportional representation electoral systems enhance the likelihood of women's achieving success through electoral projects, which enhance their opportunities to participate in official politics.

ism, except to point up their presumedly 'natural' apathy. Feminist political scientists challenge these free-market assumptions and conclude that the **political opportunity structure** differs for women and men. For example, Gelb (1989), in a comparison of women's political activism in the US, the UK and Sweden, demonstrates how the range of party ideologies and the structure of electoral and legislative systems affect the opportunities for women as a group to undertake different kinds of political actions. Other analysts (for example, Randall 1987) argue that participation, especially in formal politics, is partly a matter of choice, with women finding local, less structured politics especially attractive.

Both opportunities and choices may change for differently-located women. Some women may choose to "do politics" outside of the official arenas of politics because they believe there is little real opportunity for them to make a difference inside. But we must not assume that opportunity structures and choices are fixed: women collectively can change the opportunity structures they face through the choices they make, and their choices may change when the opportunities available to them are changed. Women increasingly understand that the citizen's right

> We must . . . insist on our right to participate fully in public life, but must at the same time challenge its very shape and underlying logic. Angela Miles, 1982

to participate is not just a matter of fitting into the political system as it exists. It is also a matter of transforming political systems both from within and without.

Representation

Although I explored women's suspicion of the concept and practice of *representation* earlier in this chapter, its centrality to all modern forms of democracy requires brief consideration of efforts to bridge between feminist ideas and the mainstream paradigm. Feminists have taken three main approaches to the issue of representation: (1) demanding that women be included among those who are representatives; (2) insisting that the practice of democratic representation must be improved; or (3) rejecting the possibility of authentic representation altogether.

Most representative arrangements were devised before women gained the right of equal citizenship, but they have consistently made an issue of their exclusion from full and equal participation in political life. Worldwide, women constitute no more than 10 percent of all national legislatures and less than 5 percent of the senior staff in international organizations. Pateman (1988) notes that this inequality hasn't threatened the legitimacy of political regimes, however, because they were designed to exclude women. That is, the theories of representation accepted in the field don't consider the exclusion of half the population from decision-making roles sufficient to delegitimize representative democracies. Indeed, mainstream political scientists argue, "No one . . . has demonstrated that differences between representatives and the represented have an impact on actual behaviour or public policy" (Jackson and Atkinson 1974).

Many women find this conclusion counterintuitive, which is why they undertake *electoral projects* to get more women elected. And as discussed in Chapter 3 and in more detail later, research by feminist political scientists shows that women legislators are more likely to represent women's identities, needs and interests than are male legislators.

Women have tried to reform the practice of *representation*. In the early twentieth century, for example, many feminists supported the recall of legislators by the electorate and other devices of direct democracy, such as **referendums, initiatives** and **direct primaries.** Political parties have been the central organizers of representation. Over recent decades, however, they have declined as instruments of public policy and in public credibility, so much so in many countries that many citizens no longer think of their party as representing their interests or identity over a long period of time. Many women, especially in the anglo-American democracies, suspect parties of corruption, and, indeed, they have been part of the apparatus of unequal rule, with party **gatekeepers** often excluding women from participation in anything but support roles. In some countries, including Canada and Germany, women have tried to create women's parties but the **electoral systems** have posed formidable barriers to such ventures. In general, therefore, feminist approaches that aim to reform representation must deal with the issue of political parties, perhaps by creating some other structure that can organize support for the election of more women as generators of public policy. Many women consider movement organizations more effective structures than political parties for representing their interests.

Some women think women as a group have no fixed interests that can be represented in politics. French feminist Chantal Mouffe (1992), for example, believes that democracies can and must be transformed into movements of grassroots groups in which individuals can speak for themselves, avoiding the problem of those who assert a right to speak for others. In practice, some women argue for the decentralization of political decision-making to permit more women to become directly involved in articulating their needs and interests. Minority women, in particular, argue against the presumption that majority women can represent them or that women from a single minority can speak for all minority women.

For some women, these difficulties with democratic representation are reason enough to avoid involvement in anything but grassroots collectives. For others, the issue of representation poses a challenge, both for democracy and for feminist organizations, that deserves their attention.

Discrimination, Oppression, and Marginalization

Perhaps no concept used by feminists has caused so much controversy as the idea that women are oppressed. The distinction between *discrimination* and *oppression* is important. So is the concept of *marginalization.*

Discrimination and Oppression

While earlier feminists argued women were disadvantaged or discriminated against, radical feminists used the language of oppression and the goal of liberation. Gerda Lerner defines *oppression* as a "forceful subordination" (1986:233). The term implies victimization. Indeed, dictionary definitions stress cruelty and harshness, as in "to govern harshly, to treat with continual cruelty or injustice" (*Oxford,* Third edition).

Not surprisingly, then, the claim that women as a group were oppressed by men as a group was a radical claim, one which many men and some women rejected. It also raised the question of a hierarchy of oppression: who was more oppressed. Were blacks more oppressed because of racism or were women more oppressed because of their sex? Could affluent, majority women be said to be oppressed? Poor white women questioned the idea that affluent minority women, such as professionals with power over their lives, could be oppressed. 'Third world' women rejected the assumption that any 'first world' women could be considered oppressed. Reform-minded women in affluent countries rejected the term because it cast them as victims, while they wished to develop a sense of women's history as actors and achievers. In short, this politically potent concept opened a can of worms. Yet milder terms, such as *subordination, discrimination* and *marginalization,* implied a less serious condition, one that could be (and was) trivialized by male authorities.

The work of feminist historians and philosophers has begun to develop a vocabulary to express women's actual experiences of subordination and disadvantage. Lerner, for example, demonstrates that some women have always benefited from the subordination of most women under patriarchal rule. She concludes that viewing women as a group only as victims is misleading and ahistorical:

> While all women have been victimized in certain aspects of their lives and some, at certain times, more than others, women are structured into society in a way that they are both subjects and agents . . . . [T]he 'dialectic of women's history', the complex pull of contradictory forces upon women makes them simultaneously marginal and central to historical events (1986:234).

This important insight parallels that of Sanday (1981), who argues on the basis of her anthropological research, that male dominance and female power almost always co-exist and that power is rarely a zero-sum game in which men have all the power and women have none. This insight is important in feminist recon-structions of the concept of oppression, in particular because it means that women can be *both* oppressed (subject) and oppressor (agent) at the same time; that is, individual women can experience and practice aspects of oppression simultaneously.

Feminist philosopher Iris Marion Young (1990) develops this basic insight in her essays on "The Five Faces of Oppression" (see Exhibit 12). Young insists that *oppression* must be a central category of political discourse if theorists are to understand the emancipatory movements of disadvantaged people. But

Exhibit 12. The Five Faces of Oppression.

Exploitation	• Occurs "through a steady transfer of the results of the labor of one social group to benefit another" (p.49).
Marginalization	**• Occurs when a "whole category of people is expelled from useful participation in social life and thus potentially subjected to severe material deprivation and even extermina-tion" (p.53).**
	• "Marginalization does not cease to be oppressive when one has shelter and food" (p.55).
Powerlessness	• Occurs because "the powerless are situated so that they must take orders and rarely have the right to give them" (p.56).
Cultural imperialism	• "Involves the universalization of a dominant group's experience and culture, and its estab-lishment as the norm"; "the dominant group constructs the differences that some groups exhibit as lack and negation. These groups become marked as Other" (p.59).
Violence	• Suffered by "many groups, which means "they must fear random, unprovoked attacks on their persons or property, which have no motive but to damage, humiliate, or destroy the person" (p.61).

Source: Iris Marion Young 1990.

"[e]ntering the political discourse in which oppression is a central category involves adopting a general mode of analyzing and evaluating social structures and practices which is incommensurate with the language of liberal individualism" (Young 1990:39). Within mainstream political science, this discourse of oppression makes little sense. The myth of democratic control allows mainstream political scientists to disallow oppression as a phenomenon currently experienced in liberal democracies (although they admit that oppression may have been experienced somewhere else or in the past). Likewise, they rule out the possibility of unjust rule as a reality in modern democracies, where outcomes are considered the will of the people. Young argues the central importance of persuading people that the discourse of oppression makes sense out of much of actual social experience.

The first thing Young wishes to convey is the systemic, group-based character of oppression as opposed to the individualist basis of the traditional liberal idea of discrimination. But methodological individualism is basic to the methodology of mainstream political science, which understands groups as collections of individuals with shared characteristics. There is no sense of groups as communities that share a common identity and seek to reproduce and preserve that identity.[24]

One of Young's key points is the need to understand the collective identities involved in nationalism, ethnicity, race and so on in order to comprehend the mechanics of oppression and how it differs from the idea of discrimination based on individual identities. Group differentiation in itself is not, she notes, oppressive. Not all groups experience oppression. Nor is a group treated the same way over time. (In Canada and the US, for example, Catholics experienced some aspects of oppression in the nineteenth century, which do not exist now.) To Young, the existence of oppression depends on whether or not a group is subject to one or more of the conditions listed in Exhibit 12. People may not suffer all five conditions because oppression is not an all-or-nothing experience. But the framework makes it possible to determine empirically if people are more or less oppressed and to understand how someone can be both oppressed (subject) and oppressor (agent) at the same time.

As I described earlier, feminists have stretched the liberal concept of discrimination by developing the idea of *systemic discrimination*. Young's account, however, recalls that the harshness and severity associated with the stronger term *oppression* may be appropriate in describing women's lives in some circumstances. Even affluent women of the majority culture are beaten or killed by their husbands and sexual partners, a fact that cannot be captured by the term *discrimination*.

The fact that some women are oppressed to the point of death does not, however, negate the fact that some women oppress other women because of their race, class, ethnicity or some aspect of their personal status.

Marginalization

The term *marginalization* is of particular value. Historically, societies have justified the denial of equal rights to those marginalized for whatever reason. Societies today marginalize the poor, the aged, the disabled, the ill, children, people of different races and ethnicities, gays and lesbians and women who remain primarily in the domestic realm.

Marginalization is increasing as those unable to keep up the pace on the fast track of the market find themselves blamed for their circumstances and face a loss of both employment and social benefits. It is crucial that the discourse developed for feminist political science includes concepts that capture these experiences and their implications for women's politics. Feminist political science needs all of these concepts and must develop them with precision and accuracy to account for women's lives.

Interests, Needs, Rights

Just as it is important for feminist political scientists to have a vocabulary in which they can discuss women's victimization when it occurs, it is also important to have a vocabulary to use in exploring women's capacity to act or *agency*. The set of concepts I present here is a beginning in that task, although women have only recently come to explore their agency in areas beyond asserting their autonomy in relation to reproduction.

Feminist political scientists have engaged in considerable discussion of whether it is appropriate to assert that women have *interests* in common. US feminist political scientist Virginia Sapiro (1991), for example, argues that women do have interests in common because they are women, interests that can be advanced or represented in politics. Scandinavian feminist political scientists Helga Hernes (1987), Drude Dahlerup (1986b) and Anna Jønasdøttir (1988) believe that a women-centred analysis of politics can use the concept of interests if it is redefined. Others, such as Irene Diamond and Nancy Hartsock (1981) and Rosalind Petchesky (1984, 1990) identify major limitations for women in the conventional theory of interests derived from liberalism, which also includes the concept of rights. Many racial and ethnic minority women object to the use of interest theory, which assumes a single set of interests can be attributed to all women as a homogenous category, as has happened when majority feminists assert that a particular change (abortion rights, for example) is "in the interests of women".

Conventional interest theory is especially fraught for women. First, there is the distinction between *objective* and *subjective* interests. As Jønasdøttir asks, "Can we claim that women have certain objective interests regardless of what women themselves think?" (1988:36). Conflicts between feminists and anti-feminists raised this question—for example, when feminists try to explain why all women do not see such things as easier divorce or reproductive freedom as in their interests.

There is also controversy about what is in the *public interest,* a term that is increasingly set against *special interests.* Considerable debate has arisen about whether it is appropriate even to invoke the notion of a public interest, which is like the older idea of a common good. Many feminists, eager to avoid the controversy of interests and rights, use instead the discourse of *needs* and *entitlements.* Others have resisted this usage, however, largely because the concept of interests assumes a condition of human agency. Many beings have needs and may even be said to be entitled to have those needs fulfilled. But only human agents are thought to have interests that emerge out of their experiences and are shared to the extent that those lived experiences are shared.

The simple idea of men and women as two separate interest groups, which characterizes some feminist ideology and some aspects of male-centred social science ("what do women want?"), cannot serve as the basis for a feminist political science. The idea of women's interests must be contextualized to take into account different kinds of experience. But it may also be important to view reproductive and sexual relationships, conventionally understood as private, as involving potential conflicts of interest between women as a group and men as a group; that is, women share at least *some* interests across class, race, ethnic and other boundaries as do men.

Politics involve women in making choices, however: they can choose to join forces with other women around shared issues of sex and gender or contribute to political solidarity around the interests common to their class, race, ethnic or linguistic community. Women may choose to avoid heterosexual relationships and so have less in common with other women in relation to the consequence of such relationships. Other women may choose not to bear children and thus have little in common with women who are mothers. As long as interests are understood to involve choices, rather than necessity,[25] however, a redeveloped concept of interests is useful, particularly as feminist political science explores in detail how different kinds of patriarchies limit women's choices and constrain their rights to make them.

Swedish feminist icon Eva Moberg stresses the idea that women have a responsibility to have an interest in the public realm, just as men have a responsibility to be more interested in the private, domestic realm. This concept of responsibility helps bridge the gap between conventional interest theories and the modified theories developed by feminist political science. The idea that women have a responsibility to bring their ideas and insights into politics also underlies feminist efforts to bring the ethic of care into the political arena. Women's concerns for peace and their development of ecology and ecofeminism reflect this idea that women have a special responsibility to maintain peace and protect the natural environment.

Freedom, Diversity, and Identity

As already noted, the concept of *freedom* has become an almost totally

masculinized idea in western political thought, meaning *freedom from* constraints—an autonomy in which no dependence on another is required or
recognized. Although this hard-shelled individualism is attractive to some
feminists, eager to escape the responsibility of nurturing and the restrictions of
dependence, most women have as their goal interdependence among equals,
rather than the absence of links or dominant/subordinate relationships with
women on top.

The discourse of freedom, however, was shaped mainly by the experiences (or
fantasies) of elite men, who conceptualized it in a way few women could
experience. As a consequence, few women have tried to reconceptualize the
concept.

Three other concepts we have explored—liberation, autonomy and choice—
are, however, touch on the idea of freedom. Each is more limited than the
expansive concept of freedom. What first marked explorations of these three
ideas was their application primarily to the realm of sexuality and reproduction.
The idea of sexual liberation was first embraced by feminists, who were
primarily interested initially in freedom from reproduction. Later they were
criticized because the practice of sex without consequences became problematic.

It is in women's exploration of diversity or difference and in the development
of **identity politics** that other major aspects of the concept of freedom have
begun to be redeveloped. Mainstream political science has no comparable
concepts. Although both diversity and identity politics are also aspects of male-
centred politics, they usually go unrecognized because most men who create
political science see themselves as the norm. It is "others" who are characterized
by difference, therefore, or who engage in identity politics, if such things are
recognized at all. But while the fragmentation of political man into more specific
identities, such as black men, aboriginal men or gay men, has yet to affect
mainstream political science in any significant way, it is a major aspect of
feminist political science.

The concept of difference challenges many assumptions of mainstream
political science more profoundly than other concepts presented. The mainstream assumes that political actors have stable identities that shape how they
behave politically and what their interests are. It also assumes that difference is
like a suit of clothes that can and should be shed when people enter elite-level
politics. Even acknowledged differences are assumed to be assimilable; that is,
anyone who wishes to be part of the political elite can and must check his or her
sex, race or ethnicity at the door.

The rules and norms of the political realm are shaped by those who hold
power, and, as Hannah Pitkin argues, to have needs met at all, people who are
"different" must

"[A]cknowledge the power of others and appeal to their standards, even as we try to get them to acknowledge our power and standards. . . . We are forced to transform 'I want' into 'I am entitled to', a claim that becomes negotiable by public standards (1967:347).

When women manifest their female identities in the public realm, they challenge the norms of that realm in a major way. But difference is difficult to understand and act on, as majoritarian feminists have discovered. Women can listen and explain, but ultimately acknowledging difference and respecting identity require we change both how we think and how we act. This is the basic challenge of feminism to both patriarchies and mainstream political science.

Conclusion

For women to act and be recognized as sexed and gendered individuals in politics, men must accept women's right to define politics differently and structure political activity differently. Similarly, for racial, ethnic and other minorities to have their differences and identities recognized, majorities must recognize their rights to define and structure politics in a different way.

Developing ways to help people understand how to achieve this situation will be a major contribution of feminist political science. The key concepts that can be used as a bridge are the nexuses of Exhibit 8:

- Patriarchy, power/empowerment, authority.
- Equality and equity, democracy, consensus.
- Citizenship, participation, representation.
- Discrimination, oppression, marginalization.
- Interests, needs, rights.
- Freedom, diversity, identity.

These concepts are not the only ones feminists have been reworking from a women-centred perspective, but they are central, and each represents contested ground. When feminist political scientists assert and demonstrate that all existing and known states are and have been patriarchal, they challenge the discipline's most fundamental views about its field. And it is a fundamental principle that she who would change how people view the world must define her terms.

Further Reading

Feminist Critiques of Western Political Thought

Clark, Lorraine, and Lynda Lange. 1979. *The Sexism of Social and Political Theory: Women and Reproduction from Plato to Nietzsche.* Toronto: University of Toronto Press.

Coole, Diane. 1988. *Women in Political Theory.* Brighton: Wheatsheaf.

Elshtain, Jean, ed. 1982. *The Family in Political Thought.* Brighton: Harvester.

Okin, Susan Moller. 1979. *Women in Western Political Thought.* London:

Virago.

Pateman, Carole. 1988. *The Sexual Contract.* Cambridge: Polity Press.

Feminist Political Theory

Bryson, Valerie. 1992. *Feminist Political Theory: An Introduction.* London: Macmillan.

Collins, Patricia Hill. 1989. *Black Feminist Thought.* London: Unwin Hyman.

Eisenstein, Zillah. 1981. *The Radical Future of Liberal Feminism.* New York: Longman.

hooks, bell. 1984. *Feminist Theory: from margin to center.* Boston: South End.

Jaggar, Alison. 1983. *Feminist Politics and Human Nature.* Brighton: Harvester.

Jones, Kathleen. 1994. *Compassionate Authority.* New York: Routledge.

O'Brien, Mary. 1981. *The Politics of Reproduction.* Boston: Routledge.

Tong, R. 1989. *Feminist Thought.* London: Unwin Hyman.

Questions for Discussion

1. What are the core ideas that shape how mainstream political science thinks about politics?
2. What do we mean when we say that political concepts are "contested"?
3. How do the ideas of contemporary radical feminism differ from those of earlier feminists?
4. Why and how do feminists challenge mainstream political science's understanding of concepts such as power, equality, representation and participation?
5. How does the concept of systemic discrimination help build a bridge between mainstream political science and feminism political analysis?

Notes

1. Recall from Chapter 1 that you may prefer to turn now to another chapter. However, all students may find this one relevant in its explanations of why the world is the way it is.
2. The ideas that motivated earlier waves of feminists were often different. Many early (1870–1920) feminists in North America, for example, were motivated by the idea that it was their duty to get the vote in order to clean up politics, then deeply corrupted by the liquor interests. Others sought the vote in order to protect their families and communities.
3. A caveat. If you already learned about the sweep of this thought, you will notice that I often do not use chronological order here. You can learn that order from many other books, if you wish. My purpose in this text is to emphasize particular concepts and examples.
4. An extensive and fascinating literature is the argument between feminist and anti-feminist political theorists about whether Plato, who wrote about women as rulers

116

in *The Republic,* was making a feminist or an anti-feminist case. While I can't explore this debate here, I can point you to the work of Okin (1979) and Bloom (1968), which outlines the two positions.

5. The Athenian democracy was limited in scope: the "people" (citizens) did not include women, slaves or foreigners. It was a direct *democracy* that is, all citizens gathered to discuss political matters, and most offices were filled from among them by lot, not by professional politicians or representatives.

6. Rousseau, who sought political equality among men, is taught, but he also advocated excluding women from citizenship.

7. Maintaining order and legitimizing authority has not been easy, and many women and men have resisted over the centuries. When disruptions of the power order required reformulations of the reasons for unequal rule, however, the issue of women's exclusion would resurface, as in seventeenth century England and during the French and American revolutions. But until the present century, the ideas of the powerless or the less powerful were rarely available.

8. I put 'man' in single quotation marks here to alert you to the fact that it is important to know if a thinker is using the term generically (to include women in his claims) or to describe only men's behaviour. For example, although Hobbes discusses the nurturant and protective relationships between women and their children, he does not explicitly construct a different male and female nature, as Rousseau does.

9. The history of political thought has probably devoted more pages to the concept of *justice* than to any other. This sketch simply touches the surface.

10. Even so, he believed that such a system would eventually deteriorate and become unjust.

11. Modern governments draw on this idea that justice and the interests of the many always differ when they declare the interests of women or the poor to be "special interests".

12. The field of feminist history is now too large for easy description. Two early works that made the case are Hartman and Banner (1974) and Bernice Carroll (1976).

13. At the time Mayo was writing (1960), many US blacks were effectively denied the vote, as were status Indians in Canada.

14. I consider these projects and their results in Chapter 5.

15. In this text, I examine only those approaches that take an explicitly political form. You can find detailed discussions of all these traditions in the texts listed for further reading at the end of the chapter.

16. In Chapter 6, I examine in more detail the major strands of feminism that affect the political positions women take with regard to public policy.

17. Some aspects of this analysis are found in the work of Virginia Woolf and other first-wave feminists. It has become part of a much wider political analysis, however, only in the current wave of mobilization.

18. When a senate committee was investigating Thomas as a nominee in 1991, Hill, a law professor, made public a charge that when the two had worked together, he had subjected her to several years of sexual harassment. The televised hearings of the committee were broadcast around the world for several days. In the end, Thomas's appointment was confirmed. In the hearings, Hill was subjected to examination of her sex life, which many feminists considered a trial of the victim.

19. A practice that is suggestive here is the tradition in some African communities of a group of women "sitting on a man"—that is, noisily demonstrating their

collective power against men who have harmed them or their interests.

20. This definition relies heavily on the historical work of Lerner (1986) and on the work of feminist anthropologists, especially Sacks (1982) and Sanday (1981).

21. Notice that an across the board 10 *percent* increase would actually increase the wage disparity. (Work out the math yourself.)

22. For a full discussion, see Vickers, Rankin and Appelle 1994.

23. Note that I write about Aristotle as taught from texts translated in the present century. New feminist translations of the ancient texts may shed a different light on these issues.

24. A full discussion of the conflict between individual and collective identities and rights is beyond the constraints of this chapter. For more discussion, see Vickers 1993 and 1994a.

25. This interpretation has important exceptions. For example, no woman will have prostate cancer, and no man uterine cancer. So "interests" may be shared across the whole class in some cases.

Chapter 5

UNDERSTANDING AND COMPARING POLITICAL SYSTEMS WITH WOMEN IN MIND

This chapter is about understanding political systems with women in mind.[1] At this point, however, we have no theory to help us assess political systems from a women-centred perspective. So we have few guides to several pressing questions: Which political systems are "good for women"? How do we evaluate political systems for women? Are all states simply instruments of patriarchy or are some potential allies for women? Are bureaucracies always bad for women or is it useful for women to develop their own machinery within government? Should women become integrated into existing political structures and try to change them, or should they build independent women's movements to struggle for change from the outside? Can they do either, or both?

To help you analyze, compare and evaluate political systems from a women-centred perspective, I provide some thinking skills and outline some feminist political scientists' recent attempts to struggle with these questions. First, I explain the importance of the comparative method. Next I look at several approaches to comparison, each of which uses a status-of-women or women's issues framework. These approaches have some advantages, if used carefully, but each involves comparing women with men, which, as we have seen, has built-in problems, mainly because it makes male political behaviour the norm. Then I develop some more women-centred approaches.

In the rest of the chapter, I show you in concrete terms how to use both the status-of-women/women's issues approach and the women-centred approaches by comparing women's politics in six different countries: Australia, Canada, Mexico, Norway, the UK and the US. All are democracies or partial democracies, a fact that simplifies comparisons. The US, Canada and the UK are toward the liberal end of the **liberal-democracy/social-democracy** continuum while Australia and Norway are closer to the social-democratic end. Mexico is a partial democracy emerging from a more authoritarian regime. It is also significantly poorer than the other five. This range will permit us to explore the implications for women of many but not all of the characteristics of political systems.

Why Compare?

Comparison is the oldest method in the western study of politics, but its standard analytic tools do not problematize institutionalized male rule. Moreover, its frameworks for comparing usually focus on the characteristics of political systems rather than on the consequences of different kinds of systems for people's lives. Nonetheless, most mainstream political scientists hold, almost as an article of faith, that democracies are better than other political systems and that 'developing' countries are best when they are moving toward democracy. The discipline's left-wing critics evaluate democracy less positively because its dependence on a capitalist economy combines supposedly equal citizenship with economic inequality. (These critics consider state-socialist regimes better able to achieve results for most people, although the early 1990s collapse of most of the regimes dampened enthusiasm). The issue of which values to use to assess political systems makes us ask how we should compare political systems from a women-centred perspective.

For half a century, mainstream political science has kept separate its analyses of *'first world'* political systems (western democracies), *'second world'* political systems (state socialist systems) and *'third world'* political systems ('developing' societies).[2] The hierarchy has always been clear. 'Third world' political systems are viewed in a welfare perspective (Karl 1995); those that are 'modernizing' and seem to be on the road to democracy are viewed as the "worthy poor" and receive aid from the affluent 'first world'; those that

> Comparative assessments are necessary if the imaginations of feminist activists are to be spurred to think about . . . what is desirable and what is possible in a more feminist world. Katzenstein and Mueller, 1987

follow the socialist path or resist 'modernization' to preserve their indigenous cultures are viewed as not deserving of aid. Only the left oppositional frameworks have attempted to explain world poverty and underdevelopment as consequences of colonialism or imperialism. Like individual inequalities, therefore, national inequalities have been largely untheorized.

Feminist political scientists trying to reinvent the field have developed their critiques of work in these three 'worlds' somewhat in isolation, just as their critiques of the subfield of international relations have been isolated from their critiques of politics within countries. In the future, feminist political science must work to integrate these disparate elements into more general feminist theories of politics. At this stage, the key is to ensure that the values used to assess the results of different political arrangements are drawn from women's experiences worldwide, not just from the experiences of majority women in the affluent 'western' countries.

Our approach to comparison from a women-centred perspective must reflect the fact that all states are **patriarchies** characterized by **institutionalized male**

rule. Yet if we simply describe all states as patriarchal (or even fraternal), we can learn little about how patriarchal politics work or what the fact of institutionalized male rule means for different women in different times and places. As Connell argues, we must compare which political systems, institutions and activities are more or less masculinized (1994:153). We must also compare the impact of the same political structures and arrangements on *differently-located* women. And we can compare the impact of the different kinds of political structures and arrangements through which patriarchal rule is realized. The key is to follow the methodological rules of *comparing women with women* whenever we can and *contextualizing for difference.*

By comparing women with women, we avoid making male political behaviour and values the norm, although we must not lose sight of the fact that men and women occupy quite different positions in all political systems. If we mainly compared women and men, for example, we would note that in the mid-1990s 18 percent of Canada's federal MPs were women, and we would then most likely try to identify the barriers that keep women from being represented in the House of Commons at the same rate as they occur in the Canadian population (52 percent). When we compare women with other women, however, we begin to ask questions such as why are 36 percent of the national legislators in Norway women, compared to 18 percent in Canada and 9 percent in Mexico.[3]

Comparison is the best approximation political scientists have to the scientist's laboratory. Scientists learn primarily through experiments that test **hypotheses.** Such comparison makes clear that while political systems seem to be 'natural', they are really 'man-made' and, therefore, not inevitable. Comparison also helps us explore how well other women are succeeding in their efforts to change their political systems or to increase women's influence on key institutions. Comparison also helps us open our imaginations to the possibilities of change and, by illuminating the ways in which one set of institutions and arrangements

> Hypothesis: A tentative explanation put forward to account for a set of circumstances; it should be testable (subject to being disproved or tentatively affirmed) to advance our knowledge.

are similar to and different from those women face elsewhere, comparison can help us understand the character of the political system in which we live.

To understand why patterns of women's politics vary across countries and evaluate what kind of political regime produces the best results for most women, we must develop such tentative explanations, which we can test by comparison. To develop tentative explanations, however, we must first be able to describe aspects of political systems accurately

> Typology: A framework in which different types of a thing are classified. A *type* is a class of things with common characteristics; it is often called an *ideal type* because it is a mental construct, which does not exist in a pure form in the world people experience.

from a women-centred perspective and categorize them by creating **typologies.** One of our first tasks in this chapter, then, is to explore which aspects of political systems and political activity we should compare in order to produce typologies useful in our efforts to compare and evaluate political systems "with women in mind".

Feminist political scientists have begun comparing many aspects of women's political experience. In the section that follows, I explore different approaches to comparison, some of which are women-focused and some of which are women-centred. I also assess them in terms of their capacity to incorporate difference and broadly held values.

What to Compare and Evaluate?

Since feminist political scientists began to compare with women in mind, many have used approaches, alone and in combination, that compare women with men. In this sections, I outline three such approaches (see Exhibit 13) and explore their advantages and weaknesses. In the next section, I present other approaches that are more fully women-centred.

Exhibit 13.
Three Approaches to Comparison with Women in Mind.

- **Results:** Compare government outputs, or assess programs, policies and entitlements presumed to benefit women (which women?).

- **Milestones:** Compare women's "firsts", such as when women won the vote, when the first woman legislator was elected (which firsts?).

- **Participation rates:** Compare participation in political activities (which?) as a proportion of key institutions and activities (for example, paid work).

Comparing Results

The most common approach to comparison with women in mind involves *evaluating results* or outputs presumed to be 'good for women'. This approach is compelling because it compares tangible policies, programs and entitlements desired by many women, usually within a women's issues framework. Yet, it is also problematic because it involves the assumption that it's possible—even easy—to identify things that are good for women across several or many countries and for differently-located women within each country.

At one level, feminists have found it fairly straightforward to identify what benefits women. For example, Nelson and Chowdhury in a forty-three-country study asked the associates writing each country's chapter to report the three most pressing political issues for the women's movements in that country. They note:

> [t]he political problems facing women . . . cluster into four topics: ensuring personal safety, security and autonomy; providing abortion, reproductive rights, and maternal and child health programs; equalizing access to public, communal and market resources for problem solving and empowerment; and remaking the political and legal rules of the game (1994:11).

This agenda of issues would gain support from many of the world's women. Certainly most would rejoice at outcomes of personal safety without threat of war, rape, battering and harassment. Consequently, a result in which these were eliminated can easily be considered good for women.

The way in which that result is to be achieved, however, could certainly raise political disagreement. For example, majority women in most liberal democracies have concluded that to ensure their security from rape and battering they need laws prohibiting all forms of physical and sexual assault (including rape in marriage) and programs that ensure the police and courts will take these matters seriously. For them, a good result is the prosecution and imprisonment of all men who assault women. Yet racial minority and aboriginal women in the same countries, while no less concerned about personal safety, may consider use of the judicial system bad if it results in imprisoning still more of their men, who are already victimized by racism and poverty. That is, they consider what is 'good for women' to be bound up with the fate of men in the community who are their fathers, brothers, husbands and sons.

Focusing on Needs

Identifying what is 'good for women' is thus one of the most difficult tasks of women's politics and feminist political science, even in a single country. UN analyses of what is required to empower women, for example, stress that women's *basic needs* must be met before issues of *access to resources,* **conscientization,** *participation* and *control* can be addressed (Karl 1995:109).

Maxine Molyneux (1985) has developed the useful idea of **practical gender needs** to describe what women actually require to perform their basic gender-assigned tasks, such as child-care services and training. In contrast, she says, are **strategic gender needs,** what women need to over-

Conscientization: The 'third world' equivalent of consciousness-raising. It involves the self-awareness that comes from recognizing that structural and institutional discrimination contribute to women's problems and that women's role in reinforcing the system affects their growth.

123

come their subordination, although this distinction is not easy to make in practice. And even this analysis is not deep enough to understand the goals of women in situations where the most *basic needs* of food, clean water and shelter are not being met.

In brief, what is 'good for women' depends on their circumstances. For those in many parts of the world, basic material needs and practical gender needs are the highest priorities.

Nor is safety always a simple matter of gaining protection from the authorities of the state. For women who are part of secure majorities who can protect themselves through state structures, 'good' results can focus on strategic gender needs. For women who are part of threatened minorities or communities without the security of a state, the concern may first be gaining collective self-determination and security.

There have been only a few systematic attempts to compare the impact on women of political systems with different types of regimes. For example, Canadian feminist political scientist Alena Heitlinger, in her ground-breaking 1979 book, *Women and State Socialism,* not only compares the Soviet Union and Czechoslovakia but also tests the left-wing hypothesis that *state socialist* regimes produce better outcomes for women than *liberal-democratic* regimes based on a capitalist economy. Heitlinger finds many manifestations of sexual inequality but concludes (surprisingly, when she wrote) that they are "not essentially different from those prevailing in Western liberal democracies"(1979:193).

This idea of convergence between the two regime types with regard to gender is based on the facts that in the communist states the sexual division of labour assigning child care and domestic work to women survived despite public services; women's *double shift* (paid work plus domestic work) continued, so women worked far more than men; sexism continued among elites, limiting women's opportunities for political participation; and political institutions remained bastions of male power. Given the radical changes in the post-soviet world, Heitlinger's analysis is light years away from the current reality in which the gains women had made in the Soviet Union and Eastern Europe (and Heitlinger does identify some) are being eroded in the struggle toward democracy and capitalism. It will be some time before anyone can assess the consequences of these changes for women.

Comparing Liberal and Social Democracies

Although comparing the impact of different regimes on outputs for women is in its infancy, several analysts have compared the results for women of liberal democracy versus social democracy. Canadian feminist leader and journalist Doris Anderson visited six western European countries, three Nordic countries and three anglo-American countries. Although she examines some aspects of the political and economic systems in each, her main comparisons revolve

Exhibit 14. Anderson's Output Indicators.

1. How well do services for women and children work? For example, are parental leave and child care available so women have a choice about whether to work outside the home?
2. How accepting of the different needs of women are the society's major institutions? For example, how is work structured?
3. How well established is the basic philosophy of equality? Can women choose to end a pregnancy? Are they safe walking on the streets?
4. Are women present in significant numbers in the "power elites"?
5. How easy or difficult is life for "ordinary women" compared with their mothers or "ordinary men"?

Source: Anderson 1991.

around five indicators that emerged from her discussions with 'ordinary women' in the twelve countries (see Exhibit 14). A comparison of results in relation to these indicators allows us "to gauge what has been accomplished" (Anderson 1991:21).

Anderson's stated assumptions are simple: that a common understanding of outcomes that benefit women is possible, and that positive outcomes can be attributed to the actions of women's movements (which she also evaluates for their effectiveness). Notice, however, that her categories include a mix of practical and strategic gender needs; except perhaps for the last category, she assumes the fulfilment of basic needs such as clean water and adequate housing. Moreover, a number of the programs or entitlements she identifies (public child care, public transport, diaper services, and so on) require a high level of affluence.

In other words, Anderson's work raises a central issue about comparing countries with different economic levels.[4] Moreover, we must consider that many of the goods and services Anderson wants are subsidized by the labour of poorer women in the society or require consumables subsidized by the cheap labour of women elsewhere in the world. Perhaps we should instead compare how societies support women in their reproductive work (see Exhibit 15) and how effectively they free women's time for economic, political and cultural activities regardless of their level of affluence.

Anderson's concept of the 'ordinary woman' also presents problems. She explores the everyday lives of women who were quite average in their societies. They were in heterosexual relationships with partners and children mostly present, and most were still in their childbearing years. Their ideas of what was good for them and other women reflected their characteristics. They were not drawn from the society's minorities or, if they were, Anderson's analysis tells

Exhibit 15. How Reproductive Work Can Be Supported.

1. Family and local community provide support on a private, *voluntary* and often reciprocal basis.
2. Women purchase services in the *market* (child care, fast food, diaper services, etc.) from individuals and corporations.
3. Women rely on *public* support directly or via transfers of funds.
4. A combination of two or three modes.
5. No support.

us nothing about how this affected what they wanted from their society.

Anderson's analysis doesn't include women facing poverty or racism (since neither the basic needs of adequate food and shelter nor the elimination of racism are noted as indicators). It also assumes heterosexism (protection from homophobia and rights for same-sex couples are not included as basic indicators).

In brief, the question of what both minority and majority women consider to be 'good' outcomes is as important within affluent countries as differences between women in affluent countries and those in the 'third world'. A wider survey of what different women consider 'good' results would have added a category of basic needs (sufficient food, shelter, and so on) appropriate support for women's reproductive work and security against racism and homophobia as a minimum. Other minority women, such as those with disabilities and the aged, might well have deemed other results essential to their well-being, which could have been incorporated into the indicators. Some feminists argue that we should choose indicators that reveal how well the most vulnerable members of a society are doing if we want to really compare which results are best for women.

Another question here is which combinations of political and economic systems provide the best basic support services for women's *practical gender needs.* Anderson believes that their provision through public institutions produces the best outcomes for women. Indeed, each year the UN Human Development Index (HDI) puts the Scandinavian countries at the top of the index (displacing countries such as Canada and Japan, which top the scale before it is adjusted to take gender equity into account). The Scandinavian social democracies have chosen to support reproduction through public institutions. Each has significant numbers of women in public life (to shape and maintain such services at high economic levels) and is largely homogenous in cultural, racial and ethnic terms, making provision of a single set of programs feasible.

Other countries with fewer economic resources and/or heterogenous populations may reject this public sector solution, however, and women in those countries may consider that other approaches to supporting reproduction produce better results for them. Some racial and ethnic minority women in Canada and the US, for example, point out that providing support services through public institutions often means standardized services, which may not be sensitive to minority cultures and languages. Aboriginal women often share this view. Others note that these systems are expensive and yet generally pay low wages to their women workers, who are often members of minority groups or 'third world' immigrants. Still others point to the vulnerability of women when they must depend on the good will of politicians and bureaucrats to preserve essential services such as child care (Gelb 1989).

Comparing results is difficult, then, especially once we move beyond the level of basic needs and practical gender needs. A question feminist political science must address is the value to women of the programs generally called the **welfare state.** We need to consider whether the important thing is for women to work energetically in politics to gain, retain or enlarge such programs or whether a model

> A woman-friendly state would enable women to have a natural relationship to their children, their work, and public life.
> Helga Hernes, 1987

based, for example, on equipping women for greater autonomy through education achieves more reliable outcomes in the long run. A method of comparing results among countries that did not assume the inevitability (or the correctness) of the welfare state approach would identify general indicators (how reproduction is supported) and then evaluate results in relation to such things as the economic level and the cultural homogeneity or diversity of the society. Using such an approach, we could associate particular patterns of support with particular political and economic systems. A society's economic level determines which options are even possible, since many need a high level of affluence if significant numbers of women are to gain support. Choosing between public and market supports for reproduction may involve similar costs, but the decision also involves whether or not particular groups of women believe they can trust the state to provide secure and appropriate services. This, in turn, reflects women's different experiences with state institutions and services and the degree to which they feel they can influence decision-makers.[5]

Comparing the Measurable: Milestones and Participation Rates

Clearly, comparisons of outcomes require the researcher to make a variety of tricky decisions. Perhaps that is why some feminists have preferred to focus on things that are indisputedly measurable. Two types of such investigation are the listing of *milestones* and the comparison of *participation rates*.

Milestones

The investigation of *milestones* involves considering when women in different countries achieved various "firsts", such as the right to vote, election to the legislature and a place in the senior bureaucracy.[6]

Most attempts to compare political systems from a women-centred perspective consider milestones important, but why they matter is rarely clear. The implicit notion is presumably that a country in which women make certain gains early will make progress early in other ways. This logic assumes that things such as achieving the vote have a power to achieve more change; an hypothesis that may be unrealistic. New Zealand, for example, was the first country to grant women (including Maori women) the right to vote in national elections (1893). Yet Norway, which did not enfranchise women until two decades later (1913), currently has a much higher proportion of women in its legislature than New Zealand does. Clearly, the difference of twenty years in achieving this milestone made little difference in terms of women's ability to challenge male rule. Nor is it clear that the factors that influence one milestone (winning the vote) are the same as those that affect another (getting more women elected to the legislature).

Analysts of milestones also tend to assume that continual (if slow) progress occurs in women's influence and political power. Yet women have lost rights they had previously won, and they have gained them without struggle. Japanese women, for example, got the vote as part of the new constitution imposed on the country after the Second World War. Spanish and German women regained the right at the same time, having lost it under facist regimes.

Nor is it clear which milestones are important or why. Many represented legal and psychological barriers that had to be broken even to begin the process of reversing male rule. For women whose political activism is primarily a matter of the survival of family or community, however, such barriers may mean little. For them, the important milestones may be the first evidence of women's involvement in political movements, strikes and protests.

The milestones generally cited relate to the male-dominated world of *official politics*. The concept of a milestone is more useful, however, when it is expanded to include marks of a society's increased willingness to acknowledge women as **social adults.** Such marks include women's legal right to be their children's guardian; to move freely within the society and beyond without male permission or a guardian; to choose if, whom and when to marry; to choose a career or occupation; and to have the same say as men concerning where to live. These more general social and legal rights are important in relation to women's involvement in politics because they mark the degree to which women are treated as people to whom societies will entrust the responsibility of making collective decisions. They are unlikely to assign societal decision-making responsibilities to those who are not permitted to conduct their own affairs or make decisions for their families or communities. Thus, milestones must include indicators of whether or not women are considered social adults.[7]

> Social adults: Those people to whom societies give the responsibility for making collective decisions. Although chronologically and biologically adults, women may not be treated as social adults, even in the family; if they are not, they are not seen as possible decision-makers.

128

Participation Rates

Another common status-of-women approach is comparing male and female *participation rates* in various activities, both political (voting, running for office) and economic.

For example, Carol Christy (1987) compares various forms of participation, including voting, party membership, campaign work and political discussion, by the male and female citizens of fourteen countries. While she includes some aspects of **informal politics,** her methodology requires that the activity be measurable, and since her focus is comparing women to men, she does not contextualize to reveal differences among women. It is possible, however, to use the study to compare women's participation rates in different countries.

Christy reports that sex differences in political participation are narrowing two to four times faster in Scandinavia and Western Europe than in Canada and the US. Yet the reason is that the initial differences between the political participation rates of men and women were much higher in Europe and Scandinavia; smaller differentials in Canada and the US mean the pace of change is slower.[8] We must also beware of assumptions that changes in participation rates always involve progress for women and that women's political equality with men is "only a matter of time" (the time-lag thesis). For example, UN data show large declines between 1987 and 1990 in women's participation as parliamentary representatives in Eastern Europe and the former USSR (see Exhibit 16). In these countries, quotas had reserved places for

Exhibit 16. Parliamentary Representation of Women in Eastern Europe and the former USSR, 1987 and 1990.

	1987 (%)	1990 (%)
Bulgaria	21	9
Czechoslovakia	30	6
Germany (GDR)	32	21
Hungary	21	7
Poland		
Upper house	—	6
Lower house	20	4
Romania	34	4
USSR		
Congress/Deputies	—	16
Soviet/Nationalities	31	14
Supreme Soviet	35	14

Source: UN 1991:33.

women, producing participation rates in which women were between 20 and 35 percent of their legislatures. The sharp declines are a consequence of open competition among parties, most of which now reject quotas as part of the old order.

Women-Centred Approaches

Comparing milestones and participation rates mainly involves comparing men and women and only secondarily involves understanding women's activism on its own terms. These approaches emphasize easily measurable and locatable activities, whereas we know that women often do politics in unconventional political arenas and in intermittent, local groups, which are harder to locate. The participation-rates approach, in particular, relies heavily on mainstream electoral research, which Chowdhury and Nelson warn us "has not been guided by questions about the nature of representation and participation that make evident women's marginality" (1994:33).

Recently, however, comparative analysis has been enhanced by two other approaches (see Exhibit 17). The first looks at how such structural things as electoral systems, legislative systems, party systems and party alignments affect women's participation in **official politics.** Focusing on the insights gained from *barriers research,* it uses the concept of the *political opportunity structure* as its organizing idea. The second general approach casts its net more broadly to compare overall patterns of women's political activism. Although it builds on the political opportunity structure approach, it does not assume that political opportunities are fixed. Instead, it compares how effectively women are accessing or changing their political opportunities. It also looks at the pattern of women's activism in arenas beyond formal politics and examines the success of women's movements in changing the society's understanding of what is political.

I examine these approaches to comparison in detail in the remainder of this chapter. To make the discussion more concrete, I also present examples from the six countries I mentioned at the beginning of the chapter. These examples provide occasions to both explain the approaches and mention some failures (including failures to apply them).

Even using indicators derived from analyses of results (the UN's HDI, in particular) and several milestones and participation rates, it is possible to create a snapshot of our six countries (see Exhibit 18). As the table suggests, however, it is not easy to find consistent correlations among the different variables. For example, Mexican women won the right to vote and run for election much later than women in the UK, yet women's participation rates in the two countries' elected legislatures bodies are about the same. Mexico's rank on the UN's HDI is significantly lower than that of the other five countries, and predictably its maternal mortality rate (one indicator of health services for women) is significantly higher. Norway has the highest rates of women economically active and

Exhibit 17. Two Women-Centred Approaches to Comparing Political Systems.

I. A Political Opportunity Approach. This approach examines:

a. *Political opportunity structures.* Compare the institutions, alignments and ideological spectrum that shape and limit the nature and pattern of women's collective political activism (barriers research).

b. *Specialized machinery.* Does government machinery for women (such as status of women councils) exist. If so, is it effective or marginalized? Is integration or specialized machinery better? How effective is the femocrat model?

II. An Approach Focused on Women's Activism. This approach examines:

a. *Openness of the political system.* Compare how much women's styles of political activism are modifying the extent to which political structures (such as political parties) and the political system generally are open to women.

b. *Strength of women's movements.* Compare the pattern of activity of women's movements (for example, autonomous or co-opted?). Compare their capacity to deal with difference and to form and sustain alliances.

c. *Redefinition of the political.* Compare if and the extent to which women's political activism is redefining what the society considers political.

d. *Changing political discourse.* Compare the extent to which women's political activism is changing the discourse of politics.

in its legislature. But Australian women have been more successful in reducing the wage gap. Economic activity, literacy and the resources for human development are all important for women's well-being. Nonetheless, women in the UK and the US still have about the same participation rates of women in their legislatures as women in Mexico.

In short, although these approaches provide some useful insights, they reveal few clear trends to show what produces good results for women. Indeed, these approaches raise more questions than they answer (although they do show that affluence helps countries provide the services women need to bridge domestic and political activities).

With the tools provided by the two newer approaches, however, we can compare our six political systems more fully from a women-centred perspective.

Exhibit 18.
Milestones, Markers and Participation Rates, 1993–94.

	Australia	Canada	Mexico	Norway	UK	US
Franchise, national or federal[a]	1902	1917	1953	1913	1928[b]	1920
Eligible for election[c]	1902	1920	1953	1907	1918	1920
Literacy rate[d]	100	98	80	99	100	99
% Economically active[e]	52	50	30	70	48	50
Income: female as % of male[f]	85-	66+	NA	63	69	59
HDI[g]	6(+1)	11(-9)	53	2(-1)	10	9(-3)
Maternal mortality[h]	8	3	82	4	6	8
% of women in						
Lower house	7	19	9	36	6	11
Upper house	25	17[i]	5	—		6

a. In some sub-jurisdictions, achieved by some women earlier (for example, 1894 in South Australia and/or some women later (for example, 1968 for aboriginal women in Quebec).
b. For women over thirty who owned property, 1918.
c. To the national or federal legislatures. Achieved earlier or later in some subjurisdictions.
d. Data may exclude immigrant and aboriginal women.
e. In the paid workforce (full- or part-time) or engaged in non-domestic economic activity, such as farming.
f. + signifies improving, - deteriorating.
g. The first number is the 1993 rank; the parenthetical number is the adjustment for gender disparity.
h. Deaths per 100,000 live births.
i. Seats by appointment.

Sources: Nelson and Chowdhury 1994; Seager and Olson 1986; UN 1996.

Political Opportunity Structures

Analysis of **political opportunities structures** has grown out of the **barriers research** feminist political scientists have been using to try to understand why women in their country were not being represented on an equal basis with men in the formal politics of their states.

Barriers research begins by assuming that women should be in all decision-making bodies in the same proportion as they are in the population. Since this situation does not exist in any country, the conclusion is that there must be barriers.

What are they? The first focus in trying to find out was mostly on male/female differences. As the field of feminist political science has developed, however, and as feminist activists increasingly have had contact with their counterparts elsewhere, the emphasis has shifted to looking at those countries, such as Norway and Sweden, where women seem to be doing well politically and identifying structural characteristics of other political systems that are then conceptualized as barriers to women achieving the same results.

I have already discussed the major weaknesses of this approach (in Chapter 3). In particular, it focuses largely on women's involvement in official politics and neglects other forms of political activism. It also implies that women have no capacity to modify the structure—that is, to create their own opportunities. Its strength, however, is its insistence that how political systems are structured makes a difference to whether or not women can exercise political power and to what extent they can use the political system to improve their lives.

Case Study and Cohort Analysis

The methods used by feminist political scientists have proved important. Until recently, most non-statistical, comparative research undertaken by feminist political scientists has taken the form of **case study analysis,** which usually involves the use of general theory to illuminate observations about a single case. This approach allows testing of existing theory. But the mainstream theory has usually not been women-centred; at best, it "includes women" in a theory that still assumes the naturalness of the private/public split.

Nor is most feminist theory suitable for this kind of research since it makes general assertions about patriarchy but has little to say about the specifics of particular political structures or systems. Indeed, there have been just two firmly held but competing assumptions: that western democracy permits women to achieve the highest status possible, and that state-socialist regimes permit women to achieve the highest status possible.[9] Testing these competing assumptions has done little to help women understand which *electoral systems* produce the best results for them, whether they can participate more effectively in *unitary* or *federal* forms of the state, and whether they should work to be integrated into *existing political systems* or develop strong, separate political movements from which they could demand change.

Most comparative research has ultimately relied on culture to explain differences in women's political activism—that is, in the final analysis, *culture* (the customs of a particular people) is assumed to explain difference. (This approach has led some western and majority feminists to attack other women's cultures as the cause of their oppression.)

Use of the concept of *gender,* which many feminists prefer because it seems not to contain essentialist assumptions, has compounded this avoidance of explicitly political explanations. Since *gender* is socially constructed, it is no surprise that Norwegians construct it differently than Mexicans or Canadians. But this approach fails to illuminate either the similarities of women's experiences in politics across many different cultures, or the differences resulting from different political arrangements shared by countries with quite different cultures.

Cohort analysis, which examines the effects of changes on succeeding cohorts (or generations) of women over time within the same country, has proved more useful than theory-driven case studies and has guided scholars to more fruitful areas of research. It does not, however, make it easier to distinguish between the effects of changes in political structures on the one hand, and economic or cultural changes on the other. But in specific cases it has worked. For example, in the early 1970s, the Norwegian women's movement lobbied successfully for structural changes in the electoral system; cohort analysis has made it possible to isolate the effects of these explicitly political changes and thus to avoid the reductionism of purely cultural or economic explanations.

Some New Work

Both case-study and cohort analysis permit the identification of some key variables that can be converted into testable hypotheses. Comparisons organized around the idea of political opportunity structures convert variables found to be key in one country or for one cohort into testable hypotheses. Most focus on parts of political systems, such as *electoral systems, party systems* and *legislative systems,* across a number of countries *(thin comparisons).* The few comparisons that attempt to compare many or all aspects of two or more political systems *(thick comparisons)* are also worth exploring to identify generalizations or key variables.

An early and ambitious project was edited by British feminist political scientists Joni Lovenduski and Jill Hills in 1981. The text covered twenty 'modern' (industrial) countries, including those with both democratic and state-socialist regimes. The study married the traditional political science tools of studying governments, legislatures, parties and elections with feminist analysis of suffrage movements and the social and economic position of women in each country. The book offered little actual comparison between or among political systems, but it made available data that others could use for comparisons. The weaknesses of the approach were that it emphasized participation in official politics almost exclusively (except for the suffrage era) and it generalized about particular cohorts of women in ways that tended to universalize their experiences. Its strength was that it encouraged comparisons among women (even though the data presented for each country compared women with men).

A number of hypotheses emerge from this project. Subsequent studies have shown that some of the trends identified are time-dated and have since been reversed. But three generalizations, which have been sustained over time, point toward the more systematic political opportunity approach:

1) Everywhere family structure affects women's participation in official politics.

2) "The higher the fewer." All twenty countries reveal a pyramid of political participation, with more women at the lower, less powerful levels and fewer women at the higher, more powerful levels.

3) When women as a group first run for office, they are often put in "lost-cause" constituencies and unwinnable positions on electoral lists.[10]

Another series of studies from about this time focuses on regional sets of similar political systems.[11] Beck and Keddie (1978) looked at the Muslim world; Haavio-Mannila et al. (1985), Hernes (1987) and Sassoon (1987) at Scandinavia; and Lovenduski (1986) at Western Europe. Notice that each considered a region composed of countries with similar cultures. The fact that so much of this research was on the Scandinavian countries reflected the early success of women's efforts to change political structures in these countries to integrate women into official politics and their early development of feminist political science.

The several useful generalizations that emerged from this work included:

1) That relationships between the private and the public realms are especially important to women's ability to participate in decision-making in official politics.

2) That women's changing relationship with welfare states is one key to their involvement in political power.

A central question was whether the welfare state is the best basis on which to rest women's political activism. But no typologies emerged from these regional studies.

Anglo-American scholars and feminist activists now began to take more note of the fact that women were "doing politics" in different ways in different parts of the world. This observation is the focus of Hester Eisenstein's 1991 book in which she compares the situations

> Femocrats: Women bureaucrats who work within government offices (including specially designated status-of-women agencies) to press for feminist goals. The strategy involves a process of consultation with women's movements and the use of conscious tactics to avoid being co-opted into bureaucratic values. The term originated in Australia.

135

in the US and Australia. Her basic theme is that US feminism should reconsider its **anti-statism** in light of the effectiveness of the Australian feminist strategy of engagement with the state through **femocrats.**

Joyce Gelb (1989) also examines the strategy of disengaging from the main structures of the state in favour of lobbying from outside and other unconventional political activities adopted by most majority feminists in the US. She compares the US strategy with women's political activism in Sweden and the UK, explicitly using the idea of the political opportunity structure. Describing Sweden as characterized by **state feminism** ("feminism without feminists"), she concludes that US women's reliance on a vigorous, autonomous women's movement produces equal, if not better, policy outcomes.

Gelb's main theoretical contribution is to show how feminist political science can use the concept of the political opportunity structure. By demonstrating how the pattern of women's political activism in each country is shaped by the institutions, alignments and ideologies available there, her analysis points to the fact that what women choose to do politically (for example, integrate or be separate) depends more on the political opportunities available than on abstract, ideological solutions.

Thus, her analysis of the opportunities available for political activism in these three countries she studied focuses on the *nature of the political system* and the *political culture,* rather than on culture per se, directing feminist political scientists to consider how different aspects of the organization of political systems affect the political opportunities for women's activism. Her analysis calls attention to the impact of a country's party system, the ideological spectrum available, and the extent to which the powers that be will tolerate protest and unconventional activity from political actors.

Corporatism [is] interest representation in which constituent units are organized into a limited number of singular, noncompetitive, hierarchically ordered, and functionally differentiated categories, recognized . . . by the state and granted a deliberate representational monopoly within their respective categories.

Pluralism [is] a system in which multiple, voluntary, competitive, self-determined groups have access to state power. Joyce Gelb, 1989

Gelb characterizes the overall pattern of women's political activism in the three countries as interest group feminism in the US, ideological or left-wing feminism in the UK and state feminism in Sweden. The key distinction between the forms of activism in the US and UK on the one hand and Sweden on the other is women's orientation to the state and their willingness to interact with the institutions of official politics such as political parties. (This typology is one of the first constructed by feminist political science.)

Gelb also identifies the difference between a *corporatist* and a *pluralist* governmental system as particularly important in creating or limiting opportunities for women to participate.[12] In **corporatist systems,** interest representation is highly centralized with monopolies, so if women are not present in the corporate structures, they can be shut out of decision-making even if they are represented in the legislature. Norway, Australia, Mexico and the UK in our set of countries are corporatist or neo-corporatist systems. Canada and the United States have more **pluralist,** decentralized systems of interest representation, with the US system being the most open mainly because of its *congressional legislative system.*

Gelb's analysis of the impact of these two different modes of organizing the input side of political systems within democracies has provided an important tool for the evolution of feminist political science.[13] Her study makes us look behind the numbers of women in legislatures to consider if women legislators actually have the same power in each political system and if the presence or absence of women in other parts of government, such as senior levels of the bureaucracy or as politically active agents outside of government in autonomous women's movements, may be as important.

Aspects of the Political Opportunity Structure

Other major aspects of political systems have now been explored in sufficient detail to report generalizations, although not always for all six countries. Here I examine comparative research on electoral systems, governmental systems, party systems and political cultures; provide some insights derived from one or several countries on bureaucracies and courts; and outline the emerging discussions about women's relationships to different kinds of state systems (unitary versus federal) and to collective identity movements, such as nationalisms.

Electoral Systems

Considerable effort is going into understanding how different electoral systems enhance women's opportunities for or act as barriers to participation in terms of voting and running for and getting elected to office. Most research focuses on two aspects: voting[14] and getting more women elected.

Voting Participation

Some analysts highlight women's voting participation rates. In one hypothesis, drawn from mainstream political science, low female voting rates in most countries just after enfranchisement would rise as women had the right to vote longer, so eventually male and female differences in voter turnout will disappear. This hypothesis reflects the normal integration thesis (time-lag thesis) that assumes that male/female differences will disappear over time because there are no **structural** or **situational barriers** to prevent it.

Examining voting rules, however, suggests structural barriers to participation that impact differently on men than on women. Take, for example, eligibility rules. In Canada until recently, only property owners could vote in municipal elections. The eligible men greatly outnumbered the eligible women until laws were changed to mandate joint ownership of the family home and to enfranchise tenants. These changes resulted in the addition of many women to the municipal voting rolls and a consequent transformation in the conduct of municipal government, with quality of life issues now competing with issues of economic development and urban infrastructure.

Following these changes in many provinces, came a rapid influx into municipal government of women as elected representatives, municipal politics being more accessible to women than provincial or federal politics because it is cheaper and closer to home and so easier to combine with family responsibilities. It is also more accessible because political parties usually are not involved formally in municipal elections in Canada, so women face an open nomination process, not one controlled by party *gatekeepers.15*

Another example of how voting rules affect women's opportunities to participate is the method of creating the voters' list. Under some electoral systems, state officials go to residences to **enumerate** those eligible to vote. Although this approach has the disadvantage of excluding the homeless, it makes getting on the voters' list easier than systems in which potential voters must go somewhere to be **registered** as eligible to vote, which adds a step — and thus potential costs — to the effort involved in voting. Because most women face the **double-shift** of both paid work and domestic work, and most also have a safety problem entering public space, this system may reduce women's voting rates.[16]

Yet another system is compulsory voting in elections (used in Australia since 1924). Men and women vote at the same rates, partly to avoid the penalty for non-voting. But according to feminist political scientist Marion Sawer, another consequence is that "party loyalties largely determine women's as well as men's voting patterns" (1994:75). In Canada and the US, by contrast, many women have been suspicious of parties, partly because of their corruption at the time women gained the vote. As a consequence, many activist women favour working through autonomous women's organizations instead of parties to advance their views to state decision-makers (Bashevkin 1985; Vickers 1992).

Opportunities to be Elected
Because few legislatures have significant numbers of women, feminist political scientists are particularly concerned about understanding how different **electoral systems** affect women's opportunities to be elected.[17] US feminist political scientist Wilma Rule (1987) examines the factors affecting women's opportunities to be elected to the legislatures of twenty-three democracies and concludes the most significant is the type of electoral system.

Canadian political scientist Lisa Young, in a report (1994) on the impact of different electoral systems prepared for the new Canadian Advisory Council on the Status of Women (CACSW), concludes

> The type of electoral system is the most significant predictor of the number of women elected to legislatures in 23 democracies. Wilma Rule, 1987

that different electoral systems shape electoral outcomes primarily because of how they affect the behaviour of political parties in terms of who they choose to represent them in the electoral process.

Young points out that analysts must consider two aspects of electoral systems: how the country is divided for elections, and how the process of selecting candidates is organized. There are two main ways of organizing elections: **single-member electoral systems** in which the jurisdiction is divided into electoral districts ("ridings", "constituencies"), each of which can elect only one member, and **proportional representation (PR) systems,** in which more than one person is elected to represent a large geographic region. Young concludes that single-member systems present barriers to electing women:

- Because each party nominates only one candidate in each electoral district, there is no opportunity for "ticket balancing", or ensuring that . . . [women] are among the party's candidates.
- Because nomination practices tend to be highly decentralized in single-member systems, it is difficult for parties to impose affirmative action measures . . . particularly . . . where the party is likely to win.
- The logic of a single-member system requires that the party nominate the most appealing (or least offensive) candidate. Consequently, party members may believe they are taking an electoral risk if they deviate from the norm of the white, male, professional candidate (1994:ii).

The logic of PR systems is basically the reverse. Ticket balancing is possible (given a large electoral district and a multimember list), and it is electorally desirable since voters can see when a party's list of candidates excludes whole categories of voters, such as women. Affirmative action is easier with a centralized process of list creation, rather than district-by-district nominations.

There are two kinds of PR: list systems, which give parties control over who is on the list, and systems that permit voters to add and subtract names from party lists or change the order of names on them. Norway operates with a party-list system of PR.[18] Provided political parties are open to women's participation and enough women are active within parties to enforce ticket balancing, this electoral system appears to provide the fewest barriers to women's election.

The second dimension of electoral systems is how the vote is recorded. In a first-past-the-post or **plurality system,** the candidate with the largest number of votes wins, even though more people may have voted against than for that individual. In contrast, the **single-transferable vote system (STV)** allows voters to record their second choices, which will be transferred if their first choice fails. These different ways of counting votes appear to affect women's opportunities only to the extent that they are part of a PR or a **single-member electoral system.** In Australia, for example, election to the senate is by a PR system with an STV. In 1993, women were 21 percent of Australia's elected senators. By contrast, the Australian House of Representatives, elected through a single-member majority system that uses an alternate vote to achieve majorities, had only 8 percent women elected in the same year.

In our six countries, the electoral systems used in Norway and for the Australian senate present the fewest barriers to women's opportunities to be elected to legislative office. Canada, the US and the UK with single-member, plurality electoral systems present the most difficult structural barriers. In Mexico, the dominance of the Party of Revolutionary Institutions (PRI) long prevented the emergence of many of the features of more decentralized party systems and party competition so it could have run significant numbers of women candidates had it chosen to. The development of serious electoral competition, however, may now limit the willingness of the parties to run women if they believe electors will reject them.

Government Systems
In addition to the corporatist/pluralist organization of interest articulation, the organization of the institutions of government shapes women's opportunities for political activity. Two basic modes of organizing democratic governments are the **parliamentary system** (also called the *Westminster system),* which fuses the executive and legislative body (or bodies) with the executive controlling the legislature but not the judiciary; and the **congressional system,** in which powers are separated among the executive, each legislative body and the judiciary.

Parliamentary systems are marked by *party discipline* (exercised with varying degrees of severity) because the executive's continuing control of the legislature (and usually staying in power) depends on members' supporting their party. Elected members are limited in proposing or voting for legislation to benefit women that the party leadership doesn't favour. In congressional systems, party discipline is weak since each institution is its own power centre. The executive may not even be of the same party as dominates the legislature and, given fixed terms of office, nothing depends on sticking to the party line. This situation permits legislators to introduce legislation even if their party disapproves. In such a system, however, party control of the legislative business is modified (and sometimes replaced) by seniority, which favours long-sitting (usually male) members.[19] Moreover, in parliamentary systems, individual members are largely immune from lobbying, which instead focuses on the cabinet and senior bureaucracy, where most policy decisions occur. In congressional systems, on the other hand, individual members are wide open to lobbying, and their power to respond to it is considerable, especially since cabinet members are not elected.

These two government systems exist in their purest forms in the UK, which has the "mother of parliaments," and in the US, which invented congressional government. Canada, Australia and Norway have parliamentary systems that have been somewhat modified: in Norway, by the tripartite corporatist system in which policy decisions are more often made by designated representatives of labour, business and the bureaucracy, than by the legislature; in Canada, by the existence of a federal state form and a written constitution that gives the courts the power to regulate which level of government is empowered to act and apply the *Charter of Rights and Freedoms;* and in Australia, by the existence of an elected senate, which can produce conflicts between two groups of elected members, each claiming to represent 'the people'.

Nonetheless, the basic government forms do shape women's opportunities. Basing women's activism primarily on lobbying government from outside has less value in a parliamentary system than in a congressional system. The combination of a parliamentary system and corporatism makes it especially important that women be on the inside within political parties to open channels of interest representation and the bureaucracy if women's views, interests, needs and values are to be considered.

Party Systems

In 1993, UK feminist political scientists Joni Lovenduski and Pippa Norris produced a collection of essays covering eleven countries, including all of our countries except Mexico. Although their conclusions focus mainly on the effects of electoral and governmental systems on the election of women legislators, territory we have already explored, they also reach some conclusions about the ways in which political parties and party systems shape and limit women's political activism.

Because political parties are the basic organizers of elections, they are also the major **gatekeepers** in the process of candidate selection.[20] Thus, political parties are both potential allies for women and potential gatekeepers, limiting their involvement in official politics.

Norris argues that *legislative competition* (the number of people competing for party nominations and election) affects women's recruitment, and, in turn, that the role and vitality of political parties af-

> Gatekeepers: Individuals or institutions that control access to particular activities and institutions. In official politics, for example, parties determine who their candidates will be in elections or on their electoral lists; in this way, key party officers act as gatekeepers.

fect legislative competition. Her hypothesis is that "where legislative competition is weak, 'out-groups' seeking entry stand a better chance of getting elected. Where competition for seats is strong, 'out-groups face more difficulties challenging the status quo" (1993:315). Cross-cultural differences in women's recruitment into legislatures may also reflect differences in legislative competition. A finding in some individual countries is that high levels of incumbency (measured by the proportion of new members after each election) pose a barrier to change. In the US House of Representatives and the British House of Commons, for example, more than 90 percent of incumbents who run again are usually elected. In the UK, Norris says, "good Conservative open seats may sometimes attract 200–300 applicants and even hopeless seats draw many who want campaign experience" (1993:317). As she notes, however, this situation is a far cry from the Canadian one in which even safe seats attract far fewer potential candidates, "lost-cause" candidacies may be filled without a contest, and electoral turnover is considerable.

The role and vitality of political parties varies quite significantly even among

Exhibit 19. Party Systems and Competition.

Party Type	Few parties	Many parties	
Catch-all, centrist	US	Canada	
Ideologically polarized	UK	Australia	Norway
		Mexico	

our six countries (see Exhibit 19). In Norway, for example, parties are the main game in town for anyone seeking involvement in politics, and they are well regarded by most progressive women. In Canada, on the other hand, many women are turned off political parties although, unlike their US counterparts, most are not disaffected by other aspects of official politics. Perhaps one reason is that Canadian political parties seem little differentiated from one another and are often less important in policy development than other organizations and arenas. In Australia, as I noted earlier, women voters seem as vitally connected to political parties as male voters, perhaps because of compulsory voting and vigorous parties.

Overall, a jurisdictions' party system is characterized by the extent of party competition and the range of parties available. Where parties are ideologically polarized, women's involvement may be enhanced because the stakes are higher than with catch-all (omnibus) parties that are not ideologically differentiated. The existence of many ideologically differentiated parties may foster the most involvement by women in official politics. Diane Sainsbury argues (1993) that increased competition, combined with the growth of new parties, would provide the most opportunity for women candidates. Yet, party competition may not always work to women's advantage if running women candidates is seen as potentially affecting a fiercely contested outcome, which may occur in Mexico as genuine party competition develops. And, as Norris (1993) notes, France has a multiparty, ideologically organized system but of the countries she studied it also had the fewest women in office (5.5 percent in 1991).

At this time, then, the impact of party systems on women's opportunities is not as clear as the impact of electoral systems and government systems. Nonetheless, all factors affecting competition for political office are important, and party systems have an impact that needs to be examined further. To date, however, feminist political scientists have been focused on the **electoral project** and the role of parties in the struggle to get more women elected as legislators. From Australia, however, we have the insight that women may be equally influential in femocrat positions within the bureaucracy. In Canada, it is clear that having women in senior positions in the courts is also important. In other words, restricting our study of women's activism to electoral politics limits our insights.

Political Cultures

Ironically, although feminist political scientists have had recourse to *culture* as an explanation for differences in patterns of women's activism, they have paid little attention to the impact of *political cultures.* Mainstream political science has explored this aspect of the puzzle—for example, through the comparative project reported by Almond and Verba in *The Civic Culture* (1963), in which political values and attitudes were studied in five countries including the US, the UK and Mexico. This study has been severely criticized, including by feminist political scientists, for setting the US as the pinnacle of democracy. Nonetheless, it established a comparative method that focused on both men's and women's attitudes and values concerning politics. What no mainstream study has done, however, is link characteristics of political cultures with women's opportunities to participate. In this subsection, I show such influences for our six countries (see Exhibit 20).

Because early feminist analysis relied on abstract theory drawn almost entirely from the US or the UK, it involved little sense of the impact of a country's general political culture on women's activism and little exploration of the women's political cultures that emerge because women live in a different political world than men do (McCormack 1975). Yet, as I explored in a comparison of the political values of the Canadian and US women's movements (Vickers 1992), each feminist movement incorporates aspects of the overall political culture of the country in which it developed. The anglo-Canadian movement focuses on the state, although it is distrustful of political parties. The franco-Quebec movement trusts the Quebec state but is ambivalent about the

Exhibit 20.
Political Culture and Women's Political Opportunities.

Country	Orientation
Australia	• State-focused.
	• Impeded by ethos of "mateship".
Canada	• State-focused with francophone Quebec women attached to Quebec government, anglophone women to federal level.
Mexico	• Deeply class-divided and ideologically organized.
	• Suspicious of state corruption, political violence.
Norway	• Integrated into official politics and parties.
	• Cultural emphasis on equality and avoiding conflict.
UK	• Deeply class-divided and divided by feminist ideology.
	• Suspicious of the state except at local level.
US	• Majority of women suspicious of the state.
	• Strong majority women's movement.
	• Deeply divided by race.

federal state. The majoritarian US movement is much less trusting of the state, although US women and blacks, who are often forced to rely on state programs, are more supportive of state activism than white men (the original rugged individuals?).

"Radical movements in Australia", notes Australian feminist political scientist Marion Sawer, "have traditionally sought to satisfy their demands through new state structures" (1994:76). She interprets the women's movement femocrat strategy as consistent with that approach. Nonetheless, she also wonders if the pervasive culture of male bonding in its various forms ("mateship") hasn't "locked women out" of Australian politics despite a surface appearance of inclusion. She concludes that the new culture of bureaucratic and economic rationalism means "the political environment has become increasingly unfriendly to the feminist enterprise .... The entire political spectrum has moved to the right, and there has been an increasing commitment to the market as the ultimate arbiter of value" (Sawer 1994:89).

This rightward shift in the balance of political cultures, which is noted everywhere in the 'developed' world, reflects in part the collapse of the Soviet Union and its empire. Countries like Norway with broad social support for equality have resisted it more than others. Yet the social democracies reflect their own cultures. For example, feminist political scientist and junior secretary of state Helga Hernes describes Norway as a patriarchal guardian state in which "[w]omen have been the objects of welfare policy and not its creators" (cited van der Ros 1994:530). Economic change and the movement to larger political units such as the European Union (EU) threaten the benefits of even a guardian state without offering the prospect of transforming its weaknesses. Van der Ros concludes that in countries such as Norway "women's integration in the political system and in the central and local bureaucracies will not make it easy for politicians to reverse hard-won victories" (1994:542). Despite this optimism, she notes that Norwegian women have paid a price for their integration. Given their society's emphasis on equality and its disapproval of open conflict, women and their political culture must largely avoid confrontation; one result is a relatively weak autonomous women's movement. Nonetheless, the crisis centre movement emerged in the late 1970s. Although small, volunteer and largely unsuccessful in getting the broader society to grapple with the issue of violence against women, the movement marks a departure from the emphasis on cooperation (van der Ros 1994).

Women in the UK encounter a political culture deeply class-divided and ideologically polarized. By the end of the 1970s, UK women had split into *radical-feminist* and *left-feminist* wings with little capacity for countrywide action except on individual issues. Neither wing was oriented toward official politics, and women's involvement in UK politics was quite low. Since then, during the long period of Conservative rule, many feminists have become active in local politics to establish programs for women.

A major hurdle for UK women has been the challenge of racial diversity resulting from the presence in the country of many people from Britain's previous colonies ("the Empire strikes back"). The vitality of the movements of racial and ethnic minority women contesting the deep racism and ethnocentrism of British society contrasts with the present weakness of majority women's organizations. Nonetheless, within their confrontational political culture, majority women continue to work with some success in actions such as the women's anti-nuclear peace movement.

Mexican women, like their British counterparts, are affected by the deep class and ideological divisions. They also share a deep cynicism about government generally, given widespread government corruption, election rigging and violence against political opponents as the long-ruling (Party of Revolutionary Institutions) PRI resists the movement toward a genuinely competitive political system. Mexican women's late achievement of political rights and middle-class women's low rate of participation in the paid workforce weaken their capacity for political activism. In a country where abortion remains illegal (women are jailed for trying to end a pregnancy) and both rape and battering are endemic with little recourse to the police and courts, feminist social scientist Eli Bartra concludes that women must become involved in a fundamental transformation of state politics (1994). Race conflict remains a feature of politics largely unrecognized by most Mexican women. The struggles of indigenous peoples for self-determination are vigorously resisted by Mexican governments and the political culture is based on a myth of racial and ethnic homogeneity.

Other Dimensions

Although the work is not yet well developed, feminist political science has begun to explore how women's political opportunities are shaped by other aspects of political structures and alignments, such as the relative openess to women of the *bureaucracy* and the judiciary, the presence of *federalism,* nationalism and the impact of *globalization* in transnational political units (for example, the European Union).

The Bureaucracy and the Judiciary

Two areas that need more exploration are the place of women in various state bureaucracies and judiciaries, including their openness to women and the development of *status-of-women* and *femocrat* structures.

Looking at our six countries, we can see that women now play a significant role in the public administrations of Australia and Norway. In the former, the femocrat model, analyzed by H. Eisenstein (1991), Watson (1990) and Sawer (1994), works on a strategy of feminist bureaucrats who become strategically central in the bureaucracy but remain separate and are not co-opted. In Norway, by contrast, the strategy is full integration of women in all aspects of the public service (see Katzenstein and Skejie 1990). In Canada, both patterns are evident, although debate is emerging about the utility of *status-of-women agencies,* which are neither strategically central nor integrated (Rankin 1996).

Because bureaucracies differ in their openness to new groups, structural reform and innovation, they will be an important area for future comparisons. Future discussions can be built on the concept of **representative bureaucracy,** which emerged in Canada as scholars assessed the federal government's efforts to recruit more francophones in order to make the bureaucracy more representative of the population. (One useful comparative source is Savage and Witz 1992.)

Another important area for feminist political science will be the responsiveness of judicial systems to women as judges and to feminist understandings of the law. This relationship is especially important where the judiciary adjudicates between levels of government or administers a bill or charter of rights. For example, the presence of self-identified feminist judges as one-third of the Supreme Court of Canada was important when that court struck down the country's abortion law as violating women's rights under the Canadian *Charter of Rights and Freedoms.*

Federalism

Feminist political scientists also have begun to explore how **federalism** is a structural barrier to women's opportunities for political activism. Albertan Linda Trimble argues that federalism, as currently practised in Canada, greatly complicates women's ability to lobby the state for change because the division of powers is complex, frustrating and ultimately illogical. What she calls "marblecake federalism" leads to "multiple and overlapping jurisdictions which are difficult for women with little power and money to negotiate" (1991:87). Federal states emphasize spacially-organized differences, yet women are dispersed throughout the population, making it difficult for them to introduce sex/gender issues into politics.

Comparing the attachment of anglo-Canadian women to the federal government with franco-Quebec feminists' attachment to the Quebec state, I conclude that which government does what matters to women, whose geographic mobility is often constrained by their husbands' earning power, and especially Quebec francophone women, who want to live in a French-speaking environment (Vickers 1991, 1994b). Many Quebec feminists advocate dismantling federalism because they believe that if government decisions are taken close to home, women who are usually more tied to home by the existing sexual division of labour will have more opportunity to influence them (Maillé:1991). By contrast, Shelagh Day, a constitutional lawyer and feminist leader, argues that outside of Quebec women fear a further devolution of powers to the provinces:

> For those who are disadvantaged, even though we feel we are running in circles, resort to another level of government is always useful. This may *not* be efficient, but it is nonetheless the reality that women [outside of Quebec] . . . cannot depend on any one elected government to hear or address our problems (1991:98).

Similar debates have emerged among women considering the advantages and disadvantages of entry into the EU. In the UK, many women saw opportunities in the EU parliament and used the leverage of EU policy in domestic politics. On the other hand, a majority of Norwegian women opposed their country's entrance into the EU, fearing a levelling of services to the lowest common denominator and a loss of influence in the wider political system. Similarly, many Canadian women fear that Canada's entry into the North American Free Trade Agreement (NAFTA) will result in a deterioration of social services, although Mexican activists hope to use their country's membership strategically to raise Mexican standards. As globalization proceeds, the emergence of larger political and economic units will become a crucial issue for feminist political science to explore further.

Nationalist Movements

The relationship between women's political activism and *nationalism* is a final dimension of the structure of opportunities that feminist political science is beginning to compare. Although radical feminism has appropriated much of the theory and language of national liberation movements, it has also developed the view that such movements gain collective freedom at the expense of women's equality. Yet although some nationalist movements constrain women's behaviour by limiting their sexual and reproductive partners and encouraging reproduction, others provide space within which women's autonomous political activism can emerge (West 1997).

Because the ideas that have dominated contemporary feminist scholarship emerged largely from the imperialist and neo-imperialist countries (the US, the UK and France), explorations of the relationships between feminism and nationalism have been conducted primarily by feminists in the 'third world' and in those countries created by competing colonial powers, such as Canada.

Kumari Jayawardena (1986) demonstrates the indigenous character of feminisms in Asia, the Middle East and Africa and explores their complex relationships with nationalisms, some of which are 'modernizing' and some of which are against 'modernization'. Lois West, in an exploration of feminist nationalist social movements (1992, 1997), argues against universalism and for a gendered understanding of different cultural movements. Valentine Moghadam (1994) examines the relationship between sex/gender and national identity in five predominantly Muslim countries where religious fundamentalism shapes the character of the national movements.

The relationships between feminism and the manifestations of collective identity, including race, ethnicity and faith, in combination with nation, will be central themes in the next phases of development of feminist political science.

Making New Opportunities

Work based on comparing aspects of the political opportunity structure helps us understand how effectively women are fitting into existing political structures and processes. A second women-centred approach, by contrast, compares how effectively women are *changing the opportunities* they encounter, either by using existing processes and structures more effectively or creating new ones (look back at Exhibit 17).

Openness of Political Institutions

Women are less likely to develop alternate political institutions where the existing ones are relatively open and willing to accommodate women's different needs and styles. Of the political systems in our six countries, that of Norway has been the most open to women and those of the UK and Mexico the most resistant to the changes needed to truly integrate women. Norwegian political parties began to change in the 1970s (Skejie 1988, 1993), accommodating women in their meeting times and styles and ultimately adopting quotas to ensure that most parties' lists of candidates are 40 percent women.

Overall, the degree to which an existing political structure can become open to women depends on its relative power and the role it plays in the broader social pattern of status and wealth. Where holding office provides status and access to wealth, as in the UK and Mexico, there is more competition, and male aspirants are less willing to let women in. Where electoral outcomes depend on the integration of women, however, central authorities may mandate change.

Clearly, the degree of openness depends on variables not yet studied cross-culturally. It seems likely, however, that resistance to the integration of women is greatest in the more powerful political systems (for example, the US) and structures.

Women's Movements

Feminist political science has also begun to compare the character and effectiveness of women's movements. Vicky Randall (1987) attempts a worldwide synthesis. In it, she endorses Lovenduski's thesis that the prerequisite for the emergence of a women's liberation movement is a full array of liberal-democratic political rights.

Lovenduski's study of feminism in thirteen European and Scandinavian countries (1986) focuses on women's policy demands and achievements, with two generalizations that can be tested. First, distinguishing between women's reform movements and women's liberation movements, she hypothesizes that the latter are only possible in advanced, stable democracies. Second, she argues that women predominate in informal, grassroots political activities, where there are no gatekeepers, mainly because they have been excluded from participating in official politics.[21]

Katzenstein and Mueller's 1987 study compares women's movements in five European countries plus the US and the UK, looking at the relationships between movements and other political organizations and institutions, and at feminist consciousness and policy outcomes. They focus on the tension between opportunities to form alliances with other political institutions (parties, unions) and the degree of autonomy women's movements are prepared to forego to gain alliances. An important generalization from their project is: "[t]here is no simple linear relationship between the level of movement organizing and government response to feminist activity" (Katzenstein and Mueller 1987:13). The authors also conclude that, in Western Europe at least, parties of the left have been more supportive of feminist concerns than parties of the centre or the right, although leftist parties' insistence that their own ideological concerns come first makes their alliances with feminist movements problematic.

Gisela Kaplan's 1992 study compares western European nations within a geopolitical typology. She divides fourteen of them into four categories: the progressive north (the Nordic countries); the conservative, Germanic countries; countries of "fringe upheavals and creative traditionalism" (the Netherlands and France); and the radical and revolutionary south (Portugal, Spain, Greece and Italy). She tests hypotheses based on key variables (religion, wealth, population density, age of nation-state) to explain the character and vigour of women's movements. Rejecting the idea that any single variable is key, she proposes a complex, multivariable hypothesis: *the see-saw effect*, which she believes occurs because capitalism's "need for inequality" militates against women's ever achieving equality on all fronts at the same time. After women achieved some minimum level (not defined) in one area of equality, their gain is counterbalanced by a backlash of inequality somewhere else. She asserts that only a radical transformation can achieve a thoroughgoing feminist victory.

Each of these comparative studies is somewhat constrained by its focus on women's movements only in the developed democracies of Western Europe, the United Kingdom and the United States. The exclusion of more anglo-American democracies and the new emerging democracies elsewhere will challenge these ideas as universally applicable, although they will remain useful as regional comparisons. Jane Jacquette, a US feminist political scientist, introduces a focus on Latin America (1989). Like Kaplan's analysis, which looks at the experiences of European women across time, Jacquette's typology compares the pattern of women's activism before, during and after transitions to democracy. She argues analysis of women's political role during the transitions raises important new issues of feminist theory and practice.

She notes, for example, that examination of the century-long history of women's movements in Latin America shows women were often enfranchised by conservatives (in Chile, Brazil and Peru) who intended to use the female vote to counter the growing radicalism of the male electorate. Since 1975, however, Latin America has entered a new era of women's mobilization, especially in the cities.

In the five countries she examines, Jacquette identifies three distinct patterns of women's mobilization that have combined to give women's movements a recognized role in the transitions to democracy: women's human rights groups; feminist groups largely of middle-class women; and organizations of poor urban women. Jacquette concludes the new wave of feminism in countries such as Argentina, Chile and Uruguay has been shaped by women's role in opposition to military dictatorships. In other words, as military authoritarian rule depoliticized men and restricted citizen rights, it also mobilized normally apolitical women against the military regimes and patriarchy in general. For example, discussions of violence against women in the prisons have made it acceptable to talk about violence against women at home and in the streets.

Conclusion

Comparison of women's movements and their relationships to other political structures develops the capacity of feminist political science to move beyond the spurious universalism of early work to consider effective strategies for achieving change. The four major measures of the relative effectiveness of women's movements are their achievements in terms of results; their ability to form and sustain alliances; their ability to deal with difference; and the degree to which they are successfully changing their society's definition of the political and reshaping political discourse, which is best measured by the degree to which the private/public split and the sexual division of labour are problematized, rather than considered natural. Large-scale comparative projects, such as that initiated by Nelson and Chowdhury (1994), will make it possible to develop typologies of women's movements that move beyond the geographic or cultural.

What I hope I have shown you in this chapter is the great importance of comparison in the development of feminist political science and in our ability to explain variations in women's politics. The ideological opposition to feminist approaches, which now characterizes much of the mainstream discipline, is most easily challenged if the seeming 'naturalness' of unequal rule can be disrupted. If Norwegian women can achieve a legislature that is almost 40 percent women, there is no reason for women in other countries to accept less. If Canadian and Quebec women can disrupt the male-centred presumptions of constitutional 'experts', women elsewhere may be able to challenge the view that constitutions are a male affair. In short, by widening our horizons and comparing our achievements with those elsewhere, we can also widen our intellectual resources.

Further Readings

Anderson, Doris. 1991. *The Unfinished Revolution: The Status of Women in Twelve Countries.* Toronto: Doubleday Canada.

Jacquette, Jane S., ed. 1989. *The Women's Movement in Latin America: Feminism and the Transition to Democracy.* New York: Unwin Hyman.

Jayawardena, Kumari. 1986. *Feminism and Nationalism in the Third World.* London: Zed.

Kaplan, Gisela. 1992. *Contemporary Western European Feminism.* New York: New York University Press.

Lovenduski, Joni. 1986. *Women and European Politics: Contemporary Feminism and Public Policy.* Amherst: University of Massachusetts Press.

Nelson, Barbara, and Najama Chowdhury, eds. 1994. *Women and Politics Worldwide.* New Haven and London: Yale University Press.

Randall, Vicky. 1987. *Women and Politics: An International Perspective.* Second edition. Chicago: University of Chicago Press.

Questions for Discussion

1. What are the main benefits of making comparisons with women in mind? What are the main difficulties?
2. Why has it been difficult to develop women-centred typologies in comparative politics?
3. What is problematic about comparisons based on outcomes or results? How can we ensure that such comparisons take into account the needs and interests of minority and marginalized women?
4. Do you consider mobilizing to achieve changes in the electoral system a good strategy for women in your country, province or state? Why or why not?
5. How can we best compare women's movements cross-culturally? What is the value in considering the experiences of 'non-western' women?

Notes

1. As explained in Chapter 1, you may be reading this chapter immediately after Chapter 3, especially if you are in a course that focuses on comparative studies. The book is organized to let you make this kind of jump. I hope, however, that you will find time to leaf through Chapter 4 to get a grasp of some important theoretical points.
2. See Chapter 2, note 4, for an explanation of my use of these terms. Notice that the mainstream ignores the 'fourth world', which is how some aboriginal scholars describe the world's indigenous peoples.
3. These percentages are 1994 (for the lower houses in the cases of Canada and Mexico) and are rounded to the nearest whole number. The full comparisons are given later in this chapter.
    All of the statistics in this chapter are from Nelson and Chowdhury 1994, unless otherwise specified. This otherwise excellent text does not provide data on minority populations.
4. It is also important to remember that, within the most affluent of countries, even basic needs are not fulfilled for all groups of women.
5. I further explore these debates concerning public policy in Chapter 6.
6. The other most frequently cited milestones are the right to run for office; access to the legal profession; women's becoming "legal persons" able to be appointed to office and to sign contracts; the first women in the cabinet, judiciary, police and senior bureaucracy; the first women to serve as a party leader, general and head of government.
7. Because women have been excluded until recently from employment in the agencies and disciplines responsible for cross-country analysis, comparisons on all indicators are very difficult. Such things as the UN's HDI are proxies.
8. Notice the potential for misinterpretation here, which is a classic error in using statistics. If women's wages are $4 an hour and men's $10 and they rise, respectively, to $8 and $15, the rise for women is 100 percent and for men only 50 percent. But the absolute gap, which is huge, has actually increased.
9. Note that both express eurocentric (though competing) values. As a consequence,

'third world' feminists often write of **hegemonic feminism.**

10. There is some evidence to suggest this phenomenon ceases as the proportion of women elected increases.

11. A type of study sometimes called the *most similar systems approach* to comparison.

12. Gelb relies on Schmitter (1984). Her categories are somewhat sharply drawn, although, in her analysis, she writes about a continuum with corporatism at one end and pluralism at the other.

13. Subsequent analysts have faulted her negative assessment of the Swedish system as US-biased.

14. Women still do not have the right to vote in several countries (Kuwait and the United Arab Emirates) or received it only very recently. The focus on national milestones has also hidden the fact that ethnic and racial minority women were often excluded from the vote when it was granted to majority women. In both Canada and Australia, for example, aboriginal women (and men) living on reserves did not gain the right to vote until the 1960s, although in Canada those who 'lost their status' by leaving the reserve were often enfranchised against their will. And Canadian women with cognitive disabilities were denied the vote until 1993.

15. The absence of political parties from municipal politics in Canada was a 'reform' supported by suffrage-era feminists.

16. It also kept blacks, male and female, from voting in the southern US for many years after they were legally enfranchised.

17. For example, the relatively high levels of women elected to Scandinavia's legislatures seems to be the result of two things: these countries' electoral systems of proportional representation in large, multimember constituencies and the fact that many of their parties have adopted quotas, putting women in significant numbers and in high positions on the party lists presented to the electorate (Rule 1987).

18. Although women's lists were presented by women's organizations in the decades immediately after enfranchisement in Norway, a women's party did not emerge. Women's lists continue to exist in Iceland.

19. Until recently, most women legislators began their legislative careers after their families were grown, and thus later than men, so the seniority system has worked against them. Since women usually outlive men, however, this may change.

20. Except in the US where primaries give this role to voters in some states, and in some countries' municipalities where political parties are not directly involved in organizing elections.

21. These hypotheses badly need testing since they reflect the assumptions, common to hegemonic feminism, that western women are 'more advanced' than 'third world' or indigenous women.

Chapter 6

WHAT DO WOMEN WANT?
WOMEN-CENTRED APPROACHES
TO PUBLIC POLICY

In this chapter, I focus on what women hope to achieve through their participation in *formal* and *informal politics.1* Because women's lives everywhere differ from men's lives, their take on *public policy* issues also often differs. There are also important differences in the lives of women within the same country and, especially, between women in rich and poor countries. That political institutions everywhere are still controlled by men and are (more or less) masculinized in their values and operating norms makes all the more important the question of which political projects women choose to pursue. Politics is far less often a career for women than for men. But women everywhere are mobilizing and organizing to achieve or resist change in three sectors:

> We want a world where inequality based on class, gender and race is absent from every country, and from the relationships among countries. We want a world where basic needs become basic rights and where poverty and all forms of violence are eliminated. Mission statement, DAWN (Development Alternatives for a New Era), as cited in Côrrea 1994

- The politics of the affluent, mature democracies.
- The less affluent countries, in which survival and 'development' are the collective goals that shape most women's agendas.
- The interactions between and among countries — in foreign policy, international politics and international institutions.

Recall from Chapter 3 that women are differently related to their states than men and that only the methodological rule of **contextualizing** gives us any hope of understanding the impact of difference. We should always assume that *differently-located* women may have a relationship to the state that differs from that of majority women[2] and that women in different countries face different circumstances.

I wish I had room here to discuss the substance of the many concrete projects

154

and issues that constitute *women's politics*. Instead, I give you information that will help you explore them yourself. In the first section, I briefly describe the assumptions underlying male-centred approaches to public policies,[3] and in the second I look at the challenges offered by the major strands of **feminist ideology.**

> Feminist ideologies: Various theories about the origins of the inequality between the sexes. Although each assumes such inequality is unjust and should be changed, each offers a different set of ideas about its origins, how it can be eliminated and what kind of society should be established in its place.

In the third section, I explore the basic issues that shape women's politics in the affluent liberal and social democracies of the 'first world'. A key idea here is that women have both interests in common and interests in conflict in politics. I explore this thesis by discussing briefly the rise of anti-feminist women's groups whose values and interests differ from feminist agendas on some issues but converge with them on others. I apply these insights to a discussion of the role of welfare states in women's equality agendas in affluent 'first world'[4] countries and explore the impact of economic restructuring and globalization on state-supported equality.

In the fourth section, I move the discussion of women's views on public policy issues to the less affluent countries of the 'third world'. I outline the different approaches to what the international community calls 'the women-in-development problem', which arose because most programs of 'development' or 'modernization' have worsened, not improved, women's abilities to feed, clothe and shelter themselves and their children. And I consider if we can bring together the approaches of women in the affluent democracies with the approaches of women in the other countries of the world.

In the final section, I look at women's agendas for international politics. The centuries-old women's peace movement and the newly emerging ecofeminist movement with its struggle for sustainable development illustrate the potential for women's political activism worldwide. Women also play a major role in international human rights movements and in the international movement for women's rights and empowerment. I explore the international movement for reproductive autonomy and security against violence to illustrate that women are intensely involved in movements for change in the global system, especially through the structures of *international civil society,* although they are largely excluded from the official politics of the international arena. Women from 'third world' countries play a central role in these activities largely because the poverty of their countries makes their movements more self-reliant, less dependent on the state and, hence, less fearful of the consequences of offending it in the international arena. Indeed, it is in the international arena that women's political activism shows the greatest potential.

Challenging the Male Monopoly

Male dominance in the institutions of collective decision-making means that men enjoy a monopoly on making societal decisions about what is 'right', 'for the best' or 'the most efficient' and what ought to be 'on the agenda', 'top priority', 'trivial' or 'marginal'. The consequence for women is that the operational norms of collective decision-making reflect men's experiences, especially the experiences of affluent men, mainly from each country's majority race and culture, who dominate judiciaries, governments and bureaucracies.

As we saw in Chapter 2, the 'average citizen' in political culture is a *rational, autonomous, self-interested man*; an idea that is then used as the reference point in the creation of **public policy** as it is developed by governments, economists, political scientists, international organizations or aid agencies. This approach is based on a methodological presumption that women's needs and interests are either identical to men's or do not have to be explicitly taken into account when making policy choices; that is, it reflects the premise that the sexes have similar needs and values and that women do (or should) act like men when they enter the public sphere as workers and citizens.

> Public policy: Actions governments (including all levels and institutions) choose to take and those they choose not to take.

The idea that men's and women's lives are (and will likely remain) sufficiently different to require different logics of analysis, which women must articulate, has not penetrated the consciousness of academics, the media and decision-makers, is rejected by them without serious scrutiny or is used in a stereotyped way to legitimize inequality. Especially revealing on this point is feminist political scientist Sandra Burt's (1995) analysis of the articles published in *Canadian Public Policy* between 1975 and 1993. Only six out of the 509 articles (1 percent) dealt with 'women's issues' narrowly conceived to include child care, affirmative action, male violence and prostitution, and only ten others included any discussion at all of women's interest in other issues. Everything from free trade to the delivery of social services—policies that demonstrably affect women and men differently and on which Canadian women's movements articulated public policy positions—were explored "without regard for such a possibility" (Burt 1995:361).

The voices of women's organizations are rarely heard, however, because public policy analysis and collective decision-making are considered too important to be left to amateurs and because 'ordinary citizens' are considered public-policy amateurs, whose opinions are not defined as knowledge and are sought only in polls or ballot boxes. Moreover, any feminists who are qualified in a policy field find their views ignored or treated as biased or pleading for 'special interests'.

Why do mainstream policy analysts[5] ignore the consequences for public policy of sex/gender differences, assuming that men and women are basically interchangeable despite extensive evidence to the contrary (or that women's interests don't matter)? In addition to the general reasons for blindness to gender differences, it is also the case that contemporary feminists have not made a clear and consistent case that men and women differ in important ways that should be taken into account in determining policies, programs and entitlements.

For example, feminists sometimes demand that women be treated identically with men, as in demands for equal rights, and sometimes that women be treated differently, as in demands for state-funded programs to support women's reproductive activities (see Vickers 1984). While both demands are appropriate, on the surface they are contradictory. Male 'experts' use such surface contradictions to characterize women's demands as inconsistent since the hallmark of modern, rational expertise is the even-handed application of a single set of rules.

Moreover, some feminists resist the idea that various currently-existing differences between men and women may be unassimilable (have differences that cannot be absorbed into the 'norm'); that is, that they are more than the result of social construction in which the men in power created men's and women's lives differently to benefit and privilege men.[6] Feminists also disagree on whether the differences that currently exist between men's and women's lives can or should be eliminated.

Relevant to public policy choices are the differences that now exist between men's and women's lives, some of which have continued for several millennia. Refusing to acknowledge differences weakens the basis for arguing in favour of policies that take into account women's continuing reproductive responsibilities in an affirmative way.

Acknowledging the significance of difference in men's and women's life experiences is difficult for many women because they know such differences, reified as natural or divinely sanctioned, have been the basis for excluding women from political life and for policies that denied equal rights to women. This is the Catch 22 of feminist policy analysis: how can we demand appropriate treatment, which recognizes most women's distinctive reproductive responsibilities and sexual lives, without undercutting the argument for identical treatment by the state in terms of rights, status and opportunities? If we are unable to deal with this conceptual challenge, we will also fail to deal with differences among women effectively and fairly.

And dealing with difference among women is vitally important. Indeed, western feminists' refusal to establish their visions on the basis of the existing division of labour between the sexes provokes conflict with less privileged women in other parts of the world and with poor, minority and aboriginal women within the 'first world'. Women struggling to gain basic needs or survive in the face of repressive regimes or racism may experience community and family solidarity as critical tools for survival and empowerment. Women in more affluent countries, especially if they are part of majority populations, may experience family and community as barriers to equality, rather than supports for achieving their goals. We must explore this contradiction and its reflection in competing visions of what equality should be like in practice.

How Feminist Ideologies See Public Policy

Many forms of feminist thought analyze the causes of male dominance and women's experiences within patriarchal society; fewer have developed into *ideologies* (organized sets of ideas and beliefs) that women use in practical politics, formal or informal, to support changes for which they are working. This distinction is important because some academic forms of feminist theory cannot easily play a role in practical politics.[7] In this discussion, I consider only theories that take ideological form in practical politics.

The Goals of Early Feminism

In the US, the word *feminism* was first used in the 1910s.[8] US feminist historian Nancy Cott tells us that at this time: "[f]eminism ask[ed] for sexual equality that include[d] sexual difference. It aim[ed] for individual freedoms while mobilizing sex solidarity. It posit[ed] that women recognize their unity while it [stood] for diversity among women" (1987:5). Its key assumption was that "[m]en and women are alike as human beings, and yet categorically different from each other; their sameness and differences derive from nature *and* culture, how inextricably entwined we hardly know" (Cott 1987:5).

Thus, these early US feminists, who sought the right to vote and other changes, based their demands on a platform of equal rights argued simultaneously with the thesis that women brought a special perspective to public policy because of their actual or potential maternal roles. Women, especially those who entered the helping professions and politics in this era, believed they could generalize this special sensibility by applying it to the whole community instead of a single family.[9]

This reform-minded feminism was eager to release women's individuality from "specialization by sex" (Cott 1987:6) — what we now call *sex stereotyping* — but its advocates wanted the vote mainly to achieve urgently needed social reforms, especially curbing the widespread abuse of alcohol that blighted the lives of so many. Working women also had practical goals to achieve with the vote, although they were often discour-

> That feminism is a theory about equality appears most visibly in its goal; as many have argued, feminism can be seen as a demand to extend to women the individualistic premises of the political theory of liberalism . . . . Yet feminism is also about sexual differences, as can be seen in its method of mobilization, for it posits that women, *as* women, will feel the collective grievances to push forward toward equality. Nancy Cott, 1987

aged from seeking it by male socialists, who insisted women's position was identical to men's (Newton 1995).

Although women of this era demanded an end to discrimination in terms of rights and opportunities, few expected the differences in men's and women's lives to disappear. Given the lack of reliable contraception and the high standing then accorded to motherhood, women demanded equality between the sexes while assuming the continued domesticity of the mainly middle-class majoritarian women who shaped the ideology. The poor, often racial and ethnic minority women working in factories and as domestics in the homes of their more affluent sisters, of course, never shared in that unity. They were always in a conflict of interest with those who employed them or whose labour produced goods kept cheap by affluent women's power as consumers.

The Goals of Majority Women

As Cott argues, women had a "circumstantial unity" as long as they remained bound in fact and in sentiment to a "women's sphere" in the family (1987:7). Once many women moved out of the family for education, paid work and political activity, conflicts of interest emerged to challenge the assumption of a shared experience that could sustain a common political agenda. Thus, contemporary feminist ideologies can make different assumptions about women's goals. Women of racial and cultural majorities in the affluent democracies have created three broad ideological positions: liberal feminisms, left-wing feminisms and radical/cultural feminisms[10] (see Exhibit 21).

Exhibit 21. Women and Public Policy: Three Contemporary Feminist Views.

	Liberal Feminisms	Left Feminisms	Radical/cultural Feminisms
Basis of women's inequality?	• Discrimination	• Exploitation	• Sex/Gender arrangements
	• Sexism	• Private families	
How can the state help?	• Pass laws	• Cannot	• Cannot
	• Educate	• Must transform the system	
Is women's fate different from men's?	• Not in the public realm; only in family	• No	• Yes

Note: This simplified chart does not reflect the many different versions of each ideology.

Liberal Feminism

Of these three majority feminisms, only **liberal feminism** accepts in theory the idea that state action can help women achieve their equality goals. That is, *in theory,* unlike many radical/cultural and left-wing feminists, liberal feminists believe getting women elected, lobbying or voting can be effective in attacking the basic causes of women's inequality. Liberal feminists do not believe that transforming or transcending existing political and economic systems is required before significant changes for women can occur.

Consequently, the term *liberal feminist* is often used simply to mean any feminist willing to engage in the politics of the state. This usage is confusing and inaccurate, however, especially in countries with socialist governments. Nor does it help people distinguish among different kinds of liberal feminism,[11] which range from the position that "the system is basically okay, it just needs to include women" to advocacy of changes in legal rights, education, culture, and programs to address *systemic discrimination* and support women's reproductive responsibilities. And, in practical terms, some feminists who espouse left-wing and radical/cultural ideologies work with liberal feminists to achieve concrete policy goals through state action.

Moreover, the basic contrast implicit in the terms *liberal* and *radical* feminism may not even be valid. US feminist political theorist Zillah Eisenstein argues that liberal feminism has a radical potential because of the contradiction at its base "between liberalism (as patriarchal and individualist in structure and ideology) and feminism (as sexual egalitarian and collectivist) [that] lays the basis for feminism's movement beyond liberalism" (1981:3). This radical potential is evident in such things as the shift in practical liberal feminist politics from the constrained concept of discrimination to the concept of structural or systemic discrimination and the evolution of the concept of equal pay for equal work into concepts such as pay equity or comparable worth.[12]

This radical potential may be limited, however, as non-feminist liberals increasingly turn to neo-liberalism, the early form of liberalism that rejects government activism (thereby abandoning liberalism's nineteenth and twentieth activist forms). This turning of liberalism in on itself has forced many liberal feminists to align their analyses more with those of their left-wing feminist colleagues.

Nonetheless, liberal feminism has been successful in the affluent democracies as the basis for political advocacy for much of the twentieth century. Women now enjoy equal civil and political rights everywhere in those countries. Their education levels have soared, and their employment in paid work increases constantly. Their electoral projects have borne some fruit. While powerful democratic states such as the US, France, Germany and the UK have been the most resistant to women's efforts to achieve economic and political equality, women in the Nordic and southern European countries, Canada, Australia and New Zealand have had better results in influencing their less powerful states.

160

Left-Wing Feminisms

Left-wing feminisms (including *working-class feminism, union feminism, socialist feminism* and *Marxist feminism*) emphasize the material causes of women's inequality and work for public programs to socialize child care and domestic work and help women move into paid employment. The main focus of those left-wing feminists willing to work within existing states is **welfare state** programs to support women as workers, particularly those that help reconcile conflicts caused by the sexual division of labour in both the private and the public realms.

Despite Marxists' underlying belief that the state would "wither away", left-wing values and goals look to the state, rather than to the family, community or market, as the source of support for women in resolving the contradiction between their reproductive and productive roles. Policies of particular concern are **affirmative action** (pay equity, employment equity), child care, labour laws, parental and maternity leave, free trade and unemployment insurance. Social democratic governments have established such public policies and programs partly in response to left-wing feminists. These governments have been less effective in dealing with issues such as violence against women and girls (rape, incest, battering), sexuality and cultural issues such as pornography.

Left-wing feminisms often do not include these issues in their analyses (although socialist feminists borrow heavily from cultural feminism for analyses of these concerns). Left-wing feminisms have been weak in dealing with differences among women, such as race, nationality, religion, ethnicity and language.

Left-wing feminists in some countries believe women's equality requires a large welfare state to provide programs to support women's reproductive activities while they are in the paid workforce.[13] Thus their current preoccupation is the consequences for the affluent democracies of economic restructuring as neo-liberal regimes hollow out the welfare state by targeting such programs for elimination, rather than providing them for all citizens (Brodie 1995, 1996).

According to Isabella Bakker, a Canadian feminist political economist (1994, 1996), capitalism is being restructured from a Keynesian welfare state to a neo-liberal state in which the role of government in economic management will be much reduced. She identifies some consequences for women:

- A reduction in the public sphere, reducing public sector jobs for women, who have long relied on them for employment more than men.
- A reduction in universal public sector services, on which women have depended more than men.
- The privatization of many functions, either by returning them to the family (where women are expected to provide child care, elder care, care for the sick, and so on without pay), to the community or the market.

Such a shift threatens to marginalize those women's movements that were deeply engaged with welfare states. It has also led some feminists to react with a kind of "nostalgic welfarism" that "glorifies the postwar welfare state and reads any deviation from past experience as undesirable, disregarding that the welfare state also had negative consequences for women and other disadvantaged groups" (Brodie 1996:9).

Left-wing feminists have been particularly effective in demonstrating the gendered consequences of supposedly neutral policies, such as restructuring, globalization and freer trade. Where they are engaged with the state, most *assume* it is the best recourse for women, rather than analyzing whether it is or not.[14] Scandinavian feminists, however, have put their welfare states under the microscope, debating whether or not their patriarchal guardian states actually act in women's interests. Their conclusion is that they do so only if a **critical mass** of women is present in the centres of decision-making and administration to ensure that women's experiences, values and goals are not ignored when policies are made and economies restructured.

Radical/Cultural Feminisms

Radical/cultural feminisms focus on sex/gender arrangements as the basic cause of male/female inequality. To some radical/cultural feminists, these arrangements are based in human biology and are hard to transcend because they are reflected in all aspects of human cultures. For the most radical, the only possible response is separation into single-sex groups and the creation of a counterculture with women-only institutions.

Other radical/cultural feminists pursue grassroots cultural politics involving the provision of services to women, especially those who have experienced male violence; they also use cultural manifestations and demonstrations. The Italian women's movement, for example, achieved many significant gains from the Italian state because of a clause in its constitution that the legislature is required to discuss any bill when 500,000 registered voters sign a petition of support (Kaplan 1992:258). Movement leaders undertook mass mobilizations and demonstrations aimed at getting divorce, contraception and abortion legalized. These experiences further radicalized the movement, which declared that it would be neither peaceful nor law-abiding and that its adherents were prepared both to kill and be killed to achieve their goals.[15] And they undertook public campaigns to perform abortions without either the sanction of the state or the assistance of doctors.

This kind of radicalism has been rare elsewhere in the developed democracies. Although many radical/cultural feminists are active in demonstrations around such issues as violence against women and the cultural degradation of women in pornography, they are not commonly involved in violence or even law-breaking.

Radical/cultural feminists also focus on expanding understandings of politics ("the personal is political") and changing discourse about politics.

Differences

These three main ideological positions take somewhat different forms in different countries. Where class conflict is intense, as in Britain, for example, left-wing feminists may be more disengaged from state politics than in pluralist societies. The opportunity and desire for cooperation across ideological positions also varies widely. In some settings, for example, each ideological camp operates its own shelters for women who are victims of violence. In other settings, cooperation is possible across ideological lines but often not between women of different races or language groups.

The Goals of Minority Women

Difficulty dealing with difference, whether communal or related to personal status, has been a major problem of women's movements everywhere, especially in the liberal democracies, as they attempted to develop coherent public policy positions. The three positions we have explored to this point reflect both women's common interests (such as the fact that women of all classes, races and ages are subject to male violence) and existing conflicts of interest (between, for example, childrearing women and women without children in relation to state expenditures on child care). In some of the affluent democracies, however, serious conflicts of interests, largely unrecognized by the majority women who dominate women's movements, have resulted in the emergence of alternate visions of feminist ideology. These alternate visions reflect different values and goals and often a different conception of how equality should be realized.

> Gender politics are greatly influenced by class, race, ethnicity, sexuality, and other differences between women. Perhaps the most disappointing development in the women's movement of the 1960s and 1970s was the fragmentation that resulted from these divisions. No sooner had the slogan "Sisterhood is powerful" become established in feminist rhetoric than bitter arguments in the movement made sisterhood seem impossible. Such divisions afflicted feminist movements everywhere, although the relative influence of class, race, and sexual preference varied considerably.
> Joni Lovenduski, 1994

Two important minority women's ideologies are *womanism* and *lesbian feminism*.

Womanism

Womanism, as articulated by African-American women in the US, "asserts the inseparability of race and gender in the thought and experience of Black women and presents a view of the gender identity of Black women as ineluctably[16] located in racial and community consciousness" (Nelson and Chowdhury 1994:19). In a reaction against a notion of a single set of undifferentiated women's interests, it sees gender conflict "in terms of its racial meanings as well as its relevance for relations between men and women" (Nelson and Chowdhury 1994:19).

Community solidarity means more in this orientation than gender solidarity, a perspective found within many communities facing oppression and marginalization. Many aboriginal women in Australia, the US and Canada make the same argument while often rejecting the feminist label.

The way to deal with domestic violence[17] is one issue that has produced significant conflict between womanists and some aboriginal women on the one hand and majority, white feminists on the other. In Australia, for example, aboriginal people are ten times more likely than others to be murder victims, and domestic violence is extensive. Aboriginal women, while organizing to resist violence, have also resisted white feminists' efforts to "break the silence" on intraracial violence as long as issues of white-on-aboriginal violence and rape are trivialized and state racism and brutality are largely unchallenged (Pettman 1992). Similarly, for many womanists, the US lynch-mob culture around black-male-on-white-female rape makes some feminist activities such as Take Back the Night marches (in which women walk through areas normally considered unsafe for them) seem racist.[18] Similarly, womanists resist the covert understanding of black male sexuality that underlies some white feminist analyses, noting that they rarely deal with white-male-on-black-female rape.

A key source of counter-attack to the feminist critique of the family has come from black feminists who have vocalized their defence of the black family-household as an arena of solidarity against racism . . . .

However, one should not allow this reality—the family-household as a source of resistance to other forms of oppression—to disguise or distort the oppressive elements to women within that very institution. Gemma Tang Nain, 1991

Not all racial minority women adopt a womanist position or its equivalent. But those who espouse one of the three major strains of feminism experience difficulties when analyses do not take difference into account. Gemma Tang Nain (1991), a black feminist from the Caribbean, demonstrates that the kind of *black feminism* that has developed in the US and the UK, where black women are minorities, differs from that which has emerged where black women are part of majorities, as in her homeland of Trinidad and Tobago. She identifies four ways in which black minority and white majority women differ on public policy and political practice in the US and the UK:

- Minority black women usually experience their families (often women-led) as a refuge from racism and the basis of the household solidarity they need to survive, if not to prosper. White majority women, especially those of left-wing and radical feminist persuasions, tend to attack the family as a site of oppression.
- Minority black women assert that black men learned sexism from white men, that it was not indigenous in African cultures.
- When minority black women report violence against them by black men, they experience a sense of betraying their own people. (Such loyalty is asymmetrical, since black men perpetrating violence obviously feel no parallel loyalty to black women.)
- Majority white women's emphasis on reproductive freedoms (mainly freedom *from* reproduction) does not reflect black women's experiences (they reported being able to get abortions). They are deeply aware that majority white women's freedom from nurturing children is usually at the expense of black minority women, who are the nannies and domestics.

Nain notes that where black women are in the majority—where the effects of gender conflict are not obscured by the need for community solidarity—they tend to see these issues in ways similar to white majority women. She argues for an anti-racist feminism within which majority and minority women can develop a common framework.

Gender Gap

Gender gap analysis, an important tool feminists have developed to understand differences in political attitudes and policy choices, reveals a further problem in trying to reinvent political science without repressing differences among women and men. In the US, where the concept has also been used in practical politics by the National Organization of Women (NOW), "its primary manifestations are said to include the greater propensity of women to identify as Democrats, to vote for Democratic candidates, and to espouse more liberal views on a variety of social and political issues" (Welch and Sigelman 1989:120).

More generally, the concept of a gender gap stems from the notion, developed in the early decades of the century when women were first enfranchised, that the political values of men and women would differ significantly so that political parties would have to pursue the women's vote. These predictions (made by women seeking the vote and often also by men opposing them) were not realized because women (half the population) did not emerge immediately as a single, distinctive electoral bloc that had to be courted by the parties (Norris 1985). This non-result meant a paucity of examination of political opinions by sex, especially during the two or three decades after the Second World War, when the focus was on voting behaviour and the analysis conducted largely in the US and the UK.[19]

Renewed interest in the idea of a gender gap in political values coincided with the current remobilization of women in official politics and the emergence of feminist political science. Our ability to understand the extent to which women and men have different interests and views on some public policy issues comes from this field of research. One of the difficulties of working with gender gap analysis, however, has been its insensitivity to the effects of other aspects of difference, especially race. Because gender gap research uses statistical analysis of large samples of the general population and has focused on male/female differences, analysts have tended to overgeneralize their findings. So the finding of an ideological gender gap between US women and men has been cast as a general (even universal) finding, whereas race-sensitive research shows "almost a complete lack of differentiation between black men and women across a wide range of political attitudes" (Welch and Sigelman 1989:125).

Between white men and women in the US, the gender gap is widest in attitudes concerning violence and the use of force. But is also evident on so-called compassion issues, such as treatment of the poor, elderly and infirm. White men are now much less willing that white women to support state activism on these compassion issues. In the black population, by contrast, men and women hold very similar views, especially on issues concerning state activism.

In brief, on many (though not all) issues, black men and women in the USapproach politics as blacks. Their opinions are more liberal than the opinions of whites on the compassion issues, and black men and women support women's issues at about the same rate. It is important to understand, therefore, that research tools such as gender gap analysis can hide as much as they reveal. And exploring other gaps or cleavages within the female population is vital, especially when we know that particular communities of women have mobilized around somewhat different issues, producing distinctive ideologies.

Lesbian Feminism

In the advanced democracies, the second major feminist ideology organized around difference is **lesbian feminism**, with a lesbian defined as "a woman who has sexual and erotic-emotional ties primarily with women or sees herself as centrally involved with a community of self-identified lesbians . . . who is herself a self-identified lesbian" (Phelan 1989:9).[20] As an ideology at work in politics, this position holds that:

- Sexism and heterosexism are hopelessly intertwined.
- The oppression of women and lesbians is the prototype for all other oppressions since the oppression of women and lesbians crosses boundaries of race, class and age.
- Male violence is the major mechanism through which patriarchy is maintained so separatist women-only groups are required for living, working and doing politics.
- The heterosexual family is dangerous for girls and women.

Lesbian feminism works at both the theoretical and practical levels, challenging the concepts of family and spouse and fighting for same-sex adoption rights, same-sex benefits and state recognition of same-sex marriages. Most of this activism includes "rights talk" that could proceed within a liberal-feminist framework except for the persistent prejudice lesbians experience from hetero-sexual feminists and societies, which has led many mainstream women's movements to soft-pedal issues of lesbian rights or refuse to advocate them at all. Lesbian feminism's challenges to feminist heterosexism, its conceptions of sexuality and its analysis of the relationship between maleness and violence, however, have created a distinctive political ideology. Lesbians are in the forefront of efforts to counter rape, battering, incest and other forms of violence against women. They often provide much of the energy for the creation of women's institutions from bookstores to women's studies programs.[21]

Lesbian feminism conflicts with the ideas of many heterosexual and minority women, who understand both the family and the main sources of violence in their societies. In Canada in recent years, these conflicts have erupted within shelters. Often these shelters were the creations of lesbian feminists who built their intellectual (and diagnostic) frames on a view that male violence is endemic and that women who experience it should remove themselves from the family or heterosexual relationship. (Violence in lesbian relationships is only now being discussed openly.)

Many women from racial and ethnic minorities who work in or use the shelters reject this analysis and now demand a presence in the collectives and on the boards running the shelters, seeing them as providing a public service because they receive state funding. The functioning of many shelters has been disrupted, sometimes resulting in closure.

Parallel conflicts have arisen when women with disabilities protested lack of physical access to the shelters. Feminists in the disability rights movement have contested, for example, the values of most feminists that abortion on demand should be not just available but the obvious choice for any woman expecting a child known or thought to be disabled. Many women with disabilities reject the devaluing of their lives inherent in such values.

In both cases, a strain of feminism advances values that challenge the bottom line positions of mainstream feminisms with regard to public policy positions.

Benchmark Issues and Fracture Points

Each of the main ideological streams within feminism in the advanced democ-racies has *benchmark issues,* which have shaped its orientation to public policy, and *fracture points,* where it is vulnerable to fragmentation. The nature and histories of these issues vary from country to country. In the US, for example, the question of support for lesbian rights was a benchmark issue for liberal feminists, who struggled during the 1970s and again in the 1990s with what founder Betty Friedan called "the lavender menace" within NOW. Liberal feminists in NOW in the 1970s met the challenge by supporting lesbian rights and ensuring lesbian visibility within the organization, broadening the movement's base but alienating it further from anti-feminist women and from many traditional women who supported women's rights within a maternal feminist frame.[22] (Although lesbian rights and visibility are issues elsewhere, they have been less of a benchmark issue in countries other than the US.)

Pensions and wages for homemakers were benchmark issues for Canada's National Action Committee on the Status of Women (NAC) in the 1970s. The left-wing and liberal feminist coalition, which then dominated NAC, believed that women could be equal only by moving into the public realm of paid work, and the organization explicitly rejected the argument that housewives should receive equal economic support because the work they do is productive for society. (The wages-for-housework idea first developed in Italy to make this case within the left.) Eventually, a new coalition in NAC, which included cultural feminists, changed the institution's views on these issues. Nonetheless, the status of housewives was a benchmark issue for both liberal and left-wing feminism in Canada and influenced both the movement's public policy positions and its relationships with housewives' groups, some of which, such as Mothers Are Women, are feminist.[23]

These benchmark issues also point to the dynamic of anti-feminist opposition to the public policy positions feminists advanced. For women of middle years who choose a full-time domestic life, the mainstream feminist idea of economic independence (being in the paid workforce and not relying on a man for support) has little attraction and may cause fear. A simple conflict-of-interest analysis shows that they may lose from freer divorce and legal assumptions that women shouldn't need alimony if divorce occurs. It also suggests that they may see publicly-funded child care as taking money from their single-earner families to support a service to be used by relatively affluent two-earner families and affirmative action as threatening their household incomes and the career advancement of their husbands, brothers and sons.

Although lines of fracture operate differently in women's politics in different countries, these examples illustrate the importance of examining both common interests and conflicts of interest in our efforts to understand women's politics.

Women and Public Policies: The Affluent Democracies

When we examine public policy issues around which women in the affluent democracies have mobilized, we find no simple pattern. The reasons are numerous and complex, including different histories of women's activism in relation to their states.

Political Histories

The countries we can lump together as affluent, stable democracies, liberal or social, have quite different political histories. The specifics concerning women

differ in at least seven important ways:
- When women got the vote, and when they became eligible to run for office.
- When male/female differences in voting rates disappeared.
- When women began to be elected to public office in significant numbers.
- Whether women's political activism went through a long dormant period (as in, for example, the UK and the US) or experienced continuous organizing (as in Scandinavia).
- The pattern of women's political activism: interest group feminism (US), ideologically organized and divided (UK, Mexico), integrated into parties (Norway), **femocrat strategy** (Australia) or some combination (Canada).
- The extent to which anti-feminist (and anti-suffrage) backlashes occurred and produced enduring organizations of women opposed to feminist goals.
- The extent to which racial, ethnic and linguistic diversity exists in the society, its effect on women's capacity for political action and the relative capacity of majority women to build common agendas with minority women.

Although I lack space to outline the political histories of even a sample of the affluent democracies, I can sketch several modal experiences showing how these differences affect the range of public policy issues that concern women in various countries.

The Scandinavian Countries

In the Scandinavian countries, women gained the vote early (Sweden was last in 1921). Differences between men's and women's voting turnout had virtually disappeared by the 1950s (when US political science was just discovering women's natural apathy). Women's organizations formed in the late nineteenth and early twentieth centuries worked energetically to integrate women into existing political structures. Soon after enfranchisement, some women tried forming women's parties to get more women elected, but the failure of this strategy made most women commit to working within political parties. There was no significant anti-suffrage or anti-feminist backlash and no long dormant period. Mobilization was renewed in the 1960s, sparked by concerns about the low levels of women decision-makers. By the early 1980s, women were at least 25 percent of each of the Scandinavian legislatures (Canada had 8 percent and the UK 3 percent in the same period). The major issues revolved around programs and entitlements necessary to support women's reproductive and public responsibilities. The Scandinavian countries, pressured by women activists, have also enacted policies intended to resolve the conflicts in the existing sexual division of labour. Some women have been mobilized by women's liberation movements, especially around the issue of violence. But they are small compared to the older women's rights organizations, and they are marginalized as male violence is not part of the core movement's analysis.

One way of analyzing public policy from a women-centred perspective is to

Role equity issues address the distribution of power in society but do not disturb basic sex-role definitions. In contrast, *role change* challenges traditional sex-role ideology. Ellen Boneparth, 1982

differentiate between policies to advance *role equity* and those to promote *role change* or *transformation*. The principle is the substantial difference between programs or entitlements that achieve greater equity between the sexes — such as maternity leave and child care — and those that aspire to transform the sexual division of labour altogether by changing sex roles[24] or changing assumptions about the two sexes (such as same-sex marriage). The pattern achieved in the Scandinavian countries has largely taken the form of policies aimed at role equity, although policies providing parental leave for fathers to be care-giving parents aim at role change.

The Anglo-American Countries

The pattern of mobilization in the anglo-American democracies (the UK, the US, Canada, Australia, New Zealand) also included early enfranchisement of women, but their integration into existing political structures was much slower than in Scandinavia, as was the process of their gaining other legal rights. The UK and the US especially saw strong anti-suffrage movements and strong backlash movements (both including women) against the policy demands of women's organizations in the 1920s. Some women's organizations have maintained a continuous existence in each country, but there was a long period of dormancy or demobilization from the 1930s until the 1960s. By the 1980s, many decades after the enfranchisement, women in these countries were still not visible as political actors in legislatures.

From the 1960s on, however, revitalized women's organizations and new women's liberation groups completed the gaining of legal rights and opened up new policy concerns, especially about reproductive freedom. A second wave of backlash movements emerged in these countries in the 1980s, with anti-feminist women gaining political prominence. Lively, autonomous women's movements lost both members and momentum as a result of this backlash plus neo-liberal attacks on the welfare state and challenges from minority women.

Issues concerning violence against women (first rape and then battering, incest and harassment) remobilized many women. But new groupings emerged; for example, the issue of pornography found some feminists allied with anti-feminists in support of censoring it, while other feminists allied themselves with civil liberties activists against censorship.

Meanwhile, the process of economic restructuring and globalization is moving these countries from activist (Keynesian) states, willing to spend money on welfare programs and intervene in the economy, to neo-liberal states. Women have responded with a wave of *defensive mobilization,* struggling to retain the state employment, programs and entitlements they gained in earlier decades.

Most of the policies achieved in these countries have been aimed at role equity. The more radical elements of women's movements, however, have actively demanded more substantial role change. Issues raised by lesbian feminists and the gay rights movements have challenged the underlying assumptions about the sexual division of labour more than issues raised by mainstream liberal or left-wing feminists. Activism around these issues has also fed the backlash movements, which are markedly strong in these countries.

Other Countries

These two thumbnail sketches do scant justice to the full range of political activism undertaken by women in countries where they were enfranchised early. Each pattern, however, is quite different from that in countries where women's political activism emerged primarily after the Second World War (France, Belgium, Switzerland) or where the political mobilization of women was shaped by fascism, revolution, civil war and foreign occupation (Spain, Italy, Germany, Greece).

Although each of these countries is now an affluent democracy, not all have been stable and not all of the people within them share in their generally high levels of affluence. In particular, women's relationships with unions and parties of the left, on the one hand, and with churches and parties of the right, on the other, have affected their patterns of political mobilization in these countries in ways not seen in the Scandinavian or anglo-American democracies. Indeed, in several countries, women's enfranchisement was long delayed because each of the polarized social elements believed women's votes would change electoral outcomes.[25] Moreover, several generations of women responded to the horrors of war, civil war and revolution with political quietism.

In these contexts, issues of particular concern to women take on a different character. For example, while public programs that support women's reproductive activities may be generous, as they are in France, they may reflect *pro-natalism* on the part of the state, not a response to women's equality demands.

The postwar stabilization of the western European states, however, opened them up to the mobilization of women and the reemergence of public policy issues of concern to women as part of the 'new social movements'. Issues of reproductive freedom and access to divorce in Catholic countries were important in mobilizing women; so were issues related to violence against women. The period of mobilization was relatively short in some of these countries, however, as the political and economic changes involved in the creation of the European Union (including policy harmonization) took centre stage.

Policy Outcomes

Another approach to understanding the kinds of changes women seek in various democracies is to compare different kinds of policy outcomes.

Some feminist political scientists distinguish between policies and programs that are *women friendly* and those that are *women-focused.* The former are not designed specifically for or by women but they have positive effects for most women. Policies that increase the minimum wage or raise welfare rates are good examples because usually more women than men earn only the minimum wage and depend on welfare programs. By contrast, programs to improve the detection and treatment of breast cancer are women-focused since they are designed to prevent a harm that is (almost) exclusively suffered by women.

Analysts also find it useful to distinguish policy types along other dimensions, such as the expected durability of their outcomes and whether they are distributive or redistributive, regulatory or fundamental/constitutional in character (see Exhibit 22). For example, the achievement of constitutional protection for sex equality rights and affirmative action programs in Canada established a policy of the most durable kind, constitutions being harder to change than legislation, especially in federal states.

Exhibit 22. Four Basic Policy Types.

1. **Distributive** - Gives benefits to individuals or groups, especially in the form of government subsidies. Produces most vulnerable outcomes.	3. **Redistributive** - Transfers benefits (tangible or symbolic) from one group (for example, men) to another (for example, women).
2. **Regulatory** - Involves government regulation of the practices of groups or individuals.	4. **Fundamental/ Constitutional** - Establishes the overall rules of the game, including the distribution of powers and citizenship rights. Produces most durable outcomes.

Note that the four types are increasingly difficult to achieve; that is, distributive policies are the least difficult, constitutional policies usually the most difficult.

Most feminist demands have been for *distributive* policies, seeking to provide benefits to women without taking anything away from men. The most conflict among feminists has often been provoked by demands for *regulatory policies,* such as efforts to regulate pornography, prostitution and other aspects of the sex trade. *Redistributive policies,* which transfer benefits from one group (men) to another (women), are quite rare.

Commonalities

Important though the differences are in the patterns of issues that have mobilized women in the affluent democracies, commonalities also appear.

- The major mobilizers of women have been sex/gender issues, such as legal rights, reproductive freedom and security from violence and cultural issues, such as pornography. The reason is that majority-dominated women's movements have focused less on basic needs (food, shelter and employment) than on sex/gender and cultural issues.
- More political space is opened up for the exploration of issues involving reproduction and sexuality where an autonomous women's movement is active.
- Gender gaps persist in majority populations around issues of security (war and the use of force) and insecurity (state activism to provide support programs such as health care).
- Progress from a women's-issues approach to a more holistic, feminist approach to public policy, in which most issues are examined for their gendered impacts, has been stimulated by the efforts of the growing numbers of women legislators, bureaucrats and judges; the analyses of women's movements; and the emergence of feminist political science in these countries.

The challenge raised for feminists in the affluent democracies by economic restructuring and globalization may now divert some attention away from specific sex/gender issues (that is, women-focused issues).

Women's Politics in Less Affluent Countries

The division created by the mainstream political science paradigm between 'developed' and 'developing' societies has greatly impeded feminist public policy analysis. The very language with which women in the affluent democracies write about women elsewhere is often fraught with bias and misunderstanding. Even the general designation of where other women live (*'third world'*, *'less developed countries'*) has ideological dimensions. Descriptions of the general activity of women trying to improve their lives reflect contested ground: policy approaches changed from WID (Women *in* Development) to WAD (Women *and* Development) to WED (Women *and Environment and Alternatives to* Development). Most of this literature, until recently, was produced by development agencies, international institutions and feminist scholars in the affluent countries. The voices of women in the less affluent countries, many of whom are leaders of highly successful women's movements and organizations, were heard far less often.

Yet some of these women have developed strategies from which feminists in the more affluent countries may have much to learn as globalization proceeds. Thus, in this section, I explore public policy issues about 'women in development' and suggest how a more integrated approach can be achieved.

Some Background

The huge economic disparities between the affluent and the less affluent countries have permitted 'first world' feminists to often presume our analyses and strategies must be better than those developed by women elsewhere. (Government policy-makers have worked on the same presumption.)

The underlying assumption has been that countries that are now affluent got that way because they were smarter or harder-working than less affluent countries. This belief, which is deeply embedded in our collective psyches, ignores the centuries-old history of European conquest of other countries and the colonial systems that damaged the indigenous socioeconomic systems and the sense of self-worth of the colonized. The resulting empires were based on economic exploitation that enriched the European countries while they impoverished countries now 'underdeveloped' according to mainstream western theory.

Many Europeans and their white descendants in the settler societies (the US, Canada, Australia, South Africa, Latin America and others) continue to believe these imperial ventures were justified because white domination performed a valuable service of 'civilizing' the 'backward' peoples so conquered. An important part of the belief that non-European peoples were 'primitive' was the myth that they treated 'their' women in ways far worse than Europeans treated theirs.[26] This belief ignores the lack of rights and the harsh treatment endured by most women in Europe until the twentieth century. It also neglects the major economic roles played by women in most parts of the world. The images of Chinese women's bound feet, polygamy and harems associated non-European traditions and religions with the oppression of women while women's advancement became associated with 'modernization', which meant becoming secularized and Europeanized.

Thus, the paradigm of mainstream political science separated the politics of 'developed' and 'developing' societies and treated them quite differently. What a feminist political science needs is an approach that abolishes this artificial distinction and views women's politics everywhere within a common framework. Such a framework cannot, however, be drawn from the ideas of women living in the affluent democracies alone (their approaches do not even account for the needs, interests and values of their poor and minority compatriots). Instead, it must recognize that many of the outcomes we 'first world' feminists consider the result of our governments' greater concern for women (or better strategy on the part of women's movements) have been possible only because of the vastly greater wealth of the 'developed' countries, wealth that continues to be based on neo-colonial exploitation.

What Do Women Want?

Is There a Common Women's Agenda?

The analyses of non-European and minority women make it clear that the values and priorities that motivated the development of contemporary, western feminism cannot be assumed to be universal and that it is unjustified for white, majority feminists to believe they have the right to define women's common interests and speak for women. Western majority feminists must pay far more attention to the values, priorities and agendas of other women and recognize how we are privileged by other systems of oppression such as racism.

Yet important commonalities exist. When the researchers edited by Nelson and Chowdhury (1994:3, 7) look at patterns of women's political engagement globally, they find:

- "[I]n no country do women have political status, access, or influence equal to men's."
- Everywhere, international economic forces such as globalization and stringent macroeconomic policies, whether introduced domestically or forced on countries by international institutions such as the World Bank and the International Monetary Fund (IMF), affect men and women differently. Women experience negative consequences more than men, largely because they are concentrated in marginal, informal economic sectors and in activities that are vulnerable but nonetheless feed and shelter families. When positive gains occur, women everywhere benefit less than men.
- The changing nature of nationalisms, especially the rise of "ethnic essentialism" and the increasing influence of religious fundamentalisms, is challenging earlier trends toward universalism and secularism, which seemed to expand opportunities for women to participate in both civil society and the state.
- The power and vitality of women's political organizing are increasing everywhere. Local, grassroots movements are now more accepted as indigenous political expressions of women's interests. International feminism is reemerging vigorously. This growth has been stimulated by three basic trends: first, the collapse of the Soviet empire and the resulting crisis of the left deflated Marxist criticisms of women's movements as bourgeois or imperialist; second, feminists are learning to deal more effectively with issues of difference, to identify interests women have in common and build movements based on solidarity among equals; third, the international activities have been stimulated partly by the UN Decade for Women (1976–85) and its aftermath and partly through the expansion of women's organizations in the arena of international civil society, especially through women-led non-governmental organizations (NGOs).

Given these common circumstances, it seems reasonable to expect that women around the globe want at least some of the same things. Women in the poor countries have been fighting the effects of economic restructuring and globalization far longer than 'first world' women. Looking at women's agendas

> The political problems facing women . . . cluster into four topics: ensuring personal safety, security and autonomy; providing abortion, reproductive rights, and maternal and child health programs; equalizing access to public, commercial and market resources for problem solving and empowerment; and remaking the political and legal rules of the game. Barbara Nelson and Najama Chowdhury, 1994

globally, therefore, may produce a tougher and more far-sighted vision.

Nelson and Chowdhury (1994) identify four major areas where women in the forty-three countries in their project have demands (the specific content often differs, of course). First, women everywhere want *relief from violence* and place a high priority on the attainment of safety and security for themselves and their families. Often, the end to war is key to their security. Second, women everywhere are concerned with *reproductive rights* (more broadly conceived than the right to abortion), including a particular concern for the health of mothers and children and opposition to coerced abortions and sterilizations. Third, women are focusing attention on *equalizing strategies,* including attempts to improve their access to education, credit, land, employment, health care and other resources they need to enjoy life chances comparable to men's. Finally, women everywhere are concerned with *politics and the law, increasing women's involvement in political participation* in democratic regimes and transforming or overthrowing corrupt or brutal regimes.

Nelson and Chowdhury conclude that women's political activism does make a significant difference:

> Women's activism has demonstrated the inaccuracy of assuming that more players merely cut the political pie into smaller pieces. As often as not, increasing the number and variety of political players changes the nature of politics and generates additional political resources (1994:14).

Who is making political decisions can, therefore, make a great difference to outcomes for women.

Women-in-Development Policy Approaches

Since the Second World War, domestic and international public policy has focused on 'development', understood primarily as 'modernization' of economics and as the westernization of political cultures, including the secularization of institutions.

The world spends extensive resources trying to solve the problem of 'underdevelopment' yet all development strategies adversely affect poor women and their children. That statement surprises hearers only because they have forgotten the horrible effects of the development of capitalism in Europe, where the human costs of economic change, although partly mitigated by wealth imported from exploited colonies, were heavily (and unwillingly) subsidized by exploited men and especially women and children working in factories and mines. In brief, 'development' costs, and everywhere women and children pay.

> Women, as the group most adversely affected by the existing development strategies, will have to be in the forefront of the definition of a new self-reliant and people-centered development.
>
> Wanjiru Kirhoro, 1992

Western Approaches

Exhibit 23 outlines five major approaches to development used from the 1950s to the present day. In most, including several women-in-development (WID) approaches endorsed by many western feminists,[27] women are depoliticized. Instead of being viewed as political actors with needs, interests, goals and values to determine and express for themselves, women are most often seen as 'a problem' in the development process because they and their children are adversely affected by development, seemingly regardless of the strategies adopted. Women's fertility, in particular, is treated as a problem—a women's problem.

The *equity approach,* the first WID approach developed by 'first world' feminists, was based on a neo-colonial perception of 'third world' women as victimized by their cultural traditions. Many 'third world' feminists, however, reject the assumptions underlying modernization theories that see non-western traditions and cultures as causing women's oppression; that is, they reject the assumption that to be 'liberated', women must reject their traditional cultures and religions.

Most 'first world' feminists view women's primary goal as autonomy—independence as individuals, but most 'third world' women view it as "a self embedded in kinship (and other social) webs, as well as in the local landscape" (Apffel-Marglin and Simon

> Feminist orientalism: The assumptions made by western feminists about 'other' women not of European origin, especially those of Asian origin. They are summed up in the oppositions civilized/backward, independent/dependent, active/passive, liberated/oppressed and modern/traditional, which are assumed to distinguish 'western' and other women.

1994:33). Some 'third world' feminists use the term **feminist orientalism** to describe these assumptions, which often contain biases, conscious or unconscious, against the cultural or religious practices of othered societies or reflect

Exhibit 23. Public Policy Approaches to 'Third World' Women and Economic Development.

	Origin	When	Purpose	Results
Welfare approach	• Residual of colonial rule	• 1950s–1970s	• Bring women into development as better *mothers*	• Food aid, family planning and domestic training provided
	• EDM[a]	• Still used	• Meet PGNs[b]	• Women seen as *passive* beneficiaries
Equity Approach	• Original WID approach[c]	• 1975–85 UN Women's Decade	• Gain equity for women in development	• Women seen as *actors* in development
	• Assertion of failure of EDM[a]		• Meet SGNs[b] including equality	• Approach seen as western especially by governments
	• First-world feminists			
Anti-poverty approach	• Second WID approach[c]	• 1970s onward	• Increase productivity of poor women	• Development, not male dominance, fails women
	• Toned-down equity	• Still not popular	• Meet PGNs[b] to earn income	• *Poor women* singled out as the problem
	• Link to basic needs			
Efficiency approach	• Third WID approach[c]	• Post-1980	• Make development efficient	• Women's ability to *produce more* and extend working day is main concern
	• Assertion that economic restructuring needs women's economic contributions	• Now most popular approach	• Meet women's PGNs[b] while social services deteriorate or are not created	• Governments and multilateral agencies favour
Empowerment approach	• 'Third world' women's writings and grassroots organizing	• 1975 on	• Empower women via *self-reliance*	• At least some SGNs[b] are met
		• Still not popular	• Bottom-up mobilization	• Approach critiques EDM,[a] male dominance and colonialism

a. EDM is the Economic Development Model, also called modernization theory. It assumes that 'development' is primarily a matter of economic changes, including capitalization and industrialization, which produced affluence in the west. The model neglects the role of imperialism in the actual development of western economies.
b. PGNs and SGNs are practical gender needs and strategic gender needs.
c. WID (Women in Development) refers to early approaches to including concerns about women in development.
Source: Derived from Karl 1995:98, 99.

simple racial prejudice.[28] 'Third world' feminists critiques are also called *postcolonial,* since its basic ideas come mainly from people trying to understand and overcome biases introduced into their conceptions of themselves because of the long established dominance of colonial ideas asserting the superiority of white, eurocentric cultural practices. One mark of this underlying bias is the heavy emphasis 'first world' feminists put on the elimination of oppressive practices faced by othered women, such as genital mutilation, dowry murder and footbinding. "First world' feminists in the development field seem to ignore the oppression experienced now and in the past by western women. Instead they present a mythical norm in which all western women appear, in Audre Lorde's words, "white, thin, young, heterosexual, Christian and financially secure" (1984:116).

The ideas underlying the WID discourses give priority to experiences of sex and gender by women in the modern industrial countries and confer special importance on their values and goals. Georgina Ashworth (1995) describes their "mother knows best" approach as *maternalism* (to parallel paternalism). She argues that blindness to reality denies the "lagoons of poverty" that exist in the affluent states and constructs women in less affluent societies as if they were homogenous and voiceless. In fact, she says, they have often been more successful than their more affluent, 'first world' sisters; for example, Egypt now has more women professional engineers and Turkey more women lawyers than the UK has of either.

Ashworth also notes, however, that responses to this maternalism have also been problematic:

> [B]y projecting all the blame indiscriminately on the North [the affluent nations], elite women in the South absolve themselves of their responsibilities in the inequalities within their own society, or of their relative privilege to challenge patriarchy and to work with their compatriot women (1995:9).

Clearly, maternalism or feminist orientalism and unproductive responses to it must be transcended if we are to develop coherent, worldwide approaches to feminist public policy analysis.

Empowerment

Approaches to development created by women in the less affluent countries emphasize women's roles as political actors who have choices to make, only some of which are about economics or development. The *empowerment approach* created by women in the 'third world', for example, combines critiques of economic development theory, of structures of male dominance and of the effects of colonialism on women's capacity to provide for themselves and their children.

The empowerment approach, unpopular with governments and aid agencies, is explicitly political, arguing that women must organize collectively to gain more representation in decision-making. It stresses women's basic needs but argues that equality and empowerment must (see Exhibit 24) receive a high priority too. In this approach, the development of consciousness is important,

Exhibit 24.
Empowerment Approach: Five Levels of Equality.

1. **Welfare:** Aims at basic needs; women are passive beneficiaries.
2. **Access:** Involves resources, education, land and credit. When women recognize their lack of access, growth occurs.
3. **Conscientization:** Occurs when women recognize structural discrimination exists and their role in maintaining it.
4. **Participation:** Occurs after mobilization, when women are taking decisions equally with men. Requires women to organize and work collectively.
5. **Control:** Occurs when the balance of power between the sexes is equal; neither dominates the other. Women control their lives and their contributions are valued.

Source: UNICEF 1993:5.

and it emphasizes the training of female leaders in community, grassroots groups and NGOs as key in empowering women. In short, the analysis of women's path to equality bases it on self-organization and self-reliance, rather than on the provision of state-funded social services considered essential to women's quest for equality by most feminists in affluent democracies.

This emphasis on self-reliance may be a matter of making a virtue of necessity (the less affluent countries cannot afford extensive welfare state programs) or of a different vision. In either case, this approach to women's equality will be important for women in the affluent democracies to learn from as globalization continues, especially if it results in any significant redistribution of wealth from more to less affluent countries.

Other feminist perspectives emerging in the 'third world' deal with women and environments and sustainable alternatives to western-style economic development. Compatible with the empowerment approach, these perspectives (not outlined in Exhibit 23) have the potential to unite the concerns of women around the world, including in the postcommunist countries.

Militarism
Militarism is yet another model of development, although one rarely explicitly critiqued by feminist scholars. As Andrée Michel says:

> [F]eminist writings in the . . . industrialised nations have not addressed the processes of militarisation and the structures which generate them, either as a mode of development which affects the situation of women, or as patriarchal structures elaborated solely by men (1995:33).

By focusing heavily on the theme of equality, feminists in the affluent states have largely ignored the coercive underpinnings of development in their own and other countries. The idea of the continuum of violence, identifying violence as a feature of intersex relationships, must also be understood as an interstate phenomenon.

Militarization is rarely understood as a mode of development that affects women, yet everywhere military regimes provide the worst environments for women. Michel attributes the oversight to the virtual invisibility of women in the affluent countries in scientific, technological and policy fields that relate to the weapons of violence. Feminist peace activists have identified as a problem the vast expenditures of money spent on weapons and the research to perfect them, and they hoped for a "peace dividend" when the cold war finally ended. What is rarely analyzed is the fact that in rapidly developing countries based on the militarist mode, including Brazil, South Korea, China, Argentina and various countries in Africa, the poverty, ill health, abuse and exploitation of women and children are directly related to military rule and expenditure. UNICEF reports, for example, that in 1981 military spending in the countries of sub-Saharan Africa was 11 percent of their collective budgets while health spending was only 5 percent; low spending on health care increases infant mortality, restricts the availability of contraceptive information and harms maternal health (Michel 1995:38). (The major countries selling arms include France, the US and the UK, but sales of military materials by all western countries support 'first world' affluence to some degree.)

Nelson and Chowdhury describe the devastating impact of state militarism on the lives of women and children—deaths, famine and starvation, disease, destruction of property, kidnapping, rape and torture. They also point to the more diffuse but equally corrosive effect of "the cold winter of militarism" on everyday life "whose practices become more patriarchal as part of the *gestalt* of military rule" (1994:12).[29] Uruguayan Graciela Sapriza (1994) explains that as the public world disappears or shrinks under militarism with the banning of political parties, unions and elections, men's and women's political horizons are limited to the home and neighbourhood, where men's efforts to exercise whatever power remain to them as fathers, brothers and husbands intensify with increasing violence for the girls and women who are their daughters, sisters and wives. Even the employment that results in industrial countries from the sale of arms, technology and military know-how benefits men more since few defence-related industries and disciplines employ women (Michel 1995).

Women's Politics in the International Arena

Feminists have been a force in the international arena for several centuries, working in a variety of groups, including anti-slavery movements, anti-war movements (including the Hague Peace Conferences), the worldwide movement for the vote and international organizations such as the International Council of

Women. Since 1975, however, women's activism in the international sphere has increased significantly within international civil society and the official institutions of international politics. This change in the international environment has, in the words of long-time observer Georgina Ashworth, been an "explosion of 'the woman question' into the international public sphere" that "set off a chain of necessary reaction, of which policy makers would prefer not to think" (1995:7).

This rapid growth has at least two immediate causes: first, the development of internationally agreed-to conventions, declaring that "women's rights are human rights" that must be respected by signatory countries, created a new environment in some states and in the international arena; and second, the UN Decade for Women and its associated assemblies and plans of action created or revitalized women's movements in many countries, movements that often adopt a *strategy of internationalism,* using the documents and global public opinion to lever concessions for women out of reluctant governments and institutions of civil society.

Thus, the last two decades have seen the creation of a wide variety of women's international organizations, networks, caucuses, research and media agencies. A few of the major ones are AAWORD (Association of African Women for Research and Development), DAWN (Development Alternatives for a New Era), Entre Mujeres, FEMNET News, FINRAGE (Feminist International Network of Resistance to Reproductive and Genetic Engineering), the Global Tribunal on Women's Human Rights, the Helsinki Watch and Women's Rights Project, IBFAN (International Baby Food Action Committee),[30] ISIS International (a women's development agency), and WAND (Women and Development Unit). Meanwhile, women's political activism through international pressure groups, within the institutions of international civil society (churches, unions and so on) and in movements for (and against) change has increased significantly.

> It is now certainly time for Northern feminists to recognize that inherent sexism of masculine definition and identification of national economic and military priorities. . . . The support will come from Third World feminist enquiry, where feminists have integrated into their critique, [such a recognition] lacking a Northern feminism. Andrée Michel, 1995

Equally important have been women's efforts to transform the male-centred nature of international politics through both academic work and the work of independent, women-led agencies such as DAWN, AAWORD and ISIS. This work highlights the need for a continuity of analysis between national and international arenas and between the affluent and the poor countries. Currently, as Georgina Ashworth argues:

Foreign policy is separated from domestic policy as if a different set of values and morals are necessary. This replicates the traditional separation of the public from the private, and reinforces that separation when transposed to the international-public and the national-private (1995:7).

Women's insistence that their values be considered in international politics disrupts this ultimate private/public split. In fact, mainstream (male) commentators and aid agencies often describe women's collective actions in the international sphere as naive "do-gooding" because of women's refusal to accept that different values should apply in the international arena or in 'first world' dealings with poorer countries.

Approaches to Change

Women's efforts to change the understanding of international politics takes several approaches. One is *transformative efforts* by feminists like Jeanne Vickers and Georgina Ashworth, both activists in the international arena and authors on international politics. Often working through the UN or through international NGOs, advocates of this approach include women from the poorer nations, who envision a global feminism. They reject the field's distinctions between domestic and international politics and between 'developed' and 'developing' societies, insisting that each is part of women's politics and that common values must apply.

The second group works within the interdisciplinary field[31] of international relations and the political science subfield of international politics. Advocates of this second approach propose an alternate *world society paradigm:* "the shift in thought that has taken place is characterized by a shift from the state and its power as the unit of analysis, to the identity group to which the individual owes allegiance" (Burton 1986:47). This approach, which is not women-led and is gaining some currency in the field of international relations, does provide space for the study of women. As in the women-and-development models, however, women will likely be objects of research ("problems") within it.

More promising is an explicitly feminist approach, led by women such as V. Spike Peterson (1992) and Cynthia Enloe (1983, 1993), that explores the *gendered theory and practice of international politics,* especially concerning militarism and the conduct of foreign policy. Christine Sylvester in a 1994 volume shows how feminist scholars are "homesteading" subjects such as security and cooperation in ways that challenge the field's standard understanding of them. She also shows the potential transformative power of reinserting women into the field by asking questions such as: What were real women doing in international politics during the long decades of the realist/idealist debates? Finally, there is the work of prominent women peace activists such as Betty Reardon (1985), Director of the Peace Education Program at Columbia University and Dr. Helen Caldicott, who seek to broadly influence public opinion about the dangers of war.

Together these approaches are producing a rich literature on women's involvements in international politics. As in each country's politics, few women hold decision-making positions in official political institutions. Few countries make women their foreign affairs minister, and fewer still place women in decision-making roles in the 'security' system of bombs, missiles and other instruments of war. The military and the mainstream international media remain almost entirely male. Nonetheless, women's renewed activism in international institutions, NGOS and international movements is a major new force within international politics.

Attempts to Achieve Security and Reproductive Rights

Given our knowledge of women's agendas worldwide, it is not surprising that their needs for security and reproductive health and rights underpin two of the most vital movements in international politics. Women are outstandingly active in international campaigns against violence, in anti-war and anti-nuclear movements, in efforts to get sexual violence included in international treaties concerning refugees and in campaigns to stop the traffic in women and children for use as sex slaves. They are also vigorous in demanding (within the feminist movement, as well as society at large) the right to self-determination in reproduction.

The Search for Security

Images of women as non-violent are common in literature on international politics. Often, women are portrayed as "the moral mother" who is the victim, not the perpetrator, of violence. Women are rarely portrayed, however, as using their collective power to resolve conflicts or prevent violence against other women and their children. Miranda Davies (1994) demonstrates the effect of introducing the feminist idea of the continuum of violence into the study of international politics. The text shows that, throughout the world, women are organizing to support women's security. This image of women using their collective power to protect other women and children is a potent force in the field that has tended to view women as victims. Yet it is not new. In the introduction to her book *Women and War,* Jeanne Vickers recalls that in *Lysistrata,* Aristophanes' BC 411 play, the protagonist's name means "the one who undoes armies". Vickers summarizes the plot:

> At Lysistrata's instigation, the Acropolis and the treasury of Athens are seized by her followers on behalf of all the women of Greece, who declare a sex strike until such time as the men agree to bring the war to an end (1993:vii).

The entire continuum of violence is becoming important internationally. UN documents established gender-based violence as a development issue in 1985. Rape, wife beating, sexual slavery, sexual harassment and gang rape as an instrument of war and genocide are all subjects of national and international campaigns by women. Feminist research illustrates the interdependence among militarism, rapid industrialization in economic zones and the exploitation of women and children in the sex industries, especially through sex tourism and sexual slavery. Fuentes and Ehrenreich (1983) illustrate how young women recruited for work in economic development zones because of good eyesight, nimble fingers and pliant behaviour find themselves after a few years relegated to the sex trades, servicing domestic and foreign military and travelling businessmen. Sister Mary Soledad Perinan, who founded the Third World Movement against the Exploitation of Women (TW-MAE-W) in the Philippines in 1980, points to a *Playboy* article, "Why They Love Us in the Philippines", which describes that country as "the last frontier where you can have what you want—get a blow job, see a female boxing bout and oil wrestling, and have fun with LBFMs (Little Brown Fucking Machines)" (Perinan 1994:151). This link between the concerns of women in the affluent and less affluent countries is characteristic of the emerging global feminism and the strategy of feminist internationalism.

Violence against women is also coming to be understood internationally as a human rights issue and especially as an issue affecting refugees. Because of women's activism, the UN is now one of a growing number of international agencies concerned with domestic violence. Resolution 45/114, adopted by the UN General Assembly in 1990, resulted in a working group of experts that produced *Strategies for Confronting Domestic Violence* (1993). The United Nations Development Fund for Women (UNIFEM) produced a volume (Schuler 1992) documenting the research undertaken worldwide and puts out regular fact sheets.

Breaking the silence about domestic violence through a concerted international campaign has proved quite effective in some contexts. Women also face violence because of the actions of communities, nations and states however, and these dangers are far more difficult to resolve. Here women's movements have used many innovative techniques to draw attention both to the injustice causing the conflict and the consequences of the conflict for women and children. Not in Our Name, the US feminist peace slogan "is a powerful denunciation of foreign policies [supposedly] devised in the 'national interest', without consent or consultation with the majority of the electorate, who benefit nothing from it" (Ashworth 1995:11). Another example is the Women in Black movement; participants on both sides of critical conflicts (such as Palestine/Israel, and the former Yugoslavia) stand in silent vigil weekly in Jerusalem and other cities to mourn women war victims and protest the conflicts. Similarly, women's anti-nuclear campaigns have involved women's street theatre (for example, Canada's Raging Grannies) and peace camps in many places, the most famous of which was at Greenham Common in England.

Women are using networks as the basic structure of their efforts to make women aware of their human rights worldwide. They also engage in international efforts to release sex slaves (by buying them or helping them escape) and to force the UN to take action about the traffic in women slaves. CHANGE, an international women's network based on the strategy of "speaking truth to power", has led in the articulation of women's human rights and their betrayal of them by most international agencies, to formulate what Ashworth calls *Diplomacy of the Oppressed* (1995). She highlights feminist conflict resolution methods and bottom-up peace-making initiatives as grassroots methods of creating counterpower that women can use to effect a sea change in international politics.

The Search for Reproductive Determination

The international women's movement for reproductive determination has to work hard both to define and achieve its objectives. As Sonia Côrrea with Rebecca Reichman (henceforth Côrrea 1994) point out, women in the poorer countries have to battle repressive governments, international actors *and* often the incomprehension and arrogance of women in more affluent countries. One struggle within the international feminist movement has been over how reproductive rights ought to be formulated and who should do the formulating.

The population debates of the 1990s and earlier were based on the false premise that women's fertility, especially in the 'third world', was a barrier to economic development and the cause of worldwide environmental degradation. Not surprisingly, women from poorer countries have organized to resist this interpretation of their fertility as "the problem". They have encountered fierce resistance from the conservative population-control community, which is influenced by western economic theory and religious fundamentalism alike. Nevertheless, at least for the moment, the campaign to establish international documents on women's rights to reproductive self-determination has achieved some success (at the 1994 International Conference on Population and Development in Cairo and at the 1995 UN Fourth World Conference on Women in Beijing).

Garcia-Moreno and Claro (1994a) show how the women's health movement in the 'third world' moved the debate from *population control* (women as the problem) to *women's reproductive rights* (women as agents) by organizing isolated grassroots initiatives into national, regional and then international networks. Côrrea (1994) demonstrates, however, that this international movement first had to overcome the ideas of majority women in the affluent democracies who held that women's reproductive rights were about *not* having babies, rather than about women's rights to choose if, when and with whom to reproduce. The underlying anti-natalism that pervaded the feminism of majority women in the affluent countries reinforced the colonialist and racist presumptions that less affluent countries and peoples were poor because they could not control their fertility. 'Third world' feminists, not surprisingly, saw the poverty of their countries at least partly as the result of colonial and neo-colonial exploitation.

The agenda of the international feminist movement for reproductive rights stresses women's right to *self-determination* in reproduction, which means rejecting both the absence of contraception and safe abortion and coercive contraception or sterilization and coerced abortions. The movement emphasizes maternal health and rejects the safety testing of contraceptives on women in the 'third world', testing that often occurs without their knowledge or through monetary inducements (which are very difficult for poor women to reject). The transfer of the risks in developing reproductive technologies from women in affluent countries to usually poor, third world women shows the stark connections between women's struggles for liberation and equality around the world.

The movement argues that establishing women's rights to be reproductive decision-makers will most effectively shape populations to economies and environments since no one has a greater interest in being able to feed, house and educate children than their mothers. Women's fertility rates are the highest where intergroup conflicts are rampant and infant mortality is high. Côrrea says, "Everywhere, fundamentalism uses women's bodies as a battlefield" (1994:3). She concludes that control over women's bodies in the form of controlling their sexuality and reproduction is the goal not just of conservative religious, ethnic and nationalist forces but also of the most 'modern' development agencies, which, like western feminists, have been unwilling to trust poor 'third world' women to make their own decisions about having children.

Global reproductive rights activists insist on linking this campaign, which can be shared by women in both affluent and poor nations, with campaigns for social and economic justice. Until women in affluent nations understand the need for the links, the movement's strength and cohesion will be compromised. Where there is no welfare state to support them in old age, people have children; where infant mortality is high because of poverty or war, women choose to have more children;[32] where girls must go off to work for their husbands' families, women will try for boys. Once 'first world' feminists come to accept these choices as sensible for women in some contexts, respecting their autonomy, a stronger global movement will be possible.

Conclusion

Women's choices of political projects in the international arena are very similar to their choices in their own countries. Structured male rule in the institutions of international politics is as unwilling to take account of women's views on public policy as are political institutions within states. And just as women mobilize to achieve their goals and establish centres of counterpower within countries, so too they mobilize in the international arena. Differences among women, when unrecognized, weaken women's international movements as they do at home. But women's collective power, when brought to bear on issues, such as women's right to reproductive self-determination and to security from violence, can have significant results.

Further Reading

Public Policy within Countries

Brodie, Janine. 1995. *Politics on the Margins: Restructuring and the Canadian Women's Movement*. Halifax: Fernwood.

_____, ed. 1996. *Women and Canadian Public Policy*. Toronto: Harcourt Brace.

Gelb, Joyce. 1989. *Feminism and Politics: A Comparative Perspective*. Berkeley: University of California Press.

Gelb, Joyce, and Marian Lief Palley. 1982. *Women and Public Policies*. Princeton, N.J.: Princeton University Press.

Nain, Gemma Tang. 1991. "Black Women, Sexism and Racism: Black or Antiracist Feminism?" *Feminist Review* 37(Spring):1–22.

Welch, Susan and Sigelman, Lee. 1989. "A Black Gender Gap?" *Social Science Quarterly* 70(1):120–33.

Women's Politics and Development

Harcourt, Wendy, ed. 1994. *Feminist Perspectives on Sustainable Development*. London: Zed.

Karl, Marlee. 1995. *Women and Empowerment: Participation and Decision Making*. London: Zed.

Lourdes, Beneria, and Shelley Feldman. 1992. *Unequal Burden: Economic Crises, Persistent Poverty and Women's Work*. Boulder, Colo.: Westview.

Mies, Maria, and Vandana Shiva. 1993. *Ecofeminism*. London: Zed.

Sen, Gita, and Caren Grown. 1985. *Development, Crisis and Alternative Visions: Third World Women's Perspectives*. New York: Monthly Review.

Women's International Politics

Ashworth, Georgina, ed. 1995. A *Diplomacy of the Oppressed: New Directions in International Feminism*. London: Zed.

Côrrea, S., with R. Reichman. 1994. *Population and Reproductive Rights: Feminist Perspectives From the South*. London: Zed.

Davies, Miranda, ed. 1994. *Women and Violence*. London: Zed.

Enloe, Cynthia. 1993. *The Morning After: Sexual Politics at the End of the Cold War*. Berkeley: University of California Press.

_____. 1983. *Does Khaki Become You? The Militarisation of Women's Lives*. London: Pluto.

What Do Women Want?

Reardon, B. 1985. *Sexism and the War System*. New York: Teachers College Press.

Sylvester, C. 1994. *Feminist Theory and International Relations in a Postmodern Era*. Cambridge: Cambridge University Press.

Tickner, A. 1990. *Gender in International Relations*. New York: Columbia University Press.

Vickers, Jeanne. 1993. *Women and War*. London: Zed.

Questions for Discussion

1. Is there a common women's agenda that links efforts for change world-wide?
2. What are the most useful ways in which feminists have conceptualized public policy?
3. What do 'third world' feminists mean when they accuse feminists from the affluent democracies of *maternalism* or *orientalism?*
4. What are the important differences among the major strains of feminist ideology?
5. Why are neo-liberal attacks on the activist state so threatening to feminists in the affluent democracies?
6. What are the main WID approaches? Why have many 'third world' women criticized them? Do you agree with that criticism?
7. How would you characterize women's activism in international politics?

Notes

1. You may be reading this chapter immediately after Chapter 3. And it should be useful to you, especially if you are taking a course in public policy, development, international relations or women's studies. You may, however, find it easier to grasp some of the ideas if you first skim Chapters 4 and 5, where I explain, respectively, different kinds of feminism with their various recipes for achieving women's goals and the complexity of identifying goals that are common to majority and minority women within a single country, much less to women in different countries that have different political systems and different levels of wealth.
2. To symbolize the difference, I keep in mind that as a young woman I was encouraged to look for a policeman if I was in any kind of trouble. To me, as a white woman, the policeman was held up as a symbol of state protection. To my non-white friends and colleagues, by contrast, the police were a symbol of the state's harassing and brutalizing of first nations people and other "outsiders", such as racial minorities.
3. You may find it thought-provoking to review, in Chapters 1 and 2, my comments in the ubiquitous male-centred paradigm of mainstream political science.
4. For an explanation of my 'first world/third world' terminology, see Chapter 2, note 4.
5. And their oppositional critics. As I showed in Chapter 2, the Marxist and political

philosophy traditions of political science are as accepting as the mainstream of the private/public split and the division of labour, which leads to unequal rule between the sexes.

6. Lerner's account (1986) stresses the ahistorical fallacy of assuming that women were always victims who didn't concur in and sustain the early construction of the sexual division of labour. Even differences that are completely unassimilable, moreover, have different consequences in different times and places.

7. *Psychoanalytic feminism* and **postmodern** feminism, for example, are basically disengaged from practical politics, as is **cultural feminism** in its separatist form.

8. See Offen (1988) for an account of the use of the term in France before the 1910s. The word didn't appear in the *Oxford English Dictionary* until 1933.

9. Some people label this ideology **maternal feminism;** others call it social feminism. In fact, these labels are somewhat confusing when applied to public policy.

10. You may find it helpful to look back at Chapter 2, where I explore this typology with emphasis on the groups' willingness to work within the politics of the state.

11. In Canada, for example, there are feminists who reject significant state involvement in people's lives. Some are neo-liberals; others describe themselves as libertarian feminists. Still others call themselves conservative feminists; they believe in state intervention to support women's rights — but not to 'meddle' in the economy. See Vickers, Rankin and Appelle (1994) for a discussion of the full range of feminist ideologies in anglophone Canada.

12. In my analysis of the majority feminist movement in anglophone Canada (Vickers 1992), I find it useful to describe its operational code as radical liberalism, as distinct from the status quo liberalism that characterizes most male members of the Liberal Party of Canada.

13. Ironically, out of an ideology that traditionally viewed the liberal state as something to be transformed or transcended for women to progress, many left-wing feminists in practice place great emphasis on state action on behalf of women through extensive welfare state programs.

14. A lapse that may reflect the absence of a theory of politics in Marxism, the worldview in which these feminisms are rooted.

15. More women experienced political violence for feminist goals in Italy than anywhere else in the developed democracies.

16. *Ineluctably* means inevitably, in a manner useless to struggle against.

17. I use the term *domestic violence* deliberately here to recognize the fact that, although most adult violence in families is perpetrated by men against women, children are victims of violence from both men and women. By focusing only on patterns of adult violence (as in wife beating), we ignore female violence against children and violence by children against siblings and parents.

18. Indeed, the threat of stranger rape, which patriarchal societies use to control the mobility of women through fear, frequently contains overtly racist elements.

19. Current evidence from the US, Canada, Australia and New Zealand is that women *did* use their vote in enough of a bloc to affect some political outcomes. Women's votes were responsible for the imposition of prohibition and other limits on alcohol use, the elimination of child labour, the establishment of protective legislation for working women and the establishment of laws concerning compulsory education, clean water and pasteurized milk. That is, although not all women used their votes to achieve reforms, enough women (along with reform-minded

men) did so that many reforms women sought were implemented.

20. This complex definition reflects a reaction against the tendency to depict all feminists, especially if they advocate a separatist position as lesbians.

21. That this energy is usually attributed to feminism generally adds to lesbian invisibility.

22. The issue again became problematic in NOW in the 1990s, when a president's bisexuality was revealed.

23. NAC is an umbrella organization (that is, its members are smaller organizations). The only groups to whom it ever denied membership espoused a wages-for-housewives position. It was, however, also severely conflicted over the view that the state pension system should provide pensions for housewives. The franco-Quebec movement has been similarly challenged by these issues.

24. A revealing exercise is trying to identify clear examples of policies that would genuinely transform the sexual division of labour. Drafting women for combat would be such a policy, but allowing women to serve voluntarily in the military is not so clear cut. Neither are women's paying alimony to ex-husbands or men's right to gain custody following divorce. (The two latter instances show that little of the role change includes men assuming women's roles on more than a minor, voluntary basis.)

25. Many male socialists in Belgium, for example, opposed the vote for women because they considered 'women' as a category to be "priest-ridden" and conservative. And fascist regimes everywhere adopted an anti-feminist gender ideology.

26. These issues are developed in Chaudhuri and Strobel (1992).

27. WID strategies were developed mainly by western aid agencies under the influence of western feminism. As Exhibit 23 shows, there have been at least three WID approaches, each of which tried to fit women into western development models. By contrast, most women in the 'third world' challenge key elements of the western paradigm of development.

28. The concept is similar to that of **hegemonic feminism.**

29. A *gestalt* is a total worldview or mind picture.

30. Which supports breastfeeding worldwide and takes international action against corporations that sell cheaply or give away or products to suppress breastmilk or provide products that must be mixed with water, and hence put babies at risk (because the water supply is impure in many locales).

31. The field of international relations draws on the paradigms of history, economics and sociology in addition to that of political science.

32. In the words of Palestinian women, 'because one will surely be imprisoned and two will die". My thanks to Elissar Sarrouh for helping me understand this point.

GLOSSARY

Affirmative action Actions undertaken by governments or institutions to compensate individuals for the consequences of **systemic discrimination** against members of their sex or race.

Altruism Unselfish behaviour in which the self-interest of the actor is overruled by the needs of the person acted for.

Analysis A method of study that involves breaking things up into their component parts, rather than studying the entity as a whole.

Androcentric A male-centred bias in theory or language.

Anti-statist/state-focused Terms used to describe the orientation of women's movements in various countries. Those that are **anti-statist** are alienated from the politics of the state and limit their activities to grassroots political activism. Those that are **state-focused** are willing to interact with some or all state institutions.

Authority The recognized and legitimate right to give orders (make decisions) and make others obey them.

Barriers research Research undertaken within mainstream political science to explain the relatively small numbers of women elected to legislatures. It focuses largely on *demand-side barriers,* which limit the demand of women as candidates for legislative office. Less often studied are *supply-side variables,* which are forces that keep women from putting themselves forward as candidates. In other words, it assumes women are impeded from participating mainly by **structural barriers** and does not consider other explanations, such as women's finding other political arenas, such as local or movement politics, more attractive.

Bureaucracy A hierarchically-structured organization created to implement public policies using formal rules that, in theory, are impartial.

Case study analysis A method of analysis that usually involves using general theory to illuminate observations about a single case.

Chilly climate The effect on the working and learning environment for those excluded from an activity or discipline, when the activities and values of a dominant group are portrayed as the norm in the activity or theories of the discipline. Previously excluded groups experience this effect long after they are allowed to enter a field.

Civil society Institutions that are neither private nor part of the state. The context of the category differs from society to society. In most **liberal democracies,**

churches, unions, educational institutions and the mass media, such as newspapers and TV stations, are considered part of civil society. The institutions of the international arena, like those of a single state, can be classified as *civil* or part of political politics.

Class Originally a categorical division in society between those who owned the means of production (such as land or capital) and those who did not. This concept is key in left-wing analysis, as signalled by the terms *class consciousness* and *class conflict*. For me, however, the word involves access (or lack thereof) to economic resources, the degree to which life involves a basic struggle for survival, and the degree to which state power is organized primarily to repress challenges to the position of an owning group.

Cognitive community A group of people who interact with one another through a common set of ideas about their subject matter. They almost literally "see" their fragment of the world through the same intellectual eyes. Each new generation is socialized early into the community's worldview so that it seems natural.

Cohort analysis A technique of examining the effects of changes on succeeding cohorts of women within the same country over time. A cohort identifies persons grouped together because of a common characteristic (often statistical). For example, all women who received the right to vote when women were politically emancipated constitute a political cohort. (This is not the same as a generation—that is, a cohort of all women born in the same decade.)

Comparison Identification of the similarities and differences between and among cases. *Thick comparisons* examine many aspects of similarity and difference between a few cases. *Thin comparisons* examine a single characteristic of similarity and difference across many cases.

Congressional system A way of organizing government that involves a strict separation of powers among the executive, legislature and judiciary with no government body being able to control the others. It exists in countries such as the US and Mexico.

Conscientization The 'third world' equivalent of **consciousness-raising.** It involves the self-awareness that comes from recognizing that structural and institutional discrimination contribute to women's problems and that women's role in reinforcing the system affects their growth.

Consciousness-raising (CR) A process in which small groups of women talk about their lives. Used mainly by radical and New Left feminists, it helped reveal that their problems were shared and often structurally caused.

Consensus A general agreement of opinion, usually achieved by extensive discussion that continues until those who originally disagreed are persuaded or until a new position emerges that all participants can accept.

Contextualizing Taking into account ways in which women's (or men's) values and activity patterns differ because of differences in geographical location, class, communal affiliation (race, ethnicity, religion, nationality, language) and personal status (age, sexual orientation, disability).

Corporatism A system of representing interests in which the state recognizes a limited set of organizations, gives them a monopoly on representing interests in their sector, organizes them in a hierarchical way in functional categories and permits no competition among them for access to decision-makers. Compare to **pluralism,** a system of representing interests in which as many groups as want to compete can do so on a voluntary and self-determined basis. In such a system, the state is technically open to all groups that choose to press their case. In fact, decision-makers mainly hear the most influential interests. (Relative influence is usually determined by the size of the group represented and its level of resources.)

Counterpower The collective power women exercise by contesting male dominance through protests or longer-term actions conducted mainly through associations within civil society.

Critical mass The proportion of women members needed in an institution, such as a legislature, before the presence of women changes it so that it can respond to women's needs. What constitutes a critical mass may vary from institution to institution and country to country. The concept was developed by feminist political scientists in Scandinavia.

Cultural feminism *See* **Radical/cultural feminism.**

Democracy In theory, government or rule by the people. At a minimum, it is exercised through representatives who are chosen in periodic, open, competitive elections and who make decisions for the society as a whole after being chosen in such elections. The word is derived from Greek *demos,* "the people". *See also* **liberal democracy, direct democracy** and **representative government.**

Direct action Citizens' direct pursuit of a political goal—for example, by occupying a university building and using it as a child-care centre until university authorities agree to let it serve as a centre and to fund it. By contrast, most political action involves citizens trying to achieve their goals indirectly through political parties or pressure groups, which in turn influence decision-makers.

Direct democracy A theory and practice that rejects the use of intermediaries, such as representatives, parties and pressure groups, in decision-making. Instead, all citizens may participate directly in decision-making, with any specialized jobs (such as chair of the meeting) being chosen by lot. **Representative government,** by contrast, has elected or appointed intermediaries participate in decision-making. It rarely allows citizens to decide which policies to implement, but limits their choices to which political party forms the government or which candidate becomes their legislative member.

Direct primaries *See* **Primaries.**

Discrimination The unfair denial of equal rights to citizens because of prejudice. *See also* **Systemic discrimination.**

Double shift The fact that most women work in the paid workforce and then perform most of the child care and domestic work as well. Also called the *double day.*

Economic restructuring *See* **Globalization.**

Electoral projects Systematic efforts by women in a country, state or province to get more women elected to its legislature.

Electoral systems The rules that apply in the nomination, election and funding of political candidates for office; how people qualify to vote; and how votes are counted. In **single-member electoral systems** each electoral district, riding or constituency elects only one representative. The winner is determined by one of two basic sets of rules: the **first-past-the-post system,** in which the candidate with the most votes wins even if more voters overall opposed than supported her or him; and the **single-transferable vote system,** in which voters express first and second choices so that if no candidate wins a majority, second-choice votes are counted until someone does obtain a majority. In contrast, **proportional representation** electoral systems have multiple candidates on a list from which the electors choose. All the many kinds of PR systems are designed so that each party receives the same proportion of legislators as the proportion of votes it receives overall from the electorate. Voter eligibility can be determined through **enumeration systems,** in which each household is visited to identify those eligible to vote; **registration systems,** in which prospective voters must go to a designated location to be registered; or **permanent list systems,** in which permanent lists of electors are maintained and revised regularly by either enumerators or registration.

Enumeration system *See* **Electoral systems**.

Epistemology Any theory of how human beings know and what constitutes valid knowledge.

Equal Rights Amendment (ERA) An amendment to the US constitution pursued unsuccessfully by that country's women's movements for most of this century. It would have prevented any distinctions in treatment between men and women in any federal laws, programs or entitlements in the US.

Equal rights feminism In the early decades of the twentieth century, equal rights feminists argued for the vote on the grounds that they should be treated the same as men and enjoy rights equal to them. (For a contrast, *see* **Maternal feminism.**) Later in the twentieth century, the emphasis shifted to other legal rights.

Equality *See* **Formal equality/Substantive equality.**

Federal state A system of government in which the power of authoritative collective decision-making (of making decisions and having the power to make them stick) is divided between two levels of government, each of which has final authority in some areas of responsibility. Some responsibilities are usually shared by the two. Canada and the United States are both federal states. For the contrasting form, *see* **Unitary state**.

Feminist ideologies Various theories about the origins of the inequality between the sexes. Although each assumes such inequality is unjust and should be changed, each offers a different set of ideas about its origins, how it can be eliminated and what kind of society should be established in its place.

Feminist orientalism The assumptions made by western feminists about 'other' women not of European origin, especially those of Asian origin. They are summed up in the oppositions *civilized/backward, independent/dependent, active/passive, liberated/oppressed* and *modern/traditional*, which are assumed to distinguish 'western' and other women.

Femocrats Women bureaucrats who work within government offices (including specially designated status-of-women agencies) to press for feminist goals. The strategy involves a process of consultation with women's movements and the use of conscious tactics to avoid being co-opted into bureaucratic values. The term originated in Australia.

First-past-the-post system *See* **Electoral systems**.

Formal equality/substantive equality With **formal (legal) equality,** the state treats women exactly the same as it treats men. The contrast is **substantive equality,** in which women are treated as equal citizens but also as different when appropriate so that men and women enjoy equal results from their citizenship. Theories of substantive equality mandate the use of devices such as affirmative action, pay equity and party quotas for women candidates.

Formal politics *See* **Official politics**.

Gatekeepers Individuals or institutions that control access to particular activities and institutions. In official politics, for example, parties determine who their candidates will be in elections or on their electoral lists; in this way, key party officers act as gatekeepers.

Gender gap The differences between men and women of a particular group, in a particular country, at a particular time, concerning political values, beliefs or behaviour, especially differences in voting behaviour.

Gender needs *Practical gender needs* are what women require to perform their actual tasks in the existing division of labour (such as child-care services and training). *Strategic gender needs* are what women require to overcome their subordination.

Globalization An economic process in which barriers among nations are reduced and economic activity is organized on a global instead of a country-by-country basis. The process tends to provoke **economic restructuring,** in which each country's economy is reorganized to play a role in the global economy. The shift involves pressures to develop political structures that operate beyond the nation-state and to abandon economic ventures not considered globally competitive. It can also lead to pressures to homogenize (to the lowest common denominator) such things as employee benefits, labour laws and environmental laws between and among countries to create "a level playing field" for business.

Hegemony Dominance of ideas (or of a country) so complete that alternate visions (or leaders) are hard to conceptualize. **Hegemonic feminism** describes the dominance of western or 'first world' assumptions about what it means to be feminist and what women need to be liberated.

Hypothesis A tentative explanation put forward to account for a set of circumstances; it should be testable (subject to being disproved or tentatively affirmed) to advance our knowledge.

Identity politics Political movements organized around aspects of individuals' identities such as their sex (women's movements), race/ethnicity (nationalisms, anti-racist movements, red power, black pride), sexual orientation (gay/lesbian movements), age (Grey Panthers) or disability (movements of people with disabilities). The emphasis is on the right to self-describe or name and to portray the identity in culture and as the basis for political choices and alliances. *See also* Standpoint analysis.

Informal politics *See* **Official politics**.

Initiative/referendum Instruments intended to increase the powers of citizens and limit the powers of elected representatives. In the **initiative,** citizens petition to have policies or legislation put before the electorate in a vote. In a **referendum,** the electorate is asked to vote on a proposed policy or law, which may be initiated by the government or a citizen's initiative. The vote is often not binding on the government.

Institutionalized male dominance A situation in which male dominance is built into the institutions, laws, customs, practices and operating rules of a society. **Patriarchies** are characterized by institutionalized male dominance.

Left-wing feminism The term I use to describe a number of versions of feminism that are derived generally from Marxism or neo-Marxism. They include, among others, *Marxist feminism* and *socialist feminism.*

Legal equality *See* **Formal equality**.

Legitimize To justify; to make acceptable and in accordance with a prevailing set of rules.

Lesbian feminism Feminism organized around the ideas that sexism and heterosexism are hopelessly intertwined, that male violence is the major mechanism for sustaining patriarchy, that the heterosexual family is dangerous for girls and women, and that the oppression of women, especially lesbians, is the prototype for all other oppressions.

Liberal democracy A political system that fuses elements of **democracy** with the values, practices and legal norms of the **liberal** political system that developed in the anglo-American and some European countries from the seventeenth to the nineteenth centuries. This hybrid form has intrinsic value conflicts: for example, between democracy's primary value of equality and liberalism's primary value of freedom. In liberal-democratic theory, democracy is transmuted into **legal equality** through the right to vote and the existence of competition (or choice) among political parties. The conflict between liberal and democratic values is lessened in **social democracies,** such as those developed in Finland and Sweden, where the equality values predominate and the **welfare state** is used to compensate for many of the inequalities created by liberal values and a capitalist economy.

Liberal feminism A form of feminism that mainly operates within the framework of liberalism. It includes **equal rights feminism,** among other strains.

Liberalism A complex philosophy and ideology with economic, social, religious and epistemological dimensions. The liberal theory of government stresses five values: the human (not divine) origin of political authority; its origins in a hypothetical contract among rational men (not women) acting in their self-interest; the importance of the rule of law; the fundamental importance of property; and freedom, which is liberalism's prime value. Dante Germino says: "Liberal government is government under law for limited objectives, above all for the preservation of the lives and property of the society's members. Liberal government is rational government: government of rational men, by rational men, for rational men. The obverse of liberal government is arbitrary or tyrannical government in any of its forms" (1972:138–39). Liberalism had an activist phase in the past century as it was fused with democracy. **Neo-liberalism** involves rejection of this activism and of the welfare state devised to increase equality by regulating the market.

Liberation The act of being set free, especially from control by an authority that is considered oppressive. Calling 1960s and 1970s women's political activism the **women's liberation movement** meant adopting the idea that women were oppressed in the same way that colonized people were—that is, women as needing freeing, not just rights or an end to discrimination.

Marginalization The preclusion of individuals or a whole category of people from useful involvement in social life, requiring them to exist "on the margins" of society. Usually includes ignoring or trivializing the ideas and voices of such individuals, groups or categories.

Maternal feminism A late nineteenth- and early twentieth-century theory that women should be given the vote because they are mothers with a unique perspective on public policy. For a contrast, *see* **Equal rights feminism.**

Neo-liberalism *See* **Liberalism.**

New Left A 1960s version of left-wing ideology. In the US, it was characterized by an intense suspicion of state politics and a determination to resist any involvement in state institutions. In some other countries, such as Canada, the New Left was less anti-state but also stressed community and cultural politics.

Non-governmental organizations (NGOs) Organizations that operate in domestic or international **civil society.**

Obligation What one must do because of a law, contract (binding promise) or moral precept; one's duty.

Official politics The term I use to identify political activity that occurs within state institutions and political structures, such as parties and pressure groups designed to influence political decision-making in the state. Also called **formal politics.** The contrast is with **informal politics,** which is the term I use to identify efforts to achieve or prevent change through informal groups and movements, direct action and politico-cultural activities such as street theatre. (Other terms used by feminist political scientists to describe these activities are **unofficial politics,** *ad hoc politics* and *grassroots politics*.) Like single states, the international arena has official and informal or unofficial politics.

Oppression A system of forceful subordination that includes some or all of physical harm, marginalization, powerlessness, cultural denigration and economic exploitation.

Paradigm A set of concepts, theories and assumptions accepted and widely used by scholars in a field; includes assumptions about proper methods, units of measure, theory of knowledge, and so on. Most scientific fields have a single dominant paradigm; in the social science fields, several may compete for dominance.

Parallel vision A principle of feminist method that requires focus on women's activity *both* in traditionally male fields and in traditionally female fields and use of norms based on the view *both* from the top and from below.

Parliamentary system A way of organizing government in which the executive and the legislature are fused, so the executive controls the legislature but not the judiciary. Strict party discipline is usually required to retain executive control. In the anglo-American democracies, where it is also known as the Westminster system, it usually includes a second legislative house in which membership is sometimes elected and sometimes appointed or hereditary. The authority of the head of state is derived from the monarch.

Patriarchy As the term is used in feminist political science, political systems characterized by **institutionalized male dominance**, in which men are dominant in all state institutions and favoured by the balance of power in other important social institutions. Patriarchy is historical; that is, we know when and how it was invented. It takes different forms over time and place. All known historical states have been patriarchal in form; some non-state political systems, such as village republics, have not, however.

Permanent list system *See* **Electoral system**.

Pluralism *See* **Corporatism**.

Political culture A country's, region's or group's distinctive values and beliefs about politics and the proper limits of political action.

Political opportunity structure The alignment of political forces, structures and ideas that characterize official political systems and that enhance or deter women's political participation. For example, most **proportional representation electoral systems** enhance the likelihood of women's achieving success through **electoral projects,** which enhance their opportunities to participate in official politics.

Political philosophy A field of traditional political science that focuses mainly on the presumed eternal validity of classical, medieval and early modern political ideas.

Politics All activity aimed at changing, maintaining or restoring power relationships in a society, its communities or its institutions; usually involves activity undertaken within a collective or group context. *See also* **Official politics; Informal politics.**

Postmodernism An approach to knowledge and research based on the belief that because knowledge is socially constructed, there can be no single or master version (narrative) of any event. Postmodernism is also a cultural theory. Its proponents do not believe that any form of authentic representation is possible in art or politics because of the distortion they believe inevitably occurs.

Postmodern feminists challenge the adequacy of any representational voice; that is, they believe no woman can represent the views of other women.

Power Power over, or domination, means having the capacity (ultimately based on coercion) to make others do what one wants them to do and that which they otherwise wouldn't do. **Power to,** or capacity, is based on ability, energy, skill, leadership, affection or collective action in which coercion (or threat thereof) is not involved and in which exploitation or oppression does not result.

Practical gender needs *See* **Gender needs**.

Primaries Part of an election system whereby citizens can play a role in choosing candidates for political parties (instead of their being chosen by small groups of party members). In *direct primaries,* eligible citizens can vote for competing candidates to represent the parties in the election. In *indirect primaries,* they elect delegates who, in turn, select the candidate. Primaries are used in many US states, where they were introduced as part of the reform movement with which suffrage-seeking feminists were associated.

Proportional representation *See* **Electoral systems**.

Public policy Actions governments (including all levels and institutions) choose to take and those they choose not to take.

Radical/cultural feminism Versions of feminism based on the belief that women are oppressed by men as part of a universal **sex/gender** system maintained by culture, economic and political power and coercion (force). **Radical feminism** also holds that women were the first oppressed group and that **patriarchy** is a universal system in which men always oppress women on the basis of women's sexuality and reproductive capacity. **Cultural feminism,** which is a later variant, also involves the belief that violence, conflict and competition are part of men's nature and that peacefulness, cooperation and nurturance are part of women's nature. This form of feminism is usually alienated from the politics of the state and other male-dominated institutions. In practice, most radical/cultural feminists have organized in women-only groups that operate by consensus, designate no leaders and reject representative forms of democracy in favour of direct forms.

Referendum *See* **Initiative/referendum**.

Regimes Broad categories of types of political rule. A simple typology includes **democracies,** *authoritarian regimes* and *state-socialist regimes.*

Registration systems *See* **Electoral systems**.

Representative bureaucracy/judiciary An idea based on the argument that bureaucrats and judges cannot be fully objective and that their institutions, therefore, need to have representation of different groups on the same scale as in the society. The argument was first made in Canada to support the recruitment of a larger numbers of francophones into the federal bureaucracy. The Constitution specifies that the Supreme Court must include Quebec judges trained in that province's civil code. There is also increasing pressure to have more women judges, largely because of the critiques of male bias in the judiciary advanced by feminist scholars and activists.

Representative democracy/government *See* **Direct democracy**.

Role equity/role change Role equity issues address the distribution of power in society but do not disturb basic sex-role definitions. In contrast, *role change* challenges traditional sex-role ideology.

Sex/gender Sex identifies biological characteristics. They are, however, differently expressed in different places and times. For example, menstruation is a biological characteristic of human females. In circumstances of adequate nutrition, it is a regular occurrence of physically mature women for much of their lives. In times of nutritional inadequacy, however, it may cease or occur infrequently. Moreover, its onset and cessation vary significantly even within the same place and time. How sex is experienced also varies according to such things as class, race and sexual orientation.

Gender describes the social behaviours and roles societies (and groups within them) assign to men and women because of their sex. The characteristics of gender, therefore, also vary across cultures and time, although there are some commonalities. That women bear children is a dimension of sex; that they are assigned responsibility for childrearing is a dimension of gender. My use of the compound term **sex/gender** indicates that my approach is interactionist; that is, I assume that some aspects of sex are socially constructed, while others are not.

Sexual politics A term developed by feminists in the 1960s and early 1970s to capture the fact that relationships between the sexes involve power differentials and should be understood as political—that is, subject to political change—rather than natural or private.

Single-member electoral system *See* **Electoral systems**.

Single-transferable vote system *See* **Electoral systems**.

Situational barriers/structural barriers Different kinds of barriers to women's involvement in elite-level politics as identified by barriers research. **Situational barriers** are found in the situations of women's lives, such as family responsibilities, that keep them from undertaking a political career. **Structural barriers** are aspects of political systems, such as electoral systems or legislative systems, that make it harder for women who choose to run to be elected.

Social adults Those people to whom societies give the responsibility for making collective decisions. Although chronologically and biologically adults, women may not be treated as *social* adults, even in the family; if they are not, they are not seen as possible decision-makers.

Social democracy A political system in which the fusion of liberalism and democracy emphasizes democracy's equality values. Social democracies have developed extensive **welfare states,** designed to compensate for inequalities created by liberal values and capitalist economies. Social democracies include the Nordic countries of Norway, Sweden, Finland and Denmark.

Sovereign Supreme authority to rule; the individual or body who holds such authority.

Standpoint analysis A mode of study and undertaking research that starts from the point of view of a particular identity group. *Women-centred analysis* is a form of standpoint analysis. *See also* **Identity politics**.

State feminism The activities of government institutions that formally have the task of advancing the status of women and their rights. The term is also used by some authors to describe the approach to change adopted in, for example, Norway and Sweden, whereby women accept integration into the mainstream political system. Australia's femocrat project is a form of state feminism. (See Stetson and Mazur 1995).

Stereotype A preconceived, oversimplified idea of the characteristics of a group; it is often used to 'justify' oppression or discrimination, as in "women are too emotional to be judges".

Strategic gender needs *See* **Gender needs**.

Structural barriers *See* **Situational/structural barriers**.

Substantive equality *See* **Formal equality**.

Systemic discrimination A complex system of laws, policies and practices that are seemingly neutral in their impact but that, overall, have a disparate impact on an individual or group. Such discrimination does not rely on conscious prejudice and cannot be changed simply by people's becoming less prejudiced.

Typology A framework in which different types of a thing are classified. A *type* is a class of things with common characteristics; it is often called an *ideal type* because it is a mental construct, which does not exist in pure form in the world people experience.

Underdevelopment A term used within the dominant paradigm to describe poor countries that do not have an extensive industrial sector. The implication is that some countries may be poor because they have not undertaken development. The concept does not acknowledge the role of colonial and neo-colonial exploitation and domination in 'developing' some countries while others became 'underdeveloped'.

Unitary state A state whose government is a single level. Some powers may be delegated to local/regional governments but constitutionally they remain powers of the central government, which can reclaim them. For the contrasting form, *see* **Federal state**.

Unofficial politics *See* **Official politics**.

Welfare state A system of state-administered programs that ameliorate some of the negative consequences of capitalism. The actual bundle of programs varies considerably from country to country, but they usually include unemployment support programs, family support programs, old-age security programs and health services. Most liberal and social democracies developed welfare state programs to some degree within the past century. The current wave of **neo-liberalism** seeks to reduce them significantly.

Womanism Ideas articulated by US African American women who see racial oppression as the main struggle and white women as co-oppressors of black women and men and exploiters of black women's reproductive labour (as domestics and nannies). For these black women, community solidarity among blacks is more important than gender solidarity and the family is experienced as a refuge from racism rather than as a site of oppression.

Women's liberation movement *See* **Liberation**.

BIBLIOGRAPHY

Agnew, John A. 1987. *Place and Politics.* Boston: Allen and Unwin.

Almond, Gabriel A., and Sydney Verba. 1963. *The Civic Culture.* Princeton, N.J.: Princeton University Press.

Anderson, Doris. 1991. *The Unfinished Revolution: The Status of Women in Twelve Countries.* Toronto: Doubleday Canada.

Apffell-Marglin, Frédérique, and Suzanne L. Simon. 1994. "Feminist Orientalism and Development." In Wendy Harcourt (ed.), *Feminist Perspectives on Sustainable Development.* London: Zed.

Ashworth, Georgina, ed. 1995. *A Diplomacy of the Oppressed: New Directions in International Feminism.* London: Zed.

Bakker, Isabella, ed. 1996. *Rethinking Restructuring: Gender and Change in Canada.* Toronto: University of Toronto Press.

_____, ed. 1994. *The Strategic Silence: Gender and Economic Policy.* London: Zed.

Bartra, Eli. 1994. "Mexico: The Struggle for Life or Pulling the Mask Off Infamy." In Barbara Nelson and Najama Chowdhury (eds.), *Women and Politics Worldwide.* New Haven and London: Yale University Press.

Bashevkin, Sylvia. 1985. *Toeing the Lines: Women and Party Politics in English Canada.* Toronto: University of Toronto Press.

Beck, Lois, and Nikki Keddie, eds. 1978. *Women in the Muslim World.* Cambridge: Harvard.

Bloom, Allan. 1968. *The Republic of Plato.* New York: Basic.

Boneparth, Ellen. 1982. *Women, Power and Policy.* New York: Permagon.

Brodie, Janine, ed. 1996. *Women and Canadian Public Policy.* Toronto: Harcourt Brace.

_____. 1995. *Politics on the Margins: Restructuring and the Canadian Women's Movement.* Halifax: Fernwood.

Bryson, Valerie. 1992. *Feminist Political Theory: An Introduction.* London: Macmillan.

Burgos-Debray, Elisabeth, ed. 1984. *I, Rigoberta Menchu.* Trans. Ann Wright. London: Verso.

Burt, Sandra. 1995. "The Several Worlds of Policy Analysis: Traditional Approaches and Feminist Critiques." In Sandra Burt and Lorraine Code (eds.), *Changing Methods: Feminists Transforming Practice.* Peterborough, Ont.: Broadview.

_____. 1988. "Different Democracies? A Preliminary Examination of the Political Worlds of Canadian Men and Women." *Women and Politics* 6/4(Winter):57–79.

Burton, John. 1986. "The History of International Conflict Resolution." In Edward Azar and John W. Burton, *International Conflict Resolution.* Brighton: Wheatsheaf.

Carroll, Bernice. 1976. *Liberating Women's History.* Urbana: University of Illinois Press.

Carroll, Susan J. 1984. "Women Candidates and Support for Feminist Concerns: The Closet Feminist Syndrome." *Western Political Quarterly* 27(2):307–23.

Castro, Ginette. 1990. *American Feminism: A Contemporary History.* New York: New York University Press.

Chaudhuri, Nupur, and Margaret Strobel, eds. 1992. *Western Women and Imperialism: Complicity and Resistance.* Bloomington: Indiana University Press.

Chowdhury, Najama, and Barbara Nelson. 1994. "Redefining Politics: Patterns of

Women's Political Engagement from a Global Perspective." In Barbara Nelson and Najama Chowdhury (eds.), *Women in Politics Worldwide*. New Haven and London: Yale University Press.

Christy, Carol. 1987. *Sex Differences in Political Participation: Processes of Change in Fourteen Nations*. New York: Praeger.

Clark, Lorraine, and Lynda Lange. 1979. *The Sexism of Social and Political Theory: Women and Reproduction from Plato to Nietzsche*. Toronto: University of Toronto Press.

Cohen, Yolande. 1989. "The Role of Associations in Democracy." In Yolande Cohen (ed.), *Women and Counter-Power*. Montreal: Black Rose.

Connell, R.W. 1994. "The State, Gender and Sexual Politics: Theory and Appraisal." In H. Lorraine Radtke and Henderikus J. Stam (eds.), *Power/Gender: Social Relations in Theory and Practice*. London and California: Sage.

_____. 1987. *Gender and Power*. Stanford, Calif.: Stanford University Press.

Côrrea, S., with R. Reichman. 1994. *Population and Reproductive Rights: Feminist Perspectives From the South*. London: Zed.

Cott, Nancy. 1987. *The Grounding of Modern Feminism*. New Haven and London: Yale University Press.

Crick, Bernard. 1959. *The American Science of Politics*. Berkeley: University of California Press.

Dalherup, Drude. 1986a. "From a Small to a Large Minority. A Theory of Critical Mass Applied to the Case of Women in Scandinavian Politics." Mimeo, Aarhus: Institute of Political Science.

_____, ed. 1986b. *The New Women's Movement: Feminism and Political Power in Europe and the USA*. London: Sage.

Davies, Miranda, ed. 1994. *Women and Violence*. London: Zed.

Day, Shelagh. 1991. "Constitutional Reform: Canada's Equality Crisis." In D. Schneiderman (ed.), *Conversations Among Friends (Entre Amies): Proceedings of the Conference on Women and Constitutional Reform*. Edmonton: Centre for Constitutional Studies.

de Sève, Micheline. 1996. "Women's National and Gendered Identity: The Case of Canada." mimeo, Montreal: University of Quebec at Montreal.

Diamond, Irene, and Nancy Hartsock. 1981. "Beyond Interests in Politics: A Comment on Virginia Sapiro's 'When are Interests Interesting? The Political Representation of Women.'" *American Political Science Review* 75(3):717–26.

Douglas, Mary. 1986. *How Institutions Think*. Ithaca, N.Y.: Cornell University Press.

Dumont, Micheline. 1986. *The Women's Movement: Then and Now*. Feminist Perspectives, 5b. Ottawa: CRIAW.

Eisenstein, Hester. 1991. *Gendershock: Practicing Feminism on Two Continents*. Boston: Beacon Hill.

Eisenstein, Zillah. 1994. *The Colour of Democracy*. Berkeley: University of California Press.

_____. 1981. *The Radical Future of Liberal Feminism*. New York: Longman.

Enloe, Cynthia. 1993. *The Morning After: Sexual Politics at the End of the Cold War*. Berkeley: University of California Press.

_____. 1983. *Does Khaki Become You? The Militarisation of Women's Lives*. London: Pluto.

Ferguson, Kathy. 1984. *The Feminist Case Against Bureaucracy*. Philadelphia: Temple

University Press.

Fuentes, Annette, and Barbara Ehrenreich. 1983. *Women in the Global Factory.* Boston: South End.

Garcia-Moreno, C., and A. Claro. 1994a. "Challenge from the Women's Health Movement: Women's Rights versus Population Control." In G. Sen, A. Germain and L.C. Chen (eds.), *Population Policies Reconsidered.* Boston: Harvard School of Public Health.

_____. 1994b. In Sonia Côrrea and Rebecca Richman (eds.), *Population and Reproductive Rights: Feminist Perspectives from the South.* DAWN and Kahli for Women, London: Zed.

Gelb, Joyce. 1989. *Feminism and Politics: A Comparative Perspective.* Berkeley: University of California Press.

Germino, Dante. 1972. *Modern Western Political Thought: Machiavelli to Marx.* Chicago: Rand McNally.

Gilligan, Carol. 1982. *In a Different Voice: Psychological Theory and Women's Development.* Cambridge: Harvard University Press.

Gutman, Amy. 1980. *Liberal Equality.* Cambridge: Cambridge University Press.

Haavio-Mannila, E., et al. 1985. *Unfinished Democracy: Women in Nordic Politics.* Oxford and New York: Permagon.

Halsaa, Beatrice, Helga Marla Hernes and Sirkka Sinkkonen. 1985. "Introduction." In E. Haavio-Mannila et al. (eds.), *Unfinished Democracy: Women in Nordic Politics.* Oxford and New York: Permagon.

Hartman, Mary, and Lois Banner. 1974. *Clio's Consciousness Raised: New Perspectives on the History of Women.* New York: Harper and Row.

Hartsock, Nancy. 1983. *Money, Sex and Power: Toward a Feminist Historical Maternalism.* New York: Longman.

Heitlinger, Alena. 1979. *Women and State Socialism: Sex Inequality in the Soviet Union and Czechoslovakia.* Montreal: McGill-Queen's University Press.

Hernes, Helge. 1987. *Welfare State and Woman Power: Essays in State Feminism.* Oslo: Norwegian University Press.

hooks, bell. 1984. *Feminist Theory: from margin to center.* Boston: South End.

Jackson, Robert, and Michael Atkinson. 1974. *The Canadian Legislative System.* Toronto: Macmillan.

Jacquette, Jane S., ed. 1989. *The Women's Movement in Latin America: Feminism and the Transition to Democracy.* New York: Unwin Hyman.

Jagger, Alison, and Paula Rothenberg. 1984. *Feminist Frameworks.* Second edition. Toronto: McGraw-Hill.

Janeway, Elizabeth. 1981. *The Powers of the Weak.* New York: Morrow Cluill Paperbacks.

Jayawardena, Kumari. 1986. *Feminism and Nationalism in the Third World.* London: Zed.

Jønasdøttir, Anna. 1988. "On the Concept of Interest, Women's Interests and the Limitations of Interest Theory." In Kathleen Jones and Anna Jønasdøttir (eds.), *The Political Interests of Gender.* London: Sage.

Jones, Kathleen. 1994. *Compassionate Authority.* New York: Routledge.

_____. 1988. "Toward the Revision of Politics." In Kathleen Jones and Anna Jønasdøttir (eds.), *The Political Interests of Gender: Developing Theory and Research With a Feminist Face.* London: Sage.

Kaplan, Gisela. 1992. *Contemporary Western European Feminism*. New York: New York University Press.

Karl, Marlee. 1995. *Women and Empowerment: Participation and Decision Making*. London: Zed.

Karp, Walter. 1988. "In Defense of Politics." *Harpers Magazine* 276(1656):41–49.

Katzenstein, M.F, and C. Mueller. 1987. *The Women's Movements of the United States and Western Europe*. Philadelphia:Temple University Press.

Katzenstein, M.F., and H. Skejie. 1990. *Going Public: National Histories of Women's Enfranchisement and Women's Emancipation Within State Institutions*. Oslo: Institute for Social Research.

Kirhoro, Wanjiru. 1992. "Why African Women are Still Left Behind." *Third World Network Features* 967.

Lasswell, Harold, and Abraham Kaplan. 1950. *Power and Society*. New Haven: Yale University Press.

Lerner, Gerda. 1986. *The Creation of Patriarchy*. Oxford: Oxford University Press.

Lorde, Audre. 1984. *Sister Outsider*. Trumansberg: Crossing.

Lovenduski, Joni. 1994. "Introduction." In Marianne Githens, Pippa Norris and Joni Lovenduski (eds.), *Different Roles, Different Voices: Women and Politics in the United States and Europe*. New York: Harper Collins.

_____. 1986. *Women and European Politics: Contemporary Feminism and Public Policy*. Amherst, Mass.: University of Massachusetts Press.

Lovenduski, Joni, and Jill Hills, eds. 1981. *The Politics of the Second Electorate: Women and Public Participation*. Boston: Routledge and Kegan Paul.

Lovenduski, Joni, and Pippa Norris. 1993. *Gender and Party Politics*. London: Sage.

Mackinnon, Catharine A. 1982. "Feminism, Marxism and the State: Toward a Feminist Jurisprudence." *Signs* 7(2):515–44.

Maillé, Chantal. 1997. "Challenge to Representation: Theory and the Women's Movement in Quebec." In Jane Arscott and Linda Trimble (eds.), *In The Presence of Women: Representation in Canadian Government*. Toronto: Harcourt Brace.

_____. 1991. "The Women's Health Movement in Québec Society: An Analysis for the Purpose of the Constitutional Debate." In D. Schneiderman (ed.), *Conversations Among Friends (Entre Amies): Proceedings of the Conference on Women and Constitutional Reform*. Edmonton: Centre for Constitutional Studies.

Marchak, Patricia. 1994. "Political Economy In and Out of Time." In Terry Goldie, Carmen Lambert and Rowland Lorimer (eds.), *Canada: Theoretical Discourse*. Montreal: Association of Canadian Studies.

Mayo, Henry B. 1960. *An Introduction to Democratic Theory*. New York: Oxford University Press.

McCormack, Thelma, 1975. "Toward a Nonsexist Perspective on Social and Political Change." In M. Milman and R.M. Kanter (eds.), *Another Voice*. New York: Doubleday.

Michel, Andrée. 1995. "Militarisation of Contemporary Societies and Feminism in the North." In Georgina Ashworth (ed.), *The Diplomacy of the Oppressed*. London: Zed.

Mies, Maria. 1991. "Women's Research or Feminist Research? The Debate Surrounding Feminist Science and Methodology." In Judith Cook and Mary Margaret Fonow (eds.), Beyond *Methodology: Feminist Scholarship as Lived Research*. Bloomington and Indianapolis: Indiana University Press.

_____. 1983. "Towards a Methodology for Feminist Research." In Bowles and Klein (eds.), *Theories of Women's Studies*. London: Routledge.

Bibliography

Milbrath, Lester. 1965. *Political Participation.* Chicago: Rand McNally.

Miles, Angela. 1982. "Ideological Hegemony in Political Discourse: Women's Specificity and Equality." In Angela Miles and Geraldine Finn (eds.), *Feminism in Canada.* Montreal: Black Rose.

Millett, Kate. 1969. *Sexual Politics.* New York: Avon.

Moghadam, Valentine, ed. 1994. *Gender and National Identity: Women and Politics in the Third World.* London: Zed.

Mohanty, Chandra Tolpade. 1992. "Feminist Encounters: Locating the Politics of Experience." In Michelle Barrett and Ann Phillips (eds.), *Destabilizing Theory: Contemporary Feminist Debates.* Stanford, Calif.: Stanford University Press.

Mohanty, Chandra, Ann Russo and Lourdes Torres. 1991. *Third World Women and the Politics of Feminism.* Bloomington and Indianapolis: Indiana University Press.

Morganthau, Hans J. 1960. *Politics Among Nations: The Struggle for Power and Peace.* Third edition. New York: Alfred A. Knopf.

Molyneux, Maxine. 1985. "Mobilization without Emancipation? Women's Interests, the State and Revolution in Nicaragua." *Feminist Studies* 11(2)summer:227–254.

Mouffe, Chantal. 1993. *The Return of the Political.* London: Verso.

_____. 1992. *Dimensions of Radical Democracy.* London: Verso.

Nain, Gemma Tang. 1991. "Black Women, Sexism and Racism: Black or Antiracist Feminism?" *Feminist Review* 37(Spring):1–22.

Nelson, Barbara, and Najama Chowdhury, eds. 1994. *Women and Politics Worldwide.* New Haven and London: Yale University Press.

Newton, Janice. 1995. *The Feminist Challenge to the Canadian Left, 1900–1918.* Montreal and Kingston: McGill-Queens University Press.

Norris, P. 1985. "Women's Legislative Participation in Western Europe." *Western European Politics* 8(4):90–101.

Norris, Pippa. 1993. "Conclusion: Comparing Legislative Recruitment." In Joni Lovenduski and Pippa Norris (eds.), *Gender and Party Politics.* London: Sage.

O'Brien, Mary. 1981. *The Politics of Reproduction.* Boston: Routledge.

Offen, Karen. 1988. "On the French Origin of the Words Feminism and Feminist." *Feminist Issues* 8(2):45–49.

Okin, Susan Moller. 1979. *Women in Western Political Thought.* London: Virago.

Ortner, Sherry B. 1978. "The Virgin and the State." *Feminist Studies* 4(3):19–35.

_____. 1974. "Is Female to Male as Nature is to Culture?" In Michelle Zimbalist and Louise Lamphere (eds.), *Woman, Culture, Society.* Stanford, Calif.: Stanford University Press.

Pateman, Carole. 1989. *The Disorder of Women: Democracy, Feminism and Political Theory.* Cambridge: Polity.

_____. 1988. *The Sexual Contract.* Cambridge: Polity.

Perinan, Sister Mary Soledad. 1994. "Militarism and the Sex Industry in the Philippines." In Miranda Davies (ed.), *Women and Violence.* London: Zed.

Petchesky, Rosalind. 1990. *Abortion and Women's Choice: The State, Sexuality and Reproductive Freedom.* Revised ed. Boston: Northeast University Press.

Petchesky, Rosalind. 1984. *Abortion and Woman's Choice: The State, Sexuality and Reproductive Freedom.* New York: Longman. Boston: Northeastern University Press, Revised edition 1990.

Peterson, V. Spike. 1992. *Gendered States: Feminist (Re)Visions of International Relations Theory.* Boulder, Colo.: Lynne Rienner.

Pettman, Jan (Jindy). 1992. *Living in the Margins: Racism, Sexism and Feminism in Australia.* Sydney: Allen and Unwin.

Phelan, Shane. 1989. *Identity Politics: Lesbians, Feminism and the Limits of Community.* Philadelphia: Temple University Press.

Pitkin, Hannah. 1967. *The Concept of Representation.* Berkeley: University of California Press.

Pringle, Rosemary and Sophie Watson. 1992. "Women's Interests and the Post-Structuralist State." In Michele Barrett and Ann Phillips (eds.), *Destabilizing Theory: Contemporary Feminist Debates.* Stanford, Calif.: Stanford University Press.

Radtke, H. Lorraine, and Henderikus J. Stam, eds. 1994. *Power/Gender: Social Relations in Theory and Practice.* London: Sage.

Randall, Vicky. 1987. *Women and Politics: An International Perspective.* Second edition. Chicago: University of Chicago Press.

Rankin, Pauline. 1996. "Experience, Opportunity and the Politics of Place: A Comparative Analysis of Provincial and Territorial Women's Movements in Canada." PhD Thesis. Department of Political Science, Carleton University, Ottawa.

_____. 1989. "The Politicizing of Ontario Farm Women." In Linda Kealey and Joan Sangster (eds.), *Beyond the Vote: Canadian Women and Politics.* Toronto: University of Toronto Press.

Reardon, B. 1985. *Sexism and the War System.* New York: Teachers College Press.

Rubin, Gayle. 1975. "The Traffic in Women: Notes on the 'Political Economy of Sex'." In R.R. Reiter (ed.), *Toward an Anthropology of Women.* New York: Monthly Review.

Rule, Wilma. 1987. "Electoral Systems, Contextual Factors and Women's Opportunities for Election to Parliament in Twenty-three Democracies." *Western Political Quarterly* 40:477–86.

Sacks, Karen. 1982. *Sisters and Wives: The Past and Future of Sexual Equality.* Urbana: University of Illinois Press.

Sainsbury, Diane. 1993. "The Politics of Increased Representation: The Swedish Case." In Joni Lovenduski and Pippa Norris (eds.), *Gender and Party Politics.* London: Sage.

Sanday, Peggy Reeves. 1981. *Female Power and Male Dominance.* Cambridge: Cambridge University Press.

Sapiro, Virginia. 1991. "When are Interests Interesting? The Problem of Political Representation of Women." *American Political Science Review* 75(3):701–16.

Sapriza, Graciela. 1994. "Uruguay." In Barbara Nelson and Najama Chowdhury (eds.), *Women and Politics Worldwide.* New Haven and London: Yale University Press.

Sassoon, Anne Showstuch, ed. 1987. *Women and the State.* London: Hutchinson.

Savage, M., and A. Witz, eds. 1992. *Gender and Bureaucracy.* Oxford: Blackwell.

Sawer, Marion. 1994. "Women's Policy Machinery in Australia, Canada and New Zealand." Unpublished draft of 1996 *Femocrats and Ecorats.* Geneva: UN Research Institute for Public Development.

Schmitter, Philippe C. 1984. "Still the Century of Corporatism." *Review of Politics* 36(January): 85–131.

Schuler, M. 1994. *Freedom From Violence: Women's Strategies from Around the World.* New York: UNIFEM.

Seager, Joni and Ann Olson. 1986. *Women in the World: An International Atlas.* London: PAN Books.

Skejie, Heye. 1993. "Ending the Male Hegemony: The Norwegian Experience." In Joni

Lovenduski and Pippa Norris (eds.), *Gender and Party Politics*. London: Sage.

_____. 1988. *The Feminization of Power: Norway's Political Experience (1986–)*. Oslo: Institute for Social Research.

Smith, Dorothy. 1978. "A Peculiar Eclipsing: Women's Exclusion from Man's Culture." *Women's Studies International Quarterly* (4):281–96.

Spragens, Thomas A. Jr. 1976. *Understanding Political Theory*. New York: St. Martins.

Stetson, Dorothy McBride, and Amy G. Mazur, eds. 1995. *Comparative State Feminism*. London: Sage.

Sylvester, C. 1994. *Feminist Theory and International Relations in a Postmodern Era*. Cambridge: Cambridge University Press.

Tong, R. 1989. *Feminist Thought*. London: Unwin Hyman.

Trimble, Linda. 1993. "A Few Good Women: Female Legislators in Alberta, 1972–1991." In Catherine A. Cavanaugh and Randi R. Warne (eds.), *Standing on New Ground: Women in Alberta*. Edmonton: University of Alberta Press.

_____. 1991. "Federalism, the Feminism of Poverty and the Constitution." In D. Schneiderman (ed.), *Conversations Among Friends >>Entre Amies<<: Proceedings of the Conference on Women and Constitutional Reform*. Edmonton: Centre for Constitutional Studies.

UNICEF. 1993. "The Women's Empowerment Framework." *Women and Girls Advance* 1:1–5.

UNIFEM. 1993. *Strategies for Confronting Domestic Violence: A Resource Manual*. New York: UN Centre for Social Development and Humanitarian Affairs.

United Nations. 1996. *Demographic Yearbook, 1994*. New York: UN.

_____. 1991. *The Women's World 1970–1990: Trends and Statistics*. New York: UN.

United Nations Development Program. 1993. *Human Development Report*. New York: UNDP.

van der Ros, Janneke. 1994. "The State and Women: A Troubled Relationship in Norway." In Barbara Nelson and Najama Chowdhury (eds.), *Women and Politics Worldwide*. New Haven and London: Yale University Press.

Verba, Sidney, and Norman H. Nie. 1972. *Participation in America: Social Equality and Political Democracy*. New York: Harper and Row.

Vickers, Jeanne. 1993. *Women and War*. London: Zed.

Vickers, Jill. 1994a. "Notes Toward a Political Theory of Sex and Power." In H. Lorraine Radtke and Henderikus J. Stam (eds.), *Power/Gender: Social Relations in Theory and Practice*. London: Sage.

_____. 1994b. "Why *Should* Women Care About Federalism?" In J. Hiebert (ed.), *Canada: The State of the Federation*. Kingston: Queen's School of Public Policy.

_____. 1993. "Sexual Politics and the Master Science: The Feminist Challenge to Political Science." In Geraldine Finn (ed.), *Limited Edition: Voices of Women, Voices of Federalism*. Halifax: Fernwood.

_____. 1992. "The Intellectual Origins of Women's Movements in Canada." In C. Backhouse and D. Flaherty (eds.), *Challenging Times: The Women's Movement in Canada and the United States*. Montreal: McGill-Queen's University Press.

_____. 1991. "Why *Should* Women Care About Constitutional Reform." In D. Schneiderman (ed.), *Conversations Among Friends >>Entre Amies<<: Proceedings of the Conference on Women and Constitutional Reform*. Edmonton: Centre for Constitutional Studies.

_____. 1989a. "Feminist Approaches to Politics." In Linda Kealey and Joan Sangster (eds.), *Beyond the Vote: Canadian Women and Politics.* Toronto: University of Toronto Press.

_____. 1989b. *Getting Things Done: Women's Views of Their Involvement in Political Life.* Ottawa and Paris: Canadian Research Institute for the Advancement of Women and UNESCO.

_____. 1986. "Equality-Seeking in a Cold Climate." In L. Smyth et al. (eds.), *Righting the Balance: Canada's New Equality Rights.* Saskatoon: Canadian Rights Reporter.

_____, ed. 1984. *Taking Sex Into Account: The Policy Consequences of Sexist Research.* Ottawa: Carleton University Press.

_____. 1983/84. "Major Equality Issues of the Eighties." *Human Rights Yearbook* 1(Winter):47–72.

_____. 1983. "Memoirs of an Ontological Exile: The Methodological Rebellions of Feminist Research." In Miles and Finn (eds.), *Feminism in Canada: From Pressure to Politics.* Reprinted 1989, Second edition. Montreal: Black Rose.

_____. 1980. "Coming Up for Air: Feminist Views of Power Reconsidered." *Canadian Woman Studies* 2(4):66–71.

Vickers, Jill, and June Adam. 1977. *But Can You Type? Canadian Universities and the Status of Women.* Toronto: Clarke Irwin.

Vickers, Jill, Pauline Rankin, and Christine Appelle. 1994. *Politics As If Women Mattered: A Political Analysis of the National Action Committee on the Status of Women.* Toronto: University of Toronto Press.

Waltz, Kenneth N. 1959. *Man, the State and War.* New York: Columbia University Press.

Watson, Sophie, ed. 1990. *Playing the State: Australian Feminist Interventions.* Sydney: Allen and Unwin.

Welch, Susan and Lee Sigelman. 1989. "A Black Gender Gap?" *Social Science Quarterly* 70(1): 120–33.

West, Lois. 1992. "Feminist Nationalist Social Movements." Women's *Studies International Forum* 15(5/6):563–79.

_____. (ed.) 1997. *Feminist Nationalism.* New York: Routledge.

Yates, Gayle Graham. 1975. *What Women Want: The Ideas of the Women's Movement.* Cambridge: Harvard University Press.

Young, Lisa. 1994. *Electoral Systems and Representative Legislatures.* Ottawa: Canadian Advisory Council on the Status of Women.

Young, Iris Marion. 1990. *Justice and the Politics of Difference.* Princeton, N.J.: Princeton University Press.

_____. 1989. "Politics and Group Differences: A Critique of the Ideal of Universal Citizenship." Ethics 99(January):250–74.

 **Related titles
from Fernwood Publishing**

The Women, Gender and Development Reader
Nalini Visvanathan, Lynne Duggan, Laurie Nisonoff and Brenda Wyss (eds.)
Designed as a comprehensive reader for undergraduates and development
practitioners, this book presents the best of this discipline's now vast body of
literature. Five parts cover respectively a review of the history of the theoretical
debates, the status of women in the household and family, women in the global
economy, the impact of social changes on women's lives, and women organizing
for change.
384pp 1 895686 86 5 $29.95

Feminism and Families
The Challenge of Neo-Conservatism
Meg Luxton ed.
The absence of a specific "family politics" has ceded an important political space
to anti-feminist movements and weakened the capacity of the feminist movement
to intervene effectively in the debates and struggles of the current period. Despite
significant changes in family, domestic and interpersonal relations, the prevailing
ideology of the heterosexual nuclear family as the norm still shapes social, economic and legal practices. This book argues for feminist debates in all areas
affecting families and begins with such important areas as demographics, family
law, lesbian parenting, women's friendships, child benefit legislation, the contradictions of parenting, etc.
232pp 1 895686 76 8 $21.95

Muriel Duckworth
A Very Active Pacifist
Marion Douglas Kerans
Muriel is an extraordinary woman whose life and work has enriched many—
through her faith and her practice. A feminist, a pacifist and a compassionate
Canadian, her life is an example of what love and selfless intelligence can do."
Ursula M. Franklin C.C. FRSC
"Muriel Duckworth's unwavering commitment to the cause of peace and human
progress has inspired countless women and men. The story of her life's work will
cheer and revitalize the thousands who meet her for the first time in this book."
Alexa McDonough, leader, Canada's New Democrats
240pp 1 895686 68 7 $19.95

Women in Trouble
Connecting Women's Law Violations to their Histories of Abuse
Elizabeth Comack
These stories of women in a provincial jail address the alarming fact that 80%
report histories of physical and sexual abuse. The book raises several questions
that pertain to our efforts to respond to violence against women.
"Elizabeth allows the women in this book to speak their own truth. It's a graphic,
shocking, depressing and absolutely necessary account of the connections between
histories of abuse and trouble with the law." Karen Toole-Mitchell, *Winnipeg Free
Press.*
150pp 1 895686 61 X $14.95

Child and Family Policies
Struggles and Options
J. Pulkingham, G. Ternowetsky (eds.)
This collection addresses the changing context of Child and Family Policies which
have been ushered in by the Liberal governments Social Security Review (SSR).
The contributions analyze the implications of government policy shifts showing
how they are particularly devastating for children of low income, welfare, first
nations and single parent families.
288pp 1 895686 60 1 $21.95

Politics of Community Services
Immigrant Women, Class and the State (2nd. ed.)
Roxana Ng
"The relevance of the book continues to lie in its clearly presented methodology
which can be read by students and understood. Also, of no mean importance is the
fact that the study is focused on services to immigrant women which continues to
be an area of policy concern. If anything, the issues highlighted have more visibility today than when the research was being conducted in the early eighties." Sheila
M. Neysmith, Social Work, Univ. of Toronto
110pp 1 895686 64 4 $12.95

Strategies for the Year 2000
A Woman's Handbook
Deborah Stienstra, Barbara Roberts
How well has Canada measured up to its obligations under the two agreements it
signed during the UN Decade of Women? This book details the terms of the conventions and chronicles the progress the provincial, territorial, and federal governments have made towards fulfilling their legal obligations in areas such as women's
participation in decision-making, childcare, violence against women, and so on.
124pp 1 895686 55 5 $12.95

Smoke Screen
Women's Smoking and Social Control
Lorraine Greaves
"*Smoke Screen* challenges the established medical/health model of tobacco control. Written from a feminist perspective, Greaves argues passionately and convincingly for a woman-centred approach to smoking prevention and cessation programmes. This book is highly recommended and should be read by everyone involved in tobacco control." Amanda Sandford, Women's Development Officer at ASH (Action on Smoking and Health)
144pp 1 895686 57 1 $14.95

Thunder in My Soul
A Mohawk Woman Speaks
Patricia Monture-Angus
"Monture writes about aboriginal peoples' experiences with education, racism and the criminal justice system, without missing the cultural dilemmas, the role of women in education and the law, or the human factors that make all these experiences more complex."
S. Stiegelbauer, *Resources for Feminist Research*
273pp 1 895686 46 6 $19.95

Maid In the Market
Women's Paid Domestic Labour
Wenona Giles, Sedef Arat-Koç (eds.)
"These essays explore the topic in useful ways and offer a refreshingly nuanced assessment . . ." Margaret Conrad, *Canadian Book Review Annual*
138pp 1 895686 35 0 $ 14.95

Becoming an Ally
Breaking the Cycle of Oppression
Anne Bishop
"This book is a delight to read, its language simple and clear, its examples vivid, and its message profoundly useful. It's changed the way I look at my own oppression and the way the way I do social change work. I recommend it highly." Diana Ralph, Carleton University
". . . a book that never flinches from the hard truths of our behaviours, socially and individually, yet provides a paradigm for change."
Patricia Whitney, *Herizons*
137pp 1 895686 39 3 $14.95

Limited Edition
Voices of Women, Voices of Feminism
Geraldine Finn (ed.)
This book is an introductory text and reader for use in Women's Studies. Feminist activists, teachers, students of Women's Studies and women in the paid and unpaid labour force speak about their own experiences of feminism and the difference it has made and continues to make in their public and private lives.
399pp 1 895686 13 X $26.95

Politics on the Margins
Restructuring and the Canadian Women's Movement
Janine Brodie
"This is an important and exciting contribution to the debate about future directions for the Canadian women's movement. Every woman who is thinking about what course feminist political activism should take in this era of economic and state restructuring must read this book." Shelagh Day

"Janine Brodie's thoughtful and insightful analysis of the impact of international restructuring on the women's movement asks all the right questions. Her challenge to develop new strategies in the face of the destruction of the welfare state should be taken up by feminists everywhere." Judy Rebick
120pp 1 895686 47 4 $12.95

The University as Text
Women and the University Context
Carol Schick
This book is an excellent analysis of how male-centric approaches and methods dominate university life. "Schick effectively raises stimulating questions that challenge the status quo of university education." Britta Santowski, *Cdn. Book Review Annual*
100pp 1 895686 33 4 $12.95

Undressing the Canadian State
The Politics of Pornography from Hicklin to Butler
Kirsten K. Johnson
112pp 1 895686 48 2 $12.95

The Christmas Imperative: Leisure, Family and Women's Work
Leslie Bella
252pp 1 895686 09 1 $19.95

Feminist Pedagogy: An Autobiographical Approach
Anne-Louise Brookes
168pp 1 895686 00 8 $15.95